W9-AHJ-227

365

Favorite Brand Name ™

STIR-FRY

■ RECIPES & MORE ■

PUBLICATIONS INTERNATIONAL, LTD.

365

Favorite Brand Name ™

STIR-FRY

■ RECIPES & MORE ■

Just for
Starters

1 SPRING ROLLS

½ **pound ground pork**
1 **teaspoon KIKKOMAN® Soy Sauce**
1 **teaspoon dry sherry**
½ **teaspoon garlic salt**
2 **tablespoons vegetable oil**
3 **cups fresh bean sprouts**
½ **cup sliced onion**
1 **tablespoon KIKKOMAN® Soy Sauce**
1 **tablespoon cornstarch**
¾ **cup water, divided**
8 **egg roll wrappers**
½ **cup quick biscuit mix**
1 **egg, beaten**
   Vegetable oil for frying
   Hot mustard, tomato ketchup and
      KIKKOMAN® Soy Sauce

Combine pork, 1 teaspoon soy sauce, sherry and garlic salt; mix well. Let stand 15 minutes. Heat 2 tablespoons oil in hot wok or large skillet over medium-high heat; brown pork mixture in hot oil. Add bean sprouts, onion and 1 tablespoon soy sauce. Stir-fry until vegetables are tender-crisp; drain and cool. Dissolve cornstarch in ¼ cup water. Place about ⅓ cupful pork mixture on lower half of egg roll wrapper. Moisten left and right edges with cornstarch mixture. Fold bottom edge up just to cover filling. Fold left and right edges ½ inch over; roll jelly-roll fashion. Moisten top edge with cornstarch mixture and seal. Complete all rolls. Combine biscuit mix, egg and remaining ½ cup water in small bowl; dip each roll in batter. Heat oil for frying in wok or large saucepan over medium-high heat to 370°F. Deep fry rolls, a few at a time, in hot oil 5 to 7 minutes, or until golden brown, turning often. Drain on paper towels. Slice each roll in half. Serve with mustard, ketchup and soy sauce as desired.

Makes 8 appetizer servings

Spring Rolls

JUST FOR STARTERS

2 BLACK BEAN GARNACHAS

1 can (14½ ounces) DEL MONTE®
   FreshCut™ Diced Tomatoes with
   Garlic & Onion, undrained
1 can (15 ounces) black or pinto beans,
   drained
2 cloves garlic, minced
1 to 2 teaspoons minced jalapeño chilies
   (optional)
½ teaspoon ground cumin
1 cup cubed grilled chicken
4 flour tortillas
½ cup (2 ounces) shredded sharp Cheddar
   cheese

1. In large skillet, combine tomatoes and juice, beans, garlic, jalapeño chilies, if desired, and cumin. Cook over medium-high heat 5 to 7 minutes or until thickened, stirring occasionally. Stir in chicken. Season with salt and pepper, if desired.

2. Arrange tortillas in single layer on grill over medium coals. Spread about ¾ cup chicken mixture over each tortilla. Top with cheese.

3. Cook about 3 minutes or until bottoms of tortillas are browned and cheese is melted. Top with shredded lettuce, diced avocado and sliced jalapeño chilies, if desired.

Makes 4 servings

Prep Time: 5 minutes
Cook Time: 10 minutes

VARIATION: Prepare chicken mixture as directed above. Place 1 tortilla in dry skillet over medium heat. Spread with about ¾ cup chicken mixture; top with 2 tablespoons cheese. Cover and cook about 3 minutes or until bottom of tortilla is browned and cheese is melted. Repeat with remaining tortillas.

3 GINGERED PORK TENDERLOIN SALAD

3 pounds pork tenderloin, thinly sliced
¼ cup teriyaki sauce
3 tablespoons grated fresh ginger
3 tablespoons chopped cilantro
1 tablespoon cracked black pepper
1 tablespoon olive oil
12 artichoke bottoms, cleaned and cut into
   quarters
2 tablespoons butter
6 red potatoes, boiled, peeled and sliced
2 red onions, peeled and thinly sliced
   Dressing (recipe follows)

Marinate pork slices in teriyaki sauce, ginger, cilantro and pepper 1 hour. Drain pork from marinade and stir-fry quickly in hot oil. Sauté artichokes in butter until lightly browned. Toss pork, potatoes, artichokes and onions with Dressing. Refrigerate. To serve, arrange salad on greens-lined plates.   *Makes 12 servings*

DRESSING
1 cup olive oil
¾ cup rice vinegar
¼ cup chopped parsley
¼ cup chopped chives
2 tablespoons chopped gherkins
3 anchovies, chopped
1 tablespoon capers
2 cloves garlic, minced
2 teaspoons curry powder
   Salt and black pepper to taste

Mix all ingredients together well.
Makes about 2½ cups

Prep Time: 20 minutes

*Favorite recipe from **National Pork Producers Council***

Black Bean Garnacha

JUST FOR STARTERS

4 HOT 'N CRUNCHY THAI PORK SALAD WITH SPICY PEANUT DRESSING

3 boneless pork chops, cut into stir-fry
  strips
1 medium yellow onion, finely chopped
¼ cup lime juice
2 tablespoons plus 1 teaspoon soy sauce,
  divided
1 teaspoon ground coriander
½ teaspoon ground cumin
½ teaspoon ground ginger
¼ teaspoon ground turmeric
⅛ teaspoon ground red pepper
¼ cup peanut butter
1 tablespoon brown sugar
½ cup plain nonfat yogurt
⅛ teaspoon hot pepper sauce
1 tablespoon vegetable oil
4 cups coarsely chopped Chinese cabbage
  or shredded cabbage
¼ cup thinly sliced green onions
2 cups chow mein noodles

In small bowl, combine yellow onion, lime juice, 2 tablespoons soy sauce, coriander, cumin, ginger, turmeric and red pepper. Place pork in large resealable plastic food storage bag. Pour onion mixture over pork; seal bag. Marinate in refrigerator 1 to 2 hours.

For dressing, in small saucepan, combine peanut butter and brown sugar. Cook over low heat, stirring constantly, until well blended. Remove from heat and stir in yogurt, remaining 1 teaspoon soy sauce and pepper sauce. Return to heat. Cook and stir over low heat until just heated through. Keep warm.

Drain pork, discarding marinade. In large skillet, heat oil over medium-high heat. Cook and stir pork 2 to 3 minutes or until cooked through. Remove from heat. Add cabbage and green onions; toss to combine. Divide cabbage mixture among individual plates. Place chow mein noodles on top of cabbage mixture. Drizzle with dressing.

Makes 4 servings

Prep Time: 30 minutes

Favorite recipe from **National Pork Producers Council**

5 HAM AND GOUDA QUESADILLA SNACKS

1½ cups (6 ounces) shredded smoked
    Gouda cheese
1 cup (4 ounces) chopped ham
½ cup pitted ripe olives, chopped
¼ cup minced red onion
½ cup GREY POUPON® COUNTRY
  DIJON® Mustard
8 (6- or 7-inch) flour tortillas
  Sour cream, chopped peppers, sliced
    pitted ripe olives and cilantro for
    garnish

In small bowl, combine cheese, ham, ½ cup olives and onion. Spread 1 tablespoon mustard on each tortilla; spread about ⅓ cup cheese mixture over half of each tortilla. Fold tortilla in half to cover filling.

In large nonstick skillet, over medium heat, heat filled tortillas 4 minutes or until cheese melts, turning once. Cut each quesadilla into 3 wedges. Place on serving platter; garnish with sour cream, peppers, olives and cilantro.

Makes 24 appetizers

Ham and Gouda Quesadilla Snacks

JUST FOR STARTERS

6 CHICKEN SESAME WITH ORIENTAL CRÈME

⅓ cup reduced-sodium soy sauce
2 teaspoons minced garlic
1 teaspoon dark sesame oil
½ teaspoon ground ginger
1 pound boneless skinless chicken breasts, cut into 4×½-inch strips
6 ounces (1 carton) ALPINE LACE® Fat Free Cream Cheese with Garlic & Herbs
2 tablespoons finely chopped green onions
2 tablespoons sesame seeds, toasted
1 tablespoon extra-virgin olive oil

1. To marinate the chicken: In a small bowl, whisk the soy sauce, garlic, sesame oil and ginger. Reserve 2 tablespoons and pour the remaining marinade into a self-sealing plastic bag. Add the chicken pieces and seal the bag. Turn the bag to coat all the chicken, then refrigerate for at least 2 hours, turning the bag occasionally.

2. To make the Oriental Crème: In another small bowl, place the cream cheese. Whisk in the reserved 2 tablespoons of marinade and stir in the green onions. Cover with plastic wrap and refrigerate.

3. To prepare the chicken: Remove the chicken from the marinade and discard any remaining marinade. Spread the sesame seeds on a plate and roll the chicken strips in them until lightly coated.

4. In a large nonstick skillet, heat the olive oil over medium-high heat. Add the chicken and stir-fry for 6 minutes or until golden brown and the juices run clear when the chicken is pierced with a fork. Serve with the Oriental Crème.

Makes 24 appetizer servings

7 HOT PORK AND PEAR SALAD

1 pound pork cutlets
2 large firm pears
2 tablespoons vegetable oil, divided
¼ cup cider vinegar
2 tablespoons sugar
½ teaspoon salt
¼ cup raisins
5 to 6 cups salad greens
½ cup walnuts, toasted

Cut pork into 3×¼-inch strips; set aside. Peel and core pears; cut into 12 slices. Heat 1 tablespoon oil in heavy skillet; sauté pears until tender but firm. Remove from pan and set aside. Stir-fry pork strips, adding remaining 1 tablespoon oil if necessary, about 3 minutes or until cooked through. Remove meat from pan; pour off excess fat. Add vinegar, sugar and salt to pan juices; heat until sugar dissolves. Add pears, pork and raisins; stir to heat and mix. Place salad greens in large salad bowl; spoon pork mixture over greens and toss. Sprinkle with walnuts.

Makes 6 servings

Prep Time: 20 minutes

*Favorite recipe from **National Pork Producers Council***

Chicken Sesame with Oriental Crème

JUST FOR STARTERS

8 MEXICAN PORK SALAD

1 pound boneless pork loin, cut into 3×½×¼-inch strips
4 cups shredded lettuce
1 medium orange, peeled, sliced and cut into quarters
1 medium avocado, peeled, seeded and diced
1 small red onion, sliced and separated into rings
1 tablespoon vegetable oil
1 teaspoon chili powder
¾ teaspoon salt
½ teaspoon dried oregano leaves
¼ teaspoon ground cumin

Place lettuce on serving platter. Arrange orange, avocado and onion over lettuce. Heat oil in large skillet; add chili powder, salt, oregano and cumin. Add pork loin strips; stir-fry over medium-high heat 5 to 7 minutes or until pork is tender. Spoon hot pork strips over lettuce mixture. Serve immediately. *Makes 4 servings*

Prep Time: 15 minutes

*Favorite recipe from **National Pork Producers Council***

9 HOT CHINESE CHICKEN SALAD

8 boneless skinless chicken thighs
¼ cup cornstarch
¼ cup vegetable oil
1 large tomato, stemmed and chopped
1 can (4 ounces) water chestnuts, drained and sliced
1 can (4 ounces) sliced mushrooms, drained
1 cup coarsely chopped green onions
1 cup diagonally sliced celery
¼ cup soy sauce
⅛ teaspoon garlic powder
2 cups finely shredded iceberg lettuce
Orange slices for garnish (optional)
Hot cooked rice

1. Cut chicken into bite-size pieces; place cornstarch in shallow dish.

2. Place chicken, one piece at a time, in cornstarch. Coat evenly, shaking off excess; set aside.

3. Place wok or large skillet over high heat. (Test hot pan by adding drop of water to pan; if water sizzles, pan is sufficiently hot.) Add oil to wok, swirling to coat side. Heat oil until hot, about 30 seconds.

4. Add chicken to wok; stir-fry 3 minutes or until chicken is no longer pink in center.

5. Stir in tomato, water chestnuts, mushrooms, green onions, celery, soy sauce and garlic powder. Cover; simmer 5 minutes.

6. Place chicken mixture on lettuce-lined serving platter. Garnish with orange slices, if desired. Serve with rice.

Makes 4 servings

JUST FOR STARTERS

10 CAJUN CHILI

6 ounces spicy sausage links, sliced
4 boneless chicken thighs, skinned and cut into cubes
1 medium onion, chopped
⅛ teaspoon cayenne pepper
1 can (15 ounces) black-eyed peas or kidney beans, drained
1 can (14½ ounces) DEL MONTE® FreshCut™ Diced Tomatoes with Garlic & Onion, undrained
1 medium green bell pepper, chopped

1. In large skillet, lightly brown sausage over medium-high heat. Add chicken, onion and cayenne pepper; cook until browned. Drain.

2. Stir in remaining ingredients. Cook 5 minutes, stirring occasionally.

Makes 4 servings

11 CHINESE PORK SALAD

1 pound pork strips
½ cup Oriental stir-fry sauce
½ red onion, peeled and thinly sliced
2 packages (10 ounces each) frozen snow peas, thawed and drained
1 can (8 ounces) mandarin oranges, drained
1 can (3 ounces) chow mein noodles

Marinate pork in stir-fry sauce. In large nonstick skillet, stir-fry pork and onion over medium-high heat 4 to 5 minutes. In large bowl, toss pork mixture together with remaining ingredients. *Makes 4 servings*

Prep Time: 5 minutes
Cook Time: 5 minutes

*Favorite recipe from **National Pork Producers Council***

Hot Chinese Chicken Salad (page 12)

JUST FOR STARTERS

12 APPLE CINNAMON QUESADILLAS

Spiced Yogurt Dipping Sauce (recipe follows)
1 medium McIntosh apple, cored and chopped
¾ cup no-sugar-added applesauce
⅛ teaspoon ground cinnamon
4 (6-inch) flour tortillas
¼ cup (1 ounce) shredded reduced-fat Cheddar cheese
Nonstick cooking spray

1. Prepare Spiced Yogurt Dipping Sauce. Set aside.

2. Combine apple, applesauce and cinnamon in small bowl; mix well.

3. Spoon half of apple mixture onto 1 tortilla; sprinkle with half of cheese. Top with another tortilla. Repeat with remaining tortillas, apple mixture and cheese.

4. Spray large nonstick skillet with cooking spray; heat over medium heat until hot. Cook quesadillas, one at a time, about 2 minutes on each side or until golden brown. Cut each quesadilla into four wedges. Serve with Spiced Yogurt Dipping Sauce. Sprinkle with additional cinnamon, if desired. *Makes 4 servings*

SPICED YOGURT DIPPING SAUCE
½ cup vanilla low-fat yogurt
2 tablespoons no-sugar-added applesauce
Dash ground cinnamon

1. Combine yogurt, applesauce and cinnamon in small bowl; mix well. Refrigerate until ready to use.
Makes about ⅔ cup

13 JONES® HAM STIR–FRY PASTA SALAD

¾ pound JONES® Ham, cut into ½-inch cubes
4 tablespoons vegetable oil, divided
4 cups shredded cabbage
1 red bell pepper, cut into thin strips
6 ounces snow peas, cut into halves
2 cloves garlic, crushed
½ teaspoon minced fresh ginger
3 tablespoons soy sauce
3 tablespoons dry sherry
1 tablespoon cider vinegar
½ teaspoon hot pepper sauce
6 ounces macaroni, cooked and drained

Heat 2 tablespoons oil over medium heat in wok or large skillet. Add cabbage, bell pepper and snow peas. Stir-fry 3 minutes; remove from wok. Add remaining 2 tablespoons oil to wok. Add garlic and ginger; sauté 30 seconds. Add ham; stir-fry 3 minutes. Add soy sauce, sherry, vinegar and pepper sauce.

Stir constantly and bring to a boil. Reduce heat and simmer 1 minute. Remove from heat; add pasta and vegetables, tossing to coat. Serve chilled. *Makes 6 servings*

Apple Cinnamon Quesadillas

14 CRAB CAKES WITH TOMATO SALSA

CRAB CAKES
- 1 pound crabmeat, cleaned
- 1 tablespoon FILIPPO BERIO® Olive Oil
- 1 onion, finely chopped
- 1 cup fresh white bread crumbs, divided
- 2 eggs, beaten, divided
- 2 tablespoons drained capers, rinsed and chopped
- 2 tablespoons mayonnaise
- 1 tablespoon chopped fresh parsley
- 1 tablespoon ketchup
  Finely grated peel of ½ lemon
- 1 tablespoon lemon juice
  Salt and freshly ground black pepper
  Additional FILIPPO BERIO® Olive Oil

TOMATO SALSA
- 3 tablespoons FILIPPO BERIO® Olive Oil
- 4 large tomatoes, finely chopped
- 2 cloves garlic, crushed
- ¼ cup lemon juice
- 4½ teaspoons sweet or hot chili sauce
- 1 tablespoon sugar
  Salt and freshly ground black pepper

For Crab Cakes, place crabmeat in medium bowl; flake finely. In small skillet, heat 1 tablespoon olive oil over medium heat until hot. Add onion; cook and stir 3 to 5 minutes or until softened. Add to crabmeat. Gently mix in ½ cup bread crumbs, 1 egg, capers, mayonnaise, parsley, ketchup, lemon peel and 1 tablespoon lemon juice. Shape mixture into 8 round cakes; cover and refrigerate 30 minutes.

Meanwhile, for Tomato Salsa, in medium skillet, heat 3 tablespoons olive oil over medium heat until hot. Add tomatoes and garlic; cook and stir 5 minutes. Add ¼ cup lemon juice, chili sauce and sugar; mix well. Season to taste with salt and pepper.

Dip crab cakes into remaining beaten egg, then in remaining ½ cup bread crumbs. Press crumb coating firmly onto crab cakes.

In large nonstick skillet, pour in just enough olive oil to cover bottom. Heat over medium-high heat until hot. Add crab cakes; fry 5 to 8 minutes, turning frequently, until cooked through and golden brown. Drain on paper towels. Season to taste with salt and pepper. Serve hot with Tomato Salsa for dipping.

Makes 8 crab cakes

15 COCKTAIL FRANKS OLÉ!

- 2 teaspoons vegetable oil
- 2 cloves garlic, minced
- 1 can (10 ounces) diced tomatoes with green chilies, undrained
- 1 can (16 ounces) vegetarian refried beans
- 1 package (12 ounces) HEBREW NATIONAL® Cocktail Beef Franks
- ⅓ cup chopped fresh cilantro
- ⅓ cup sliced green onions, with tops
  Finely chopped jalapeño peppers (optional)
  Tortilla chips

Heat oil in medium saucepan over medium heat. Add garlic; cook and stir 2 minutes. Stir in tomatoes with chilies, beans and cocktail franks. Bring to a boil. Reduce heat. Cover; simmer 5 minutes or until heated through. Stir in cilantro, green onions and jalapeño peppers to taste, if desired. Simmer, uncovered, 5 minutes. Transfer mixture to serving platter. Serve with tortilla chips. *Makes 12 appetizer servings*

Crab Cakes with Tomato Salsa

JUST FOR STARTERS

16 KIELBASA TOMATO SALAD

1 pound BOB EVANS FARMS® Kielbasa Sausage
1 pound tomatoes, cut into wedges
1 large red onion, chopped
1 red bell pepper, chopped
1 yellow bell pepper, chopped
3 green onions with tops, cut into ½-inch pieces
½ cup chopped fresh parsley
⅓ cup balsamic vinegar
2 teaspoons salt
1 teaspoon chopped fresh rosemary
1 teaspoon chopped fresh thyme
1 teaspoon black pepper
½ cup olive oil
Fresh rosemary sprig (optional)

Cut sausage kielbasa into ½-inch rounds; place in medium skillet. Cook over medium heat until browned, turning occasionally. Remove sausage to large glass bowl. Add tomatoes, red onion, bell peppers and green onions to sausage; toss lightly. Combine all remaining ingredients except oil and rosemary sprig in small bowl. Whisk in oil gradually until well blended. Pour over sausage mixture; cover and refrigerate 2 hours or until chilled. Garnish with rosemary sprig, if desired. Serve cold. Refrigerate leftovers.

Makes 8 side-dish servings

17 PECAN–PORK SALAD WITH HONEY–BALSAMIC DRESSING

4 boneless pork chops
Salt and black pepper
2 teaspoons vegetable oil
2 cloves garlic, minced
¼ cup honey
3 tablespoons balsamic vinegar
4 cups torn iceberg lettuce, Boston lettuce or Bibb lettuce
1 cup sliced fresh strawberries
½ cup sliced celery
¼ cup chopped pecans

Heat large skillet over medium-high heat. Season chops with salt and pepper; brush with a little oil. Cook, turning occasionally to brown evenly, until chops are just done. Remove chops from skillet and reserve. Add any remaining oil to pan; quickly sauté garlic until tender, about 1 to 2 minutes, stirring constantly. Stir in honey and vinegar; cook and stir 1 minute or until heated through. In large bowl, toss together lettuce, strawberries, celery and honey mixture. Divide lettuce mixture among individual plates. Slice each pork chop and fan over salads. Sprinkle with pecans.

Makes 4 servings

Prep Time: 20 minutes

Favorite recipe from **National Pork Producers Council**

Kielbasa Tomato Salad

JUST FOR STARTERS

18 "CRAB" & CUCUMBER NOODLE SALAD

8 ounces uncooked vermicelli
3 green onions and tops
¼ pound imitation crabmeat, shredded
1 cucumber, halved, seeded and cut into julienne strips
2 tablespoons chopped fresh cilantro
2 tablespoons vegetable oil
2 tablespoons minced fresh ginger root
2 large cloves garlic, minced
3 tablespoons KIKKOMAN® Lite Soy Sauce
3 tablespoons distilled white vinegar
2 teaspoons sugar
4 teaspoons Oriental sesame oil

Cook vermicelli according to package directions, omitting salt; drain. Rinse with cold water; drain thoroughly. Separate white parts of green onions from tops; chop whites. Cut tops into thin strips. Combine vermicelli, crabmeat, cucumber, cilantro and green onion tops in large bowl. Heat oil in small skillet over medium heat. Add whites of green onions, ginger and garlic; stir-fry 1 minute. Remove pan from heat; stir in lite soy sauce, vinegar, sugar and sesame oil until sugar dissolves. Pour over vermicelli mixture and toss to combine. Cover and refrigerate 1 hour, tossing occasionally.

Makes 6 servings

19 ORIENTAL BEEF SALAD

1 pound boneless beef sirloin or top round steak, cut ¾ inch thick
¼ cup dry sherry
¼ cup reduced-sodium soy sauce
1 tablespoon cornstarch
3 tablespoons vegetable oil, divided
8 ounces mushrooms, sliced
1 package (6 ounces) frozen snow peas, thawed
4 cups thinly sliced lettuce
Crisp chow mein noodles and red bell pepper slices (optional)

Cut beef steak into ⅛-inch-thick strips; place in medium bowl. Combine sherry, soy sauce and cornstarch in small bowl; pour over beef, stirring to coat. Heat 2 tablespoons oil in large nonstick skillet over medium-high heat. Add mushrooms and snow peas; stir-fry 3 to 4 minutes. Remove vegetables; reserve. Drain marinade from beef and reserve. Add remaining 1 tablespoon oil to skillet. Stir-fry beef strips (half at a time), 1 to 2 minutes. Return vegetables, beef and reserved marinade to skillet; cook and stir until sauce thickens. Serve beef mixture over lettuce. Garnish with chow mein noodles and bell pepper slices, if desired.

Makes 4 servings

Favorite recipe from **North Dakota Beef Commission**

"Crab" & Cucumber Noodle Salad

JUST FOR STARTERS

20 CRAB CAKES CANTON

7 ounces thawed frozen cooked crabmeat
   or imitation crabmeat, drained and
   flaked
1½ cups fresh whole wheat bread crumbs
   (about 3 slices)
¼ cup thinly sliced green onions
1 clove garlic, minced
1 teaspoon minced fresh ginger
2 egg whites, lightly beaten
1 tablespoon teriyaki sauce
2 teaspoons vegetable oil, divided
   Prepared sweet and sour sauce
   (optional)

1. Combine crabmeat, bread crumbs,
onions, garlic and ginger in medium bowl;
mix well. Add egg whites and teriyaki sauce;
mix well.

2. Shape into patties about ½ inch thick and
2 inches in diameter.* Heat 1 teaspoon oil
in large nonstick skillet over medium heat
until hot.

3. Add about half of crab cakes to hot oil.
Cook 2 minutes per side or until golden
brown. Remove to warm serving plate; keep
warm. Repeat with remaining 1 teaspoon oil
and crab cakes. Serve with sweet and sour
sauce, if desired. Garnish with cherry
tomatoes and fresh herbs, if desired.

Makes 6 servings (12 cakes)

**Crab cakes may be made ahead to this point; cover
and refrigerate up to 24 hours before cooking.*

21 SOUTH–OF–THE–BORDER SAUSAGE BALLS

1 pound BOB EVANS FARMS® Original
   Recipe Roll Sausage
½ cup dry bread crumbs
¼ cup finely chopped green bell pepper
¼ cup finely chopped onion
1 egg, beaten
3 tablespoons chopped fresh cilantro
1 tablespoon ground cumin
1½ cups chunky salsa

Combine all ingredients except salsa in large
bowl until well blended. Shape into 1-inch
balls. Cook in large skillet over medium heat
until browned on all sides, turning
occasionally. Drain off any drippings. Add
salsa; bring to a boil over high heat. Reduce
heat to low; simmer 10 minutes. Serve hot.
Refrigerate leftovers.

Makes 6 appetizer servings

Crab Cakes Canton

JUST FOR STARTERS

22 SPICY QUESADILLAS

1 package (10) ORTEGA® Soft Taco Dinner
    Kit (flour tortillas, taco seasoning mix,
    taco sauce)
1 tablespoon vegetable oil
1 pound (about 4) boneless skinless
    chicken breast halves, cut into bite-
    size pieces
1 cup (1 medium) red, green or yellow
    bell pepper strips
1 cup (1 small) quartered sliced onion
¾ cup water
½ cup (4-ounce can) ORTEGA® Diced
    Green Chiles
⅓ cup chopped fresh cilantro
1 tablespoon lime juice
2 cups (8 ounces) shredded Cheddar
    cheese, divided
    Sliced avocados (optional)
    Sour cream (optional)

HEAT oil in large skillet over medium-high heat. Add chicken, bell pepper and onion; cook, stirring occasionally, 4 to 5 minutes or until chicken is no longer pink on outside. Stir in seasoning mix and water. Bring to a boil. Reduce heat to low; cook, stirring occasionally, 5 to 6 minutes or until mixture is thickened. Stir in chiles, cilantro and lime juice.

SPREAD ¾ cup chicken mixture and 3 tablespoons cheese on 1 tortilla; place another tortilla evenly over mixture. Place quesadilla in small skillet sprayed well with nonstick cooking spray. Cook over medium-high heat 2 to 3 minutes on each side or until golden brown and cheese is melted. Repeat with remaining ingredients. Cut into wedges; serve with taco sauce, avocado and sour cream, if desired. *Makes 5 servings*

23 SHANGHAI SALAD

3 tablespoons vegetable oil
1 teaspoon minced fresh ginger
1 clove garlic, minced
1½ cups cooked flank steak or other meat,
    cut into ½-inch strips
1½ cups fresh snow peas *or* 1 package
    (6 ounces) frozen snow peas, thawed
    and drained
1 can (8 ounces) sliced water chestnuts,
    drained
½ cup green onions, cut into ½-inch pieces
2 tablespoons dry sherry
1 tablespoon soy sauce
½ teaspoon TABASCO® pepper sauce
    Shredded lettuce

Heat oil in large skillet. Add ginger and garlic; cook 1 minute. Add remaining ingredients except lettuce; stir-fry over high heat until heated through. Spoon onto bed of shredded lettuce. Serve hot with additional TABASCO® sauce, if desired.
Makes 3 to 4 servings

Spicy Quesadillas

Poultry Pleasers

24 CHICKEN WITH SNOW PEAS

1½ pounds boneless skinless chicken
  breasts, cut into bite-size pieces
3 tablespoons light soy sauce
¼ cup all-purpose flour
2 tablespoons sugar
½ teaspoon ground ginger
1 clove garlic, minced
2 tablespoons vegetable oil
4 ounces shiitake or other fresh wild
  mushrooms, cleaned, stemmed and
  cut into long thin strips
1 red bell pepper, cut into 1-inch triangles
4 ounces snow peas, trimmed
1½ cups chicken broth
1 tablespoon cornstarch
¼ teaspoon black pepper
  Hot cooked rice

1. Combine chicken and soy sauce in medium bowl; cover and refrigerate 15 minutes to 1 hour.

2. Combine flour, sugar, ginger and garlic in pie plate. Drain chicken, reserving marinade. Roll chicken in flour mixture.

3. Heat oil in wok or large skillet over high heat. Add chicken; stir-fry 3 to 4 minutes or until no longer pink in center.

4. Add mushrooms; stir-fry 1 minute. Add bell pepper and snow peas; stir-fry 1 to 2 minutes or until crisp-tender.

5. Whisk together reserved marinade, chicken broth, cornstarch and black pepper in small bowl; add to chicken mixture in wok. Cook and stir until sauce boils and thickens. Transfer to serving platter. Serve with rice. Garnish with kale leaves, if desired.   *Makes 5 to 6 servings*

Chicken with Snow Peas

POULTRY PLEASERS

25 MANDARIN ORANGE CHICKEN

2 tablespoons rice vinegar
2 tablespoons light soy sauce
2 tablespoons olive oil, divided
2 teaspoons grated orange peel
1 clove garlic, minced
1 pound boneless skinless chicken breasts,
    cut into strips
2 cans (11 ounces each) mandarin
    oranges, undrained
½ cup (approximately) orange juice
2 tablespoons cornstarch
½ teaspoon red pepper flakes
1 onion, cut into thin wedges
1 small zucchini, cut into halves and
    sliced diagonally
1 small yellow squash, cut into halves and
    sliced diagonally
1 red bell pepper, cut into 1-inch triangles
1 can (3 ounces) chow mein noodles
    (optional)

1. Combine vinegar, soy sauce, 1 tablespoon oil, orange peel and garlic in medium bowl. Add chicken; toss to coat well. Cover and refrigerate 15 minutes to 1 hour.

2. Drain chicken, reserving marinade. Drain oranges, reserving liquid; set oranges aside. Combine marinade from chicken and liquid from oranges in small bowl; add enough orange juice to make 2 cups liquid. Whisk in cornstarch and red pepper flakes; set aside.

3. Heat remaining 1 tablespoon oil in wok or large skillet over high heat. Add chicken; stir-fry 2 to 3 minutes or until no longer pink in center. Remove chicken; set aside.

4. Stir-fry onion 1 minute over high heat. Add zucchini and squash; stir-fry 1 minute. Add bell pepper; stir-fry 1 minute or until all vegetables are crisp-tender. Add orange juice mixture; stir until mixture comes to a boil. Add chicken, stirring until hot. Add oranges and gently stir. Transfer to serving plate. Top with chow mein noodles, if desired.

Makes 6 servings

26 CREAMY CHICKEN BROCCOLI SKILLET

½ cup MIRACLE WHIP® Salad Dressing
1 pound boneless skinless chicken breasts,
    cubed
1 package (10 ounces) frozen chopped
    broccoli, thawed *or* 2 cups fresh
    broccoli florets
½ pound (8 ounces) VELVEETA® Process
    Cheese Spread, cut up
    Hot cooked MINUTE® Original Rice

HEAT salad dressing in large skillet over medium heat. Add chicken; cook and stir about 8 minutes or until cooked through.

STIR IN broccoli; heat thoroughly.

ADD process cheese spread. Stir until thoroughly melted. Serve over rice.

Makes 4 servings

Mandarin Orange Chicken

POULTRY PLEASERS

27 FIRST MOON CHICKEN STIR–FRY

2 tablespoons cornstarch, divided
3 tablespoons KIKKOMAN® Soy Sauce, divided
2½ teaspoons sugar, divided
1 clove garlic, pressed
2 boneless skinless chicken breast halves, cut into 1-inch squares
¾ cup water
1 teaspoon distilled white vinegar
½ pound fresh broccoli, trimmed
2 tablespoons vegetable oil, divided
1 medium onion, chunked
1 small carrot, cut diagonally into thin slices
½ teaspoon crushed red pepper
¼ pound fresh snow peas, trimmed and cut diagonally in half

Combine 1 tablespoon *each* cornstarch and soy sauce with ½ teaspoon sugar and garlic in medium bowl; stir in chicken. Let stand 15 minutes. Meanwhile, combine water, remaining 2 tablespoons soy sauce, 1 tablespoon cornstarch, 2 teaspoons sugar and vinegar in small bowl; set aside. Remove florets from broccoli; cut into bite-size pieces. Peel stalks; cut diagonally into thin slices. Heat 1 tablespoon oil in hot wok or large skillet over high heat. Add chicken and stir-fry 3 minutes; remove. Heat remaining 1 tablespoon oil in same pan. Add broccoli, onion, carrot and red pepper; stir-fry 3 minutes. Add snow peas; stir-fry 2 minutes longer. Add chicken and soy sauce mixture; cook and stir until sauce boils and thickens.

Makes 4 servings

28 MILANESE CHICKEN & RICE SKILLET

1 pound boneless skinless chicken breasts, thinly sliced
2 tablespoons olive or vegetable oil
1 cup sliced green onions
¼ cup *each:* chopped green and red bell pepper
2 to 3 cloves garlic, minced
1 teaspoon dried oregano leaves
1 can (14½ ounces) diced tomatoes, undrained
1 can (about 14 ounces) chicken broth
¼ teaspoon ground black pepper
1 cup FARMHOUSE® Natural Long Grain White Rice
½ cup small pitted ripe olives
⅓ cup frozen peas, thawed
¼ cup grated Parmesan cheese
2 tablespoons chopped fresh basil *or* 2 teaspoons dried basil leaves
2 tablespoons chopped fresh parsley *or* 2 teaspoons dried parsley flakes

In large skillet, sauté chicken in oil until no longer pink in center. Add green onions, bell pepper, garlic and oregano; stir to coat. Add tomatoes, chicken broth and black pepper; bring to a boil. Stir in rice. Cover; reduce heat and cook 20 minutes or until most of liquid is absorbed. Stir in olives, peas, cheese, basil and parsley.

Makes 4 servings (8 cups)

First Moon Chicken Stir-Fry

POULTRY PLEASERS

29 SOUTHWEST CHICKEN AND BEANS

3 tablespoons lemon juice
2 tablespoons seasoned stir-fry or hot oil, divided
2 tablespoons finely chopped onion
1 tablespoon white wine vinegar
1 clove garlic, minced
2 teaspoons chili powder
1 teaspoon salt
½ teaspoon dried oregano leaves
½ teaspoon ground cumin
½ teaspoon black pepper
1 pound boneless skinless chicken breasts or tenders, cut into ¼-inch strips
1 medium red onion, cut into thin strips
2 large red bell peppers, cut into ¼-inch strips
1 tablespoon minced cilantro
2 cans (16 ounces each) refried beans, warmed
Tortilla chips, salsa and sour cream

1. Combine lemon juice, 1 tablespoon oil, chopped onion, vinegar, garlic, chili powder, salt, oregano, cumin and black pepper in medium bowl. Add chicken; toss to coat well. Cover and refrigerate 45 minutes to 8 hours.

2. Heat remaining 1 tablespoon oil in wok or large skillet over high heat. Add chicken mixture; stir-fry 3 minutes. Add onion strips; stir-fry 4 minutes. Add bell peppers; stir-fry 2 to 3 minutes or until vegetables are crisp-tender. Sprinkle with cilantro.

3. Serve chicken and vegetable mixture over beans with tortilla chips, salsa and sour cream on the side.

Makes 4 to 5 servings

NOTE: Seasoned stir-fry oils differ in "heat." If oil is extremely peppery, use 1 tablespoon vegetable oil and 1 tablespoon hot oil.

30 BELGIOIOSO® GORGONZOLA CHICKEN

6 boneless skinless chicken breast halves
¼ teaspoon salt
⅛ teaspoon black pepper
2 tablespoons butter
1 tablespoon olive oil
½ cup chicken stock or broth
¼ cup whipping cream
¼ cup (2 ounces) creamy BELGIOIOSO® Gorgonzola Cheese
½ cup chopped walnuts (optional)
2 tablespoons chopped fresh basil

Season chicken with salt and pepper. Pound chicken to ¼-inch thickness. Melt butter with olive oil over medium-high heat in large skillet. Add chicken and cook 2 to 3 minutes on each side or until chicken is cooked through. Set aside; cover.

Add chicken stock to skillet and cook over high heat 1 minute. Reduce heat to low and gradually add cream, stirring constantly. Blend in cheese; stir until cheese is melted and sauce is smooth. Continue cooking until sauce is of desired consistency. Pour sauce over chicken. Garnish with walnuts, if desired, and basil. Serve with wild rice.

Makes 6 servings

Southwest Chicken and Beans

POULTRY PLEASERS

31 CHICKEN WITH LIME SAUCE

4 boneless skinless chicken breast halves
3 tablespoons lime juice
1 tablespoon plus 2 teaspoons seasoned stir-fry or hot oil, divided
1 teaspoon grated lime peel
1 clove garlic, minced
½ teaspoon salt
½ teaspoon black pepper
½ cup (approximately) chicken broth
1½ teaspoons cornstarch
1 tablespoon chopped onion
1 tablespoon chopped red hot chili pepper
1 tablespoon minced cilantro (optional)

1. Place each chicken piece between two sheets of plastic wrap. Pound with mallet or rolling pin to flatten to ¼-inch thickness.

2. Combine lime juice, 1 tablespoon oil, lime peel, garlic, salt and black pepper in medium bowl. Add chicken; toss to coat well. Cover and refrigerate 15 minutes to 1 hour.

3. Drain chicken, reserving marinade. Combine marinade and enough chicken broth to make ¾ cup liquid. Whisk in cornstarch; set aside.

4. Heat remaining 2 teaspoons oil in wok or large skillet over high heat. Stir-fry onion and chili pepper 1 minute; remove from wok with slotted spoon. Set aside. Cook chicken over medium-high heat 4 to 5 minutes or until lightly browned on bottom. Turn chicken and cook 4 to 5 minutes longer or until chicken is no longer pink in center. Remove chicken from wok; keep warm.

5. Combine broth mixture and onion mixture in wok. Boil sauce until thickened, scraping bottom of wok to loosen all drippings. Pour sauce over chicken; sprinkle with cilantro and garnish, if desired.

Makes 4 servings

32 CHERRY CHICKEN

1 package (about 1½ pounds) PERDUE® Fresh Skinless Split Chicken Breasts
Salt and black pepper
2 tablespoons canola oil
1 small onion, chopped (½ cup)
1 can (21 ounces) cherry pie filling
1½ cups water
¼ cup golden raisins
2 tablespoons Cognac or brandy
1 tablespoon dry sherry
1½ teaspoons Worcestershire sauce
1 tablespoon chopped parsley

Season chicken lightly with salt and pepper to taste. In large nonstick skillet, over medium-high heat, heat oil. Add chicken; cook 4 to 5 minutes on each side or until browned. Remove chicken and set aside. Add onion to skillet; sauté about 2 minutes or until slightly softened. Stir in cherry pie filling, water, raisins, Cognac, sherry and Worcestershire; bring to a boil. Return chicken to skillet; reduce heat to medium-low. Cover and simmer 15 to 20 minutes or until chicken is cooked through.

To serve, spoon cherries over chicken and sprinkle with parsley. *Makes 4 servings*

Chicken with Lime Sauce

POULTRY PLEASERS

33 CHICKEN STIR–FRY

4 boneless skinless chicken breast halves (about 1½ pounds)
2 tablespoons vegetable oil
1 tablespoon cornstarch
2 tablespoons light soy sauce
2 tablespoons orange juice
1 bag (16 ounces) BIRDS EYE® frozen Farm Fresh Mixtures Broccoli, Carrots & Water Chestnuts
Hot cooked rice (optional)

• Cut chicken into ½-inch-thick long strips.

• In wok or large skillet, heat oil over medium-high heat.

• Add chicken; cook 5 minutes, stirring occasionally.

• Meanwhile, in small bowl, combine cornstarch, soy sauce and orange juice; blend well and set aside.

• Add vegetables to chicken; cook 5 minutes more or until chicken is no longer pink in center, stirring occasionally.

• Stir in soy sauce mixture; cook 1 minute or until heated through.

• Serve over rice, if desired.

Makes 4 servings

Prep Time: 5 minutes
Cook Time: 12 minutes

34 SANTA FE STIR–FRY

1 envelope LIPTON® Recipe Secrets® Onion Soup Mix
¼ cup olive or vegetable oil
¼ cup water
1 tablespoon lime juice (optional)
½ teaspoon LAWRY'S® Garlic Powder with Parsley
1 pound boneless skinless chicken breasts, cut into thin strips
2 cups frozen assorted vegetables, partially thawed and drained
Hot cooked rice

In large skillet, blend onion soup mix, oil, water, lime juice, if desired, and garlic powder; let stand 5 minutes. Bring to a boil over high heat; stir in chicken and vegetables. Cook, uncovered, stirring frequently, 5 minutes or until chicken is done. Serve over hot rice. Garnish, if desired, with chopped fresh parsley and lime slices. *Makes about 4 servings*

TIP: Also terrific with Lipton® Recipe Secrets® Onion-Mushroom or Savory Herb with Garlic Soup Mix.

Chicken Stir-Fry

POULTRY PLEASERS

35 CHICKEN COCONUT COLOMBO

1 pound boneless skinless chicken thighs, cut into strips
½ cup chopped onion
2 tablespoons vegetable oil
1 can (14 ounces) coconut milk
1 pound butternut or acorn squash, peeled and cut into 1-inch cubes (2½ cups)
1 tablespoon curry powder
⅛ teaspoon ground cloves
1 small DOLE® Green Bell Pepper, cut into short strips
2 medium-size firm DOLE® Bananas, sliced
2 tablespoons lime juice
Hot cooked rice

• Cook and stir chicken and onion in hot oil in large skillet over medium-high heat until chicken is browned. Stir in coconut milk, squash, curry powder and cloves. Bring to a boil. Reduce heat; cover and cook 10 to 15 minutes or until squash is tender.

• Stir in bell pepper; cook 2 minutes or until pepper is crisp-tender. Stir in bananas and lime juice. Serve over rice.

Makes 6 servings

Prep Time: 20 minutes
Cook Time: 25 minutes

36 MEDITERRANEAN TURKEY AND EGGPLANT STIR–FRY

1 pound ground turkey
1 cup thinly sliced onion
2 cloves garlic, minced
1½ teaspoons dried oregano leaves
1 teaspoon dried mint leaves
¾ teaspoon salt
¼ teaspoon black pepper
4 cups eggplant cut into ½-inch cubes
1 green bell pepper, cut into ½-inch cubes
1 tablespoon olive oil
1 teaspoon sugar
1 medium tomato, peeled and cut into wedges*
2 tablespoons feta cheese, crumbled

To peel tomato, cut a skin-deep "x" in blossom end of tomato. Drop into boiling water and blanch 15 seconds. Lift out with slotted spoon and drop into bowl of ice water. Skin will slip off easily.

1. In large nonstick skillet, over medium-high heat, sauté turkey, onion, garlic, oregano, mint, salt and black pepper 5 to 6 minutes or until meat is no longer pink. Remove turkey mixture from skillet and set aside.

2. In same skillet, over medium-high heat, sauté eggplant and bell pepper in oil 4 minutes or until vegetables are crisp-tender.

3. Combine turkey mixture with vegetable mixture. Stir in sugar and tomato. Cook mixture, over medium-high heat, 4 to 5 minutes or until heated through.

4. To serve, top turkey mixture with cheese.

Makes 4 servings

*Favorite recipe from **National Turkey Federation***

POULTRY PLEASERS

37 FESTIVE SWEET & SOUR STIR–FRY

2 cans (8 ounces each) pineapple chunks or crushed pineapple, undrained
2 medium carrots, sliced
1 medium green or red bell pepper, cut into chunks
1 medium onion, cut into chunks
2 tablespoons WESSON® Vegetable Oil
1 pound boneless skinless chicken breasts, cut into 1-inch pieces
2 jars (10 ounces each) LA CHOY® Sweet & Sour Sauce
½ cup LA CHOY® Sliced Water Chestnuts
2 tablespoons LA CHOY® Soy Sauce
Hot cooked rice

Drain pineapple; reserve 2 tablespoons juice. Cook carrots, pepper and onion in hot oil in skillet until crisp-tender. Remove vegetables from skillet. Cook chicken in same skillet until browned. Add vegetables back to skillet with sweet & sour sauce, water chestnuts, soy sauce, pineapple and reserved juice. Heat through. Serve with rice.

Makes 4 servings

Mediterranean Turkey and Eggplant Stir-Fry (page 38)

POULTRY PLEASERS

38 THAI DUCK WITH BEANS AND SPROUTS

¼ cup teriyaki sauce, divided
2 tablespoons vegetable oil, divided
1 tablespoon white wine vinegar
1 clove garlic, minced
1 pound boneless skinless duck breast, cut into ¼-inch strips
1 cup chicken broth
1 tablespoon cornstarch
½ teaspoon ground ginger
3 cups fresh green beans, stemmed and cut into halves
1½ cups bean sprouts
4 green onions with tops, cut into 1-inch pieces

1. Combine 2 tablespoons teriyaki sauce, 1 tablespoon oil, vinegar and garlic in medium bowl. Add duck; toss to coat well. Cover and refrigerate 45 minutes to 8 hours.

2. Whisk together chicken broth, cornstarch and ginger in small bowl; set aside.

3. Heat remaining 1 tablespoon oil in wok or large skillet over high heat. Drain duck, discarding marinade. Add duck to wok; stir-fry 4 minutes or until no longer pink. Remove duck from wok with slotted spoon.

4. Add green beans to liquid in wok; stir-fry 5 to 6 minutes or until crisp-tender. Add bean sprouts and onions. Stir-fry 2 minutes or until all vegetables are crisp-tender. Add chicken broth mixture and duck; stir until sauce thickens.   *Makes 4 servings*

39 CHICKEN MARENGO

2 tablespoons olive or vegetable oil
2½ to 3 pounds chicken parts *or* 1½ pounds (about 6) boneless skinless chicken breast halves
1 cup (3 ounces) sliced fresh mushrooms
½ cup chopped onion
½ cup chopped green bell pepper
1 clove garlic, finely chopped
1¾ cups (14½-ounce can) CONTADINA® Dalla Casa Buitoni Recipe Ready Diced Tomatoes, undrained
⅔ cup (6-ounce can) CONTADINA® Dalla Casa Buitoni Italian Paste with Tomato Pesto
½ cup dry red wine
½ cup chicken broth
½ teaspoon salt
⅛ teaspoon ground black pepper

HEAT oil in large skillet over medium-high heat. Add chicken; cook 3 to 4 minutes on each side or until browned. Remove chicken, leaving drippings in skillet. Add mushrooms, onion, bell pepper and garlic to skillet; cook 5 minutes. Add tomatoes and juice, tomato paste, wine, chicken broth, salt and black pepper. Return chicken to skillet; bring to a boil. Reduce heat to low; cook, covered, 30 to 40 minutes or until chicken is no longer pink in center.

SERVE over hot cooked pasta or rice.
Makes 6 servings

Thai Duck with Beans and Sprouts

POULTRY PLEASERS

40 APRICOT CHICKEN ORIENTAL

2 tablespoons butter or margarine
2 whole chicken breasts, split, skinned and
    boned
12 dried apricots, finely chopped
1 jar (10 ounces) apricot preserves
1 cup water
½ cup soy sauce
1 can (8 ounces) sliced water chestnuts,
    drained and liquid reserved
1 teaspoon ground ginger
1 teaspoon garlic powder
    Apricot Rice (recipe follows)
2 cups sliced mushrooms
1 red or green bell pepper, cut into strips
3 ribs celery, diagonally sliced
1 bunch green onions, sliced
1 package (6 ounces) frozen snow peas
    Soybean sprouts for garnish

1. Melt butter in large skillet over medium heat until foamy. Add chicken to skillet in single layer; cook 10 minutes or until chicken is browned, turning once.

2. Stir in apricots, preserves, water, soy sauce, liquid from water chestnuts, ginger and garlic powder. Simmer 25 minutes or until chicken is tender.

3. Meanwhile, prepare Apricot Rice.

4. Add water chestnuts, mushrooms, bell pepper, celery, green onions and snow peas to skillet with chicken; cook and stir 5 minutes or until vegetables are heated through.

5. Place equal amounts of rice on each serving plate. Arrange chicken and vegetables over rice. Garnish, if desired.

Makes 4 servings

APRICOT RICE
2½ cups water
¼ cup finely chopped dried apricots
¼ teaspoon salt
1 cup rice

1. Combine water, apricots and salt in medium saucepan. Bring to a boil; stir in rice.

2. Cover; reduce heat and simmer 20 minutes. Remove from heat; let stand 5 minutes.

Makes 3 cups rice

41 MAPLEY MUSTARD CHICKEN

¾ cup LOG CABIN® Syrup or LOG CABIN
    LITE® Reduced Calorie Syrup
¼ cup spicy brown mustard
2 tablespoons lemon juice
1 tablespoon vegetable oil
4 boneless skinless chicken breast halves
    Hot cooked MINUTE® Original Rice

MIX syrup, mustard and lemon juice in small bowl.

HEAT oil in large skillet over medium-high heat. Add chicken; brown on both sides. Pour syrup mixture over chicken. Reduce heat to medium; cover and cook 15 minutes or until chicken is cooked through.

SERVE chicken mixture over rice.

Makes 4 servings

Prep Time: 5 minutes
Cook Time: 25 minutes

Apricot Chicken Oriental

POULTRY PLEASERS

42 GOLDEN CHICKEN AND VEGETABLES

1 boneless, skinless chicken breast half
1 teaspoon KIKKOMAN® Stir-Fry Sauce
3 tablespoons vegetable oil, divided
1 medium onion, thinly sliced
1 large clove garlic, slivered
2 carrots, cut into julienne strips
1 stalk celery, cut diagonally into thin slices
¼ cup KIKKOMAN® Stir-Fry Sauce
1 tablespoon water
1 tablespoon sesame seed, toasted
½ teaspoon Oriental sesame oil

Cut chicken into thin narrow strips; coat with 1 teaspoon stir-fry sauce in small bowl. Heat 1 tablespoon vegetable oil in hot wok or large skillet over medium-high heat. Add chicken and stir-fry 2 minutes; remove. Heat remaining 2 tablespoons oil in same pan. Add onion and garlic; stir-fry 2 minutes. Add carrots and celery; stir-fry 2 minutes longer. Combine ¼ cup stir-fry sauce and water; add to pan with chicken and sesame seed. Cook, stirring, until chicken and vegetables are coated with sauce and heated through. Remove from heat; stir in sesame oil.

Makes 4 servings

43 TOMATO, BASIL & BROCCOLI CHICKEN

4 boneless skinless chicken breast halves
Salt and black pepper (optional)
2 tablespoons margarine or butter
1 package (6.9 ounces) RICE-A-RONI® Chicken Flavor
1 teaspoon dried basil leaves
2 cups broccoli florets
1 medium tomato, seeded and chopped
1 cup (4 ounces) shredded mozzarella cheese

1. Sprinkle chicken with salt and pepper, if desired.

2. In large skillet, melt margarine over medium-high heat. Add chicken; cook 2 minutes on each side or until browned. Remove from skillet; set aside, reserving drippings. Keep warm.

3. In same skillet, sauté rice-vermicelli mix in reserved drippings over medium heat until vermicelli is golden brown. Stir in 2½ cups water, contents of seasoning packet and basil. Place chicken over rice mixture; bring to a boil over high heat.

4. Cover; reduce heat. Simmer 15 minutes. Top with broccoli and tomato.

5. Cover; continue to simmer 5 minutes or until liquid is absorbed and chicken is no longer pink in center. Sprinkle with cheese. Cover; let stand a few minutes before serving. *Makes 4 servings*

Golden Chicken and Vegetables

POULTRY PLEASERS

44 CURRIED CHICKEN CUTLETS

4 boneless skinless chicken breast halves
½ cup all-purpose flour
1 teaspoon salt
1 teaspoon ground red pepper
1 tablespoon curry powder
2 red bell peppers, cut lengthwise into
    ¼-inch-thick slices
1 teaspoon olive oil
¼ cup lemon juice
¼ cup finely chopped fresh cilantro

1. Pound chicken breasts to ¼-inch thickness between 2 pieces of plastic wrap with flat side of meat mallet or rolling pin.

2. Combine flour, salt, ground red pepper and curry powder in shallow bowl. Dip chicken cutlets in flour mixture to coat both sides well; shake off excess flour.

3. Generously spray nonstick skillet with nonstick cooking spray; heat over medium heat. Add 2 chicken cutlets; cook 3 to 4 minutes per side. Transfer to warm plate; cover and set aside. Repeat with remaining chicken.

4. Add bell peppers and olive oil to skillet; cook and stir 5 minutes or until peppers are tender. Stir in lemon juice and cilantro; heat through. Pour sauce over chicken cutlets. Garnish with kale and fresh marjoram, if desired.   *Makes 4 servings*

45 TURKEY AND MUSHROOM SCALOPPINE

1 package (about 1 pound) PERDUE®
    FIT 'N EASY® Fresh Skinless &
    Boneless Thin-Sliced Turkey Breast
    Cutlets
  Salt and black pepper to taste
1 tablespoon vegetable oil
¼ pound cultivated wild mushrooms
    (cremini or shiitake) or white
    mushrooms, thinly sliced
1 tablespoon minced fresh chives or green
    onion tops
¼ cup Marsala or sweet vermouth
1 tablespoon reduced-calorie (stick)
    margarine (optional)
  Hot cooked noodles (optional)

Place cutlets between pieces of plastic wrap. With meat mallet or heavy skillet, pound to ⅛-inch thickness. Season with salt and pepper. In large nonstick skillet over medium heat, heat oil. Add cutlets; sauté about 30 seconds on each side or until cooked through. Remove cutlets to serving platter and keep warm.

Add mushrooms and chives to skillet; sauté 1 minute. Stir in Marsala; cook about 1 minute or until reduced to about 3 tablespoons. Remove from heat and stir in margarine, if desired. To serve, spoon mushrooms and pan sauce over cutlets and serve with noodles, if desired.
                    Makes 4 servings

Curried Chicken Cutlets

POULTRY PLEASERS

46 CHICKEN CHERRY-YAKI STIR-FRY

1 small piece (¾ inch long) fresh ginger, peeled
2 whole chicken breasts, split, skinned and boned
2 tablespoons teriyaki sauce
2 tablespoons dry sherry
1 tablespoon lemon juice
4 green onions for garnish
6 to 8 ice cubes
1½ cups tart red cherries, pitted (frozen or canned)
2 ounces Chinese rice stick noodles
Peanut or vegetable oil
1 tablespoon cornstarch
6 green onions, diagonally sliced into 1-inch pieces
2 small carrots, thinly sliced
2 cups snow peas
4 ounces sliced water chestnuts, drained
¼ cup slivered almonds, toasted

1. Cut ginger into 3 equal pieces; set aside.

2. Cut chicken into bite-size pieces; set aside.

3. Combine ginger pieces, teriyaki sauce, sherry and lemon juice in medium bowl. Add chicken, turning to coat with marinade. Cover; marinate in refrigerator 1 hour.

4. Meanwhile, to prepare green onion brushes, trim off stems (green part) of 4 onions to make 4-inch lengths. Cut each onion lengthwise into very thin strips, leaving one end uncut. Fill large bowl about half full with cold water. Add prepared green onions and ice cubes. Refrigerate until onions curl, about 1 hour; drain.

5. Thaw cherries, if frozen, in medium bowl. Drain cherries, reserving juice; set aside.

6. To prepare rice stick noodles, cut noodle bundles in half; gently pull each half apart into smaller bunches. Heat 3 inches oil in wok or large skillet over medium-high heat until deep-fry thermometer registers 375°F. Using tongs or slotted spoon, lower 1 bunch of noodles into hot oil. Cook until noodles rise to the top, 3 to 5 seconds. Remove noodles immediately to paper towels using slotted spoon; drain. Repeat with remaining bunches. Keep noodles warm until ready to serve. Drain and discard oil.

7. Drain chicken, reserving marinade. Discard ginger pieces. Blend reserved cherry juice into cornstarch in cup until smooth. Stir in reserved marinade; set aside.

8. Reheat wok over high heat. Add 2 tablespoons oil to wok, swirling to coat side. Heat oil until hot, about 30 seconds. Add chicken to wok; briskly toss and stir 2 to 3 minutes or until chicken is no longer pink in center. Remove chicken from wok; set aside.

9. Reheat wok over high heat. Add 2 tablespoons oil to wok, swirling to coat side. Heat oil until hot, about 30 seconds.

10. Add sliced green onions, carrots and snow peas to wok; briskly toss and stir 2 to 3 minutes or until vegetables are crisp-tender, adding more oil to wok if needed.

11. Stir chicken into vegetables in wok until well combined. Push chicken-vegetable mixture to side of wok; add cornstarch mixture. Cook and stir until mixture comes to a boil and thickens. Stir in cherries and water chestnuts; heat through.

12. Serve chicken-vegetable mixture over rice stick noodles. Sprinkle with almonds. Garnish with green onion brushes.

Makes 4 servings

POULTRY PLEASERS

47 ANYTIME STIR–FRY

2 tablespoons olive or vegetable oil, divided
1 pound boneless skinless chicken breasts or boneless beef sirloin or pork tenderloin, cut into ¼-inch slices
6 cups assorted fresh vegetables*
1 envelope LIPTON® Recipe Secrets® Onion Soup Mix
1¼ cups water
½ teaspoon garlic powder

*Use any of the following: broccoli florets, snow peas, thinly sliced red or green bell peppers or thinly sliced carrots.

In large skillet, heat 1 tablespoon oil over medium-high heat and brown chicken. Remove and set aside. In same skillet, heat remaining 1 tablespoon oil and cook vegetables, stirring occasionally, 5 minutes. Stir in onion soup mix blended with water and garlic powder. Bring to a boil over high heat. Reduce heat to low and simmer, uncovered, 3 minutes. Return chicken to skillet and cook 1 minute or until heated through. Serve over hot cooked rice, if desired.   *Makes about 4 servings*

Chicken Cherry-Yaki Stir-Fry (page 48)

POULTRY PLEASERS

48 CHICKEN PICCATA

1 package GALIL® Chicken Breast Cutlets
   (1½ to 1¾ pounds)
¼ cup all-purpose flour
½ cup parve bread crumbs
½ teaspoon dried basil leaves
¼ teaspoon salt
¼ teaspoon freshly ground black pepper
1 egg, beaten
3 tablespoons olive oil
¼ cup kosher dry white wine
2 tablespoons fresh lemon juice
   Lemon slices for garnish

Cut chicken breasts into halves. Place chicken breast halves between 2 pieces of plastic wrap; pound to ½-inch thickness. Place flour on small plate. Combine bread crumbs, basil, salt and pepper on another small plate. Roll each breast half in flour, then in egg. Coat with bread crumb mixture.

Heat oil in medium nonstick skillet over medium-high heat. Add chicken; cook 4 minutes. Turn; reduce heat to medium. Cook 4 to 5 minutes or until chicken is no longer pink in center. Transfer chicken to serving platter; keep warm. Add wine and lemon juice to skillet; cook and stir over high heat 2 minutes. Spoon sauce over chicken. Garnish with lemon slices, if desired. *Makes 4 servings*

49 LUSCIOUS LEMON CHICKEN

⅓ cup all-purpose flour
1 teaspoon DURKEE® Tarragon
1 teaspoon DURKEE® Garlic Powder
4 chicken breast halves, skinned and
   boned
   Vegetable oil
1 can (10¾ ounces) condensed chicken
   broth
¼ cup fresh lemon juice
1 tablespoon sugar
1 tablespoon drained capers

Combine flour, tarragon and garlic powder in small bowl. Coat chicken with 3 tablespoons flour mixture. In large oiled skillet, brown chicken on both sides over medium heat. Combine remaining flour mixture with chicken broth; stir until blended. Add to skillet with lemon juice, sugar and capers; cook, stirring occasionally until thickened. *Makes 4 servings*

Prep Time: 5 minutes
Cook Time: 20 minutes

HINT: Serve with hot fettuccine noodles.

Chicken Piccata

POULTRY PLEASERS

50 CHICKEN PICANTE

Juice from 1 lime
½ cup medium-hot chunky taco sauce
¼ cup Dijon mustard
3 whole chicken breasts, split, skinned and boned
2 tablespoons butter
Plain yogurt
Chopped fresh cilantro and lime slices for garnish

1. Combine lime juice, taco sauce and mustard in large bowl. Add chicken, turning to coat with marinade. Cover; marinate in refrigerator at least 30 minutes.

2. Melt butter in large skillet over medium heat until foamy.

3. Drain chicken, reserving marinade. Add chicken to skillet in single layer. Cook 10 minutes or until chicken is lightly browned on both sides.

4. Add reserved marinade to skillet; cook 5 minutes or until chicken is tender and glazed with marinade.

5. Remove chicken to serving platter; keep warm.

6. Boil marinade in skillet over high heat 1 minute; pour over chicken. Serve with yogurt. Garnish, if desired.

Makes 6 servings

51 ALMOND TURKEY STIR–FRY

3 tablespoons soy sauce
2 tablespoons cornstarch
¾ cup chicken broth
1 clove garlic, minced or pressed
1½ teaspoons sugar
Dash black pepper
Vegetable oil
1 cup BLUE DIAMOND® whole natural almonds
1½ cups diagonally sliced celery
1½ cups fresh asparagus cut into 1-inch diagonal slices
1½ cups thinly sliced mushrooms (about ⅓ pound)
2 cups cooked turkey cut into 1-inch strips

In small bowl, thoroughly mix soy sauce and cornstarch; blend in chicken broth, garlic, sugar and pepper. Set aside. Heat 1 tablespoon oil in large skillet or wok over medium-high heat; sauté almonds 2 to 4 minutes or until crisp, stirring often. Remove with slotted spoon and drain on paper towel. Add celery to skillet; stir-fry 2 minutes. Add asparagus and continue cooking 2 minutes longer, adding more oil if necessary. Add mushrooms and stir-fry 1 minute longer or until vegetables are crisp-tender. Add almonds, turkey and soy sauce mixture to skillet; stir until sauce comes to a boil. Serve immediately. *Makes 4 servings*

Chicken Picante

52 STIR–FRIED TURKEY WITH BROCCOLI

1 lemon
1 teaspoon dried thyme leaves
½ teaspoon salt
¼ teaspoon ground white pepper
1 pound turkey cutlets
1 pound fresh broccoli
1 cup chicken broth
1 tablespoon cornstarch
3 tablespoons vegetable oil, divided
1 tablespoon butter
¼ pound fresh button mushrooms, sliced
1 medium red onion, peeled, sliced and
    separated into rings
1 can (14 ounces) pre-cut baby corn,
    rinsed and drained*
Hot cooked rice
Lemon slices for garnish (optional)

Or substitute 1 (15-ounce) can whole baby corn, cut into 1-inch lengths.

1. Finely grate peel of lemon into large bowl. Cut lemon crosswise in half; squeeze with reamer or juicer to extract juice. Measure 2 tablespoons lemon juice. Add juice, thyme, salt and pepper to lemon peel; stir.

2. Cut turkey cutlets into 2½×1-inch strips. Add turkey to lemon mixture; coat well. Marinate 30 minutes.

3. To prepare broccoli, trim leaves from stalks; trim off tough ends. Cut broccoli tops into florets. Peel stems, then diagonally slice stems into 2-inch pieces; set aside.

4. Combine chicken broth and cornstarch in cup; set aside.

5. Place 4 cups water in wok; bring to a boil over medium-high heat. Add broccoli stems; cook 1 minute. Add florets; cook 2 minutes more or until crisp-tender. Drain and rinse with cold water; set aside.

6. Heat wok over medium-high heat until hot. Add 1 tablespoon oil and butter; heat until hot. Add mushrooms; cook and stir 2 minutes or until mushrooms are wilted. Add onion; stir-fry 2 minutes. Remove to large bowl.

7. Heat 1 tablespoon oil in wok. Fry ½ of turkey strips in single layer 1½ minutes or until well browned on all sides. Transfer to bowl with mushrooms. Repeat with remaining 1 tablespoon oil and turkey.

8. Add baby corn to wok and heat 1 minute. Stir cornstarch mixture; add to wok and cook until bubbly. Add turkey, broccoli, mushrooms and onion to wok; cook and stir until heated through. Serve over rice. Garnish, if desired.

Makes 4 to 6 servings

53 TURKEY CUTLETS DIANE

1 package (about 1 pound) PERDUE®
    FIT 'N EASY® Fresh Skinless &
    Boneless Thin-Sliced Turkey Breast
    Cutlets
Salt and black pepper to taste
2 tablespoons butter or margarine
2 tablespoons minced shallots
½ cup chicken broth or water
1 tablespoon Worcestershire sauce
1 teaspoon Dijon mustard

Season cutlets with salt and pepper. In large heavy skillet over medium-high heat, melt butter. Add shallots; sauté 1 minute. Add cutlets; sauté 1 to 2 minutes on each side or until lightly browned. Stir in remaining ingredients; cook 1 minute longer. Serve cutlets accompanied by pan sauce.

Makes 4 servings

Stir-Fried Turkey with Broccoli

POULTRY PLEASERS

54 CHICKEN WITH ORANGE AND BASIL

Nonstick cooking spray
4 boneless skinless chicken breast halves
  (1½ pounds)
¾ cup fresh orange juice
½ cup dry white wine
2 tablespoons grated orange peel
½ cup sliced red onion
1 can (6 ounces) mandarin oranges,
  drained
¼ cup sliced fresh basil leaves *or*
  2 teaspoons dried basil leaves
  Crumbled blue cheese (optional)

SPRAY large skillet with cooking spray; heat over medium-high heat. Add chicken; cook 7 to 8 minutes on each side or until chicken is no longer pink in center. Transfer to serving plate; keep warm.

COMBINE orange juice, wine and orange peel in same skillet; bring to a boil. Boil 5 minutes. Stir in onion; cook and stir about 5 minutes more or until onion is tender and sauce is reduced to about ¼ cup. Reduce heat; stir in oranges and basil. Spoon sauce over chicken; sprinkle with blue cheese, if desired.   *Makes 4 servings*

SERVING SUGGESTION: Serve with a mixed green salad and sourdough rolls.

55 LIGHTLY LEMON CHICKEN

¾ cup fine dry bread crumbs
1 tablespoon chopped parsley
2 whole boneless chicken breasts, split
  and pounded (about 1 pound)
¼ cup EGG BEATERS® Healthy Real Egg
  Product
1 clove garlic, crushed
3 tablespoons FLEISCHMANN'S®
  Margarine
1 lemon
¼ cup COLLEGE INN® Lower Sodium
  Chicken Broth

Mix bread crumbs and parsley. Dip chicken pieces into egg product, then coat with bread crumb mixture.

In skillet, over medium-high heat, cook garlic in margarine 1 minute. Add chicken and brown on both sides. Cut half the lemon into thin slices; arrange over chicken. Squeeze juice from remaining lemon half into chicken broth; pour into skillet. Heat to a boil; reduce heat. Cover and simmer 10 minutes or until chicken is tender.
                              Makes 4 servings

Chicken with Orange and Basil

POULTRY PLEASERS

56 CHICKEN BREASTS WITH SAVORY MUSTARD HERB SAUCE

2 tablespoons olive or vegetable oil, divided
1 pound boneless skinless chicken breast halves
1 medium zucchini, sliced
1½ cups sliced fresh or drained canned mushrooms
1 envelope LIPTON® Recipe Secrets® Savory Herb with Garlic or Golden Onion Soup Mix
¾ cup water
2 teaspoons Dijon, country Dijon or brown mustard

• In large skillet, heat 1 tablespoon oil over medium-high heat and cook chicken 5 minutes or until almost done, turning once; remove and keep warm.

• In same skillet, heat remaining 1 tablespoon oil over medium heat and cook zucchini and mushrooms, stirring frequently, 3 minutes. Return chicken to skillet; stir in Savory Herb with Garlic Soup Mix blended with water and mustard. Bring to a boil over high heat. Reduce heat to low and simmer, covered, 5 minutes or until chicken is no longer pink.

• To serve, arrange chicken on serving platter and top with sauce mixture.

Makes 4 servings

57 SZECHUAN STIR-FRY

1½ tablespoons peanut oil
½ teaspoon sesame oil (optional)
¼ to ½ teaspoon chili paste with garlic (optional)
1 cup broccoli florets
1 cup red bell pepper pieces (cut into 1-inch squares)
⅓ cup thinly sliced green onions
1 package (about 1 pound) PERDUE® Fresh Hot & Spicy Chicken Wings
2 tablespoons soy sauce
Hot cooked rice

In wok or large skillet, over medium-high heat, heat oils and chili paste, if desired. Add broccoli; stir-fry 2 minutes. Add bell pepper and onions; cook 1 to 2 minutes longer, stirring constantly. Add wings and soy sauce. Stir-fry 2 minutes or until wings are heated through. Serve over rice.

Makes 4 to 6 servings

58 LETTUCE WRAP

1½ tablespoons LEE KUM KEE® Hoisin Sauce
1 tablespoon LEE KUM KEE® Oyster Flavored Sauce
1 tablespoon vegetable oil
3 ounces diced onion
½ pound ground chicken or turkey
⅔ cup diced cucumber
Large lettuce leaves
Additional LEE KUM KEE® Hoisin Sauce

Combine 1½ tablespoons Hoisin Sauce and Oyster Sauce in small bowl; set aside. Heat skillet over medium heat. Add oil. Sauté onion. Add chicken, cucumber and sauce mixture. Heat through. To serve, wrap chicken mixture in lettuce leaves. Serve with additional Hoisin Sauce for dipping.

Makes 4 servings

POULTRY PLEASERS

59 GOLDEN APPLE TURKEY SAUTÉ

½ pound boneless turkey or lean pork
1 to 2 tablespoons vegetable oil, divided
1 medium green bell pepper, sliced lengthwise into thin strips
1 medium onion, sliced lengthwise into thin strips
1 Golden Delicious apple, cored and thinly sliced
3 tablespoons vinegar
2 tablespoons sugar
1 tablespoon cornstarch
2 teaspoons soy sauce
½ teaspoon salt
Dash black pepper

Remove skin from turkey; cut into 2½×½-inch strips. In large skillet, heat 1 tablespoon oil. Add turkey; cook and stir until no longer pink in center. Remove from pan. Add remaining 1 tablespoon oil to skillet, if necessary; cook and stir bell pepper and onion until crisp-tender. Return turkey to skillet; add apple and heat thoroughly. Combine remaining ingredients in small bowl. Add to turkey mixture; cook and stir until sauce thickens.

Makes 3 to 4 servings

Favorite recipe from **Washington Apple Commission**

60 CHICKEN WITH GRAPE MUSTARD CREAM

½ cup sliced mushrooms
2 tablespoons minced onion
2 tablespoons butter or margarine
1 pound boneless skinless chicken breasts
½ cup dry white wine
¼ cup heavy cream
1 tablespoon Dijon mustard
1 teaspoon dried marjoram leaves
Salt and black pepper to taste
1½ cups halved California seedless grapes
Grape clusters
Fresh marjoram leaves

Sauté mushrooms and onion in butter in nonstick skillet until tender. Place chicken breasts on top of mushroom mixture; cover and cook over medium heat 7 minutes or until surface turns white. Turn chicken and drizzle with wine. Simmer, covered, about 7 minutes or until chicken is cooked and juices run clear. Slice chicken diagonally and place on serving platter; keep warm. Add cream, mustard and seasonings to pan drippings. Cook until liquid is reduced and slightly thickened. Add halved grapes; heat thoroughly. Pour over chicken. Garnish with grape clusters and fresh marjoram.

Makes 4 servings

TIP: Serve with fresh green beans.

Favorite recipe from **California Table Grape Commission**

Chicken with Walnuts

61 CHICKEN WITH WALNUTS

1 cup uncooked instant rice
½ cup chicken broth
¼ cup Chinese plum sauce
2 tablespoons soy sauce
2 teaspoons cornstarch
2 tablespoons vegetable oil, divided
3 cups frozen bell peppers and onions
1 pound boneless skinless chicken breasts, cut into ¼-inch slices
1 clove garlic, minced
1 cup walnut halves

1. Cook rice according to package directions. Set aside.

2. Combine chicken broth, plum sauce, soy sauce and cornstarch in small bowl; set aside.

3. Heat 1 tablespoon oil in wok or large skillet over medium-high heat until hot. Add frozen peppers and onions; stir-fry 3 minutes or until crisp-tender. Remove vegetables from wok. Drain; discard liquid.

4. Heat remaining 1 tablespoon oil in wok until hot. Add chicken and garlic; stir-fry 3 minutes or until chicken is no longer pink in center.

5. Stir broth mixture; add to wok. Cook and stir 1 minute or until sauce thickens. Stir in vegetables and walnuts; cook 1 minute more. Serve with rice. *Makes 4 servings*

POULTRY PLEASERS

62 MANDARIN CASHEW CHICKEN

SAUCE
 1/2 cup syrup, reserved from mandarin
    oranges (see below)
 1/4 cup chicken broth
 2 tablespoons sugar
 1 1/2 tablespoons LA CHOY® Soy Sauce
 1 1/2 tablespoons cornstarch
 1 teaspoon rice vinegar

CHICKEN AND VEGETABLES
 1 tablespoon LA CHOY® Soy Sauce
 1 tablespoon cornstarch
 1 1/2 pounds boneless skinless chicken
    breasts, cut into thin 2-inch strips
 4 tablespoons WESSON® Oil, divided
 2 cups fresh broccoli florets
 1 teaspoon *each:* minced fresh garlic and
    ginger
 1 (8-ounce) can LA CHOY® Sliced Water
    Chestnuts, drained
 4 green onions, diagonally sliced
 1 (11-ounce) can mandarin orange slices,
    syrup drained and reserved for sauce
 1 cup roasted cashews

In small bowl, combine *sauce* ingredients;
set aside. In medium bowl, combine soy
sauce and cornstarch; mix well. Add
chicken; toss gently to coat. In large
nonstick skillet or wok, heat *3 tablespoons*
oil. Add half of chicken mixture; stir-fry until
chicken is no longer pink in center. Remove
chicken from skillet; set aside. Repeat with
remaining chicken mixture. Heat *remaining
1 tablespoon* oil in same skillet. Add
broccoli, garlic and ginger; stir-fry 2 minutes.
Stir sauce; add to skillet with water
chestnuts and green onions. Cook, stirring
constantly, until sauce is thick and bubbly.
Return chicken to skillet with orange slices
and cashews; heat thoroughly, stirring
occasionally.   *Makes 6 servings*

63 CHICKEN CACCIATORE

 1 pound boneless chicken breasts, cut into
    strips
 1 bag (16 ounces) BIRDS EYE® frozen
    Farm Fresh Mixtures Broccoli,
    Cauliflower and Carrots
 1 jar (14 ounces) prepared spaghetti sauce
 1/2 cup sliced black olives
 1/4 cup water
 1/4 cup grated Parmesan cheese

• Spray large skillet with nonstick cooking
spray; cook chicken over medium heat 7 to
10 minutes or until browned, stirring
occasionally.

• Add vegetables, spaghetti sauce, olives and
water. Cover and cook 10 to 15 minutes or
until vegetables are heated through.

• Sprinkle cheese over top before serving.
Add salt, pepper and garlic powder to taste.
                    Makes 4 to 6 servings

Prep Time: 5 to 10 minutes
Cook Time: 20 to 25 minutes

POULTRY PLEASERS

64 CHICKEN WITH LYCHEES

3 whole boneless skinless chicken breasts
¼ cup plus 1 teaspoon cornstarch, divided
½ cup tomato sauce
1 teaspoon sugar
1 teaspoon chicken bouillon granules
3 tablespoons vegetable oil
6 green onions with tops, cut into 1-inch pieces
1 red bell pepper, cut into 1-inch pieces
1 can (11 ounces) whole peeled lychees, drained
Hot cooked vermicelli (optional)
Fresh cilantro leaves for garnish

1. Cut chicken breasts in half; cut each half into six pieces.

2. Place ¼ cup cornstarch in large resealable plastic food storage bag. Add chicken pieces; close bag tightly. Shake bag until chicken is well coated; set aside.

3. Combine remaining 1 teaspoon cornstarch and ¼ cup water in small cup; mix well. Set aside.

4. Combine ¼ cup water, tomato sauce, sugar and bouillon granules in small bowl; mix well. Set aside.

5. Heat oil in wok or large skillet over high heat. Add chicken; stir-fry until lightly browned, 5 to 8 minutes. Add onions and bell pepper; stir-fry 1 minute.

6. Pour tomato sauce mixture over chicken mixture. Stir in lychees. Reduce heat to low; cover. Simmer until chicken is tender and no longer pink in center, about 5 minutes.

7. Stir cornstarch mixture; add to wok. Cook and stir until sauce boils and thickens. Serve over hot vermicelli and garnish, if desired.

Makes 4 servings

65 SPICY CHICKEN

¾ pound boneless chicken
3 tablespoons KIKKOMAN® Soy Sauce, divided
1 tablespoon cornstarch
1 tablespoon dry sherry
4 teaspoons water
2 tablespoons vegetable oil
1 teaspoon minced fresh ginger root
¾ teaspoon crushed red pepper
1 small onion, chunked
1 small red or green bell pepper, cut into matchsticks
1 small zucchini, cut into matchsticks
½ cup water

Cut chicken into thin slices. Combine chicken and 1 tablespoon soy sauce in bowl; let stand 30 minutes. Meanwhile, combine remaining 2 tablespoons soy sauce, cornstarch, sherry and 4 teaspoons water. Heat oil in hot wok or large skillet over high heat. Add ginger and crushed red pepper; cook until fragrant. Add chicken and stir-fry 3 minutes. Add onion, bell pepper, zucchini and ½ cup water; mix well. Cover and cook 1 minute, or until vegetables are tender-crisp. Add soy sauce mixture; cook and stir until sauce boils and thickens.

Makes 4 servings

Chicken with Lychees

POULTRY PLEASERS

66 CHICKEN–CUCUMBER STIR FRY

2 whole broiler-fryer chicken breasts, cut into halves, boned, skinned and cut into bite-size pieces
¼ cup water
¼ cup dry sherry
¼ cup soy sauce
2 tablespoons dark corn syrup
4 teaspoons cornstarch
1 tablespoon vinegar
¼ teaspoon red pepper flakes
⅛ teaspoon ground ginger
3 tablespoons vegetable oil
½ pound fresh mushrooms, sliced
1 bunch green onions, cut into 2-inch pieces
1 can (8 ounces) water chestnuts, drained and sliced
2 cloves garlic, minced
1 cucumber, cut into halves lengthwise, seeded and cut into thin 2-inch strips
12 cherry tomatoes, cut into halves

In medium bowl, mix together water, sherry, soy sauce, corn syrup, cornstarch, vinegar, pepper and ginger; set aside. Heat oil in wok or large skillet over medium-high heat. Add chicken; stir-fry 3 to 4 minutes or until chicken is lightly browned. Add mushrooms, onions, water chestnuts and garlic; stir-fry 3 minutes. Add cucumber and stir-fry about 1 minute or until vegetables are crisp-tender. Add soy sauce mixture and cook, stirring, until sauce thickens. Add tomatoes and heat through. *Makes 4 servings*

*Favorite recipe from **Delmarva Poultry Industry, Inc.***

67 STIR–FRIED CHICKEN WITH BLACK PEPPER SAUCE

½ cup LEE KUM KEE® Black Pepper Sauce, divided
2 teaspoons cornstarch
¾ pound boneless chicken, diced
2 tablespoons vegetable oil
¼ pound onion, diced
2 ounces red bell pepper, diced
¼ pound pineapple chunks

1. Combine ¼ cup Black Pepper Sauce and cornstarch in large bowl; add chicken. Marinate chicken 5 minutes.

2. Heat oil in wok over high heat. Add onion and cook until fragrant. Add chicken and stir-fry 2 minutes.

3. Add bell pepper, pineapple and remaining ¼ cup Black Pepper Sauce; cook until heated through. *Makes 4 to 6 servings*

68 HERBED CHICKEN WITH GRAPES

4 boneless skinless chicken breast halves (about 1 pound)
1 jar (12 ounces) HEINZ® Fat Free Chicken Gravy
½ teaspoon lemon juice
¼ teaspoon dried rosemary
¼ teaspoon dried thyme leaves
½ cup halved seedless grapes

Spray skillet with nonstick cooking spray. In skillet, brown chicken on both sides. Stir in gravy, lemon juice, rosemary and thyme. Simmer, covered, 10 minutes, stirring occasionally. Stir in grapes; heat through.

Makes 4 servings
(about 1½ cups sauce)

Chicken Provençale

69 CHICKEN PROVENÇALE

1 tablespoon olive oil
2 pounds skinless chicken thighs
½ cup sliced green bell pepper
½ cup sliced onion
2 cloves garlic, minced
1 pound eggplant, peeled and cut into ¼-inch-thick slices
2 medium tomatoes, cut into ¼-inch-thick slices
¼ cup chopped fresh parsley *or* 2 teaspoons dried parsley
¼ cup chopped fresh basil *or* 2 teaspoons dried basil leaves
1 teaspoon salt
1 cup reduced-sodium chicken broth
½ cup dry white wine
  Fresh parsley sprigs for garnish

HEAT oil in large skillet over medium-high heat until hot. Add chicken; cook 2 to 3 minutes on each side or until browned. Remove chicken from skillet.

ADD bell pepper, onion and garlic to same skillet; cook and stir 3 to 4 minutes or until onion is tender.

RETURN chicken to skillet. Arrange eggplant and tomato slices over chicken. Sprinkle with parsley, basil and salt. Add chicken broth and wine; bring to a boil. Reduce heat; cover and simmer 45 to 50 minutes or until chicken is no longer pink in center and juices run clear. Garnish with parsley sprigs, if desired.

Makes 6 servings

POULTRY PLEASERS

70 CHICKEN CORN SAUTÉ

1 tablespoon chili powder
½ teaspoon salt
4 boneless skinless chicken breast halves,
    cut into bite-size pieces (about
    1 pound)
2 tablespoons CRISCO® Vegetable Oil,
    divided
1 cup chopped onion
2 medium green bell peppers, cut into
    strips
1 medium red bell pepper, cut into strips
1 package (10 ounces) frozen whole
    kernel corn, thawed
    Hot pepper sauce (optional)

1. Combine chili powder and salt in shallow dish. Add chicken. Turn to coat.

2. Heat 1 tablespoon Crisco® Oil in large skillet over medium-high heat. Add chicken. Cook and stir until no longer pink in center. Remove to serving dish.

3. Heat remaining 1 tablespoon Crisco® Oil in skillet. Add onion. Cook and stir 2 minutes or until tender. Add bell peppers. Cook and stir 3 to 4 minutes or until crisp-tender. Add corn. Heat thoroughly, stirring occasionally. Return chicken to skillet to reheat. Season with pepper sauce, if desired.

Makes 6 servings

71 CHICKEN & FRESH GRAPEFRUIT STIR–FRY

1 SUNKIST® grapefruit
1 can (8 ounces) pineapple chunks in
    unsweetened pineapple juice,
    undrained
1 tablespoon cornstarch
1 teaspoon reduced-sodium soy sauce
2 boneless skinless chicken breast halves
    (about ½ pound)
1 medium clove garlic, minced
½ tablespoon vegetable oil
¼ pound snow peas, trimmed
2 green onions, sliced diagonally

Peel and section grapefruit over bowl; reserve juice. Drain pineapple well, reserving juice. Combine juices and add enough water to equal 1 cup liquid. Combine with cornstarch and soy sauce. Rinse chicken breast halves and pat dry; remove any excess fat. Cut across grain into thin strips. In large nonstick skillet sprayed with nonstick cooking spray, stir-fry chicken with garlic in oil over medium-high heat 5 minutes or until lightly brown. Add snow peas and cornstarch mixture; cook, stirring, until thickened. Add grapefruit, pineapple and onions; heat through. *Makes 4 (1-cup) servings*

Chicken Corn Sauté

POULTRY PLEASERS

72 SAUCY–SPICY TURKEY MEATBALLS

1 pound ground turkey
⅓ cup bread crumbs
1 egg
1 clove garlic, minced
2 tablespoons light soy sauce, divided
1 teaspoon grated fresh ginger
¾ to 1 teaspoon red pepper flakes, divided
1 tablespoon vegetable oil
1 can (20 ounces) pineapple chunks, undrained
2 tablespoons lemon juice or orange juice
2 tablespoons honey
1 tablespoon cornstarch
1 large red bell pepper, seeded and cut into 1-inch triangles
Hot cooked rice

1. Combine turkey, bread crumbs, egg, garlic, 1 tablespoon soy sauce, ginger and ½ teaspoon red pepper flakes in large bowl. Shape turkey mixture into 1-inch meatballs.

2. Heat oil in wok or large skillet over medium-high heat. Add meatballs and cook 4 to 5 minutes or until no longer pink in centers, turning to brown all sides. Remove from wok.

3. Drain pineapple, reserving juice. Add enough water to juice to make 1 cup liquid. Whisk together pineapple juice mixture, lemon juice, honey, cornstarch, remaining 1 tablespoon soy sauce and ¼ teaspoon red pepper flakes. Pour into wok. Cook and stir until sauce thickens.

4. Add meatballs, pineapple and bell pepper to sauce. Cook and stir until hot. Adjust seasoning with remaining ¼ teaspoon hot pepper flakes, if desired. Serve over rice.

Makes 4 to 5 servings

73 CHICKEN DIJON WITH WHITE WINE

2 tablespoons olive oil
6 boneless skinless chicken breast halves
Salt and black pepper to taste
1 medium onion, chopped
1 cup sliced mushrooms
2 cloves garlic, minced
1 container (6½ ounces) ALOUETTE® Garlic et Herbes
½ cup chicken broth
¼ cup white wine
1 tablespoon Dijon mustard
Fresh parsley, chopped

• Heat oil in large skillet over medium heat.

• Season chicken breasts with salt and pepper. Add to skillet; brown 10 minutes on each side, adding onion, mushrooms and garlic to skillet while chicken is browning on second side.

• In small bowl, mix Alouette® with chicken broth, wine and mustard.

• Pour Alouette® mixture over chicken and simmer 10 to 15 minutes.

• Sprinkle with parsley.

Makes 6 servings

NOTE: Any extra sauce may be served over potatoes, rice or pasta.

Saucy-Spicy Turkey Meatballs

POULTRY PLEASERS

74 SZECHUAN CHICKEN TENDERS

2 tablespoons soy sauce
1 tablespoon chili sauce
1 tablespoon dry sherry
2 cloves garlic, minced
¼ teaspoon red pepper flakes
16 chicken tenders (about 1 pound)
1 tablespoon peanut oil
Hot cooked rice

COMBINE soy sauce, chili sauce, sherry, garlic and pepper in shallow dish. Add chicken; coat well. Heat oil in large nonstick skillet over medium heat until hot. Add chicken; cook 6 minutes, turning once, or until chicken is browned and no longer pink in center. Serve chicken with rice.

Makes 4 servings

75 GINGER HOT THIGHS

2 tablespoons olive oil
1 package (about 1¾ pounds) PERDUE® Fresh Skinless Chicken Thighs
1 onion, finely chopped
4 cloves garlic, minced
¼ cup red wine
1 tablespoon grated peeled fresh ginger
1½ teaspoons ground cumin
½ teaspoon chili powder
1 tablespoon minced fresh parsley

In large nonstick skillet over medium heat, heat oil. Add chicken; cook 7 to 8 minutes on each side or until browned. In small bowl, combine onion, garlic, wine, ginger, cumin and chili powder. Add mixture to skillet; partially cover and reduce heat to medium-low. Cook about 20 to 30 minutes or until chicken is fork-tender and liquid has been reduced to a glaze. To serve, sprinkle with parsley. *Makes 3 to 4 servings*

76 YUCATAN CHICKEN STIR-FRY

4 boneless skinless chicken breast halves (about 1½ pounds)
1½ teaspoons olive or vegetable oil
1 tablespoon chili powder
1 bag (16 ounces) BIRDS EYE® frozen Farm Fresh Mixtures Broccoli, Corn & Red Peppers, thawed
½ cup tomato sauce
1½ teaspoons salt
Hot cooked rice (optional)

• Cut chicken into strips or chunks.

• In wok or large skillet, heat oil over medium-high heat 2 minutes.

• Meanwhile, coat chicken with chili powder. Add chicken to wok; stir-fry 3 to 5 minutes or until browned.

• Stir in vegetables, tomato sauce and salt. Reduce heat to low; cook 5 to 7 minutes or until vegetables are crisp-tender and chicken is no longer pink in center.

• Serve with rice, if desired.
Makes 4 servings

Prep Time: 10 minutes
Cook Time: 10 to 12 minutes

Szechuan Chicken Tenders

POULTRY PLEASERS

77 LEMON CASHEW CHICKEN STIR–FRY

1 tablespoon peanut oil
1 pound chicken tenders, cut into 1½-inch pieces
½ cup sliced mushrooms
¼ cup sliced green onions
2 cloves garlic, minced
1 cup matchstick-size carrot strips
½ cup fat-free reduced-sodium chicken broth
1 to 2 tablespoons dry sherry
2 teaspoons sugar
½ teaspoon grated lemon peel
3 tablespoons lemon juice
1 tablespoon cornstarch
⅛ teaspoon white pepper
1 package (6 ounces) frozen snow peas, thawed
3 cups hot cooked rice
⅓ cup chopped cashews

HEAT oil in large skillet over medium-high heat until hot. Add chicken; cook and stir 7 to 8 minutes or until chicken is no longer pink in center.

ADD mushrooms, onions and garlic; cook and stir 1 minute or until vegetables are tender. Add carrots, chicken broth, sherry, sugar and lemon peel; cook and stir 1 to 2 minutes more.

COMBINE lemon juice, cornstarch and pepper in small bowl; stir until smooth. Pour cornstarch mixture over chicken; cook and stir 1 to 2 minutes or until slightly thickened.

ADD snow peas; cook and stir 1 minute or until heated through. Serve over rice; sprinkle with cashews.

Makes 6 servings

78 STIR–FRIED BARBECUE CHICKEN WITH CASHEW NUTS

2 tablespoons LEE KUM KEE® Char Siu Sauce
1 tablespoon water
9 ounces chicken, cut into cubes
2 tablespoons vegetable oil
½ onion, chopped
½ green bell pepper, chopped
½ red bell pepper, chopped
2 ounces cocktail cashew nuts

1. Combine Char Siu Sauce and water in large bowl; add chicken. Marinate chicken 15 minutes.

2. Heat oil in wok; sauté onion and peppers until fragrant. Add chicken and stir-fry until cooked.

3. Stir in nuts and serve.

Makes 4 servings

Lemon Cashew Chicken Stir-Fry

POULTRY PLEASERS

79 CASHEW TURKEY STIR-FRY

1 pound turkey cutlets, cut into ½-inch strips
2 tablespoons reduced-sodium soy sauce
1 tablespoon Chinese 5-spice powder
1 clove garlic, minced
½ cup water
2 teaspoons cornstarch
1 teaspoon chicken bouillon granules
1 tablespoon vegetable oil, divided
8 green onions, bias-cut into 1-inch pieces
½ cup unsalted cashews
Hot cooked rice (optional)

1. In small bowl, combine turkey, soy sauce, 5-spice powder and garlic. Marinate 15 minutes.

2. In another small bowl, combine water, cornstarch and bouillon granules; set aside.

3. In large nonstick skillet, over medium heat, stir-fry turkey in 2 teaspoons oil 4 to 5 minutes or until no longer pink; remove and set aside. Add remaining 1 teaspoon oil. Stir-fry onions and cashews. Fold in turkey. Stir in cornstarch mixture; cook 30 seconds or until thick and bubbly.

4. Serve over rice, if desired.

Makes 4 servings

Favorite recipe from **National Turkey Federation**

80 CHICKEN WITH LIME BUTTER

3 whole chicken breasts, split, skinned and boned
½ teaspoon salt
½ teaspoon black pepper
⅓ cup vegetable oil
Juice from 1 lime
½ cup butter, softened
1 teaspoon minced fresh chives
½ teaspoon dried dill weed
Lime slices, quartered cherry tomatoes and dill sprigs for garnish

1. Sprinkle chicken with salt and pepper.

2. Heat oil in large skillet over medium heat. Add chicken to skillet in single layer. Cook 6 minutes or until chicken is lightly browned, turning once. Cover; reduce heat to low. Cook 10 minutes or until chicken is tender and no longer pink in center. Remove chicken to serving platter; keep warm.

3. Drain oil from skillet; add lime juice. Simmer over low heat 1 minute or until juice begins to bubble.

4. Stir in butter, 1 tablespoon at a time, until sauce thickens.

5. Remove sauce from heat; stir in chives and dill weed.

6. Spoon sauce over chicken. Garnish, if desired. *Makes 6 servings*

POULTRY PLEASERS

81 CURRIED CHICKEN WITH APRICOTS

12 ounces boneless skinless chicken breast meat, sliced into ½-inch strips
1 tablespoon margarine
1 cup thinly sliced green bell pepper strips (1 large)
⅓ cup finely chopped onion
¾ teaspoon curry powder
1½ cups (12-fluid ounce can) CARNATION® Evaporated Skimmed Milk
1 tablespoon plus 2 teaspoons cornstarch
1 cup (8¼-ounce can) unpeeled apricot halves in juice, drained, juice reserved
2 cups hot cooked rice
Sliced almonds, toasted (optional)

SPRAY large skillet with nonstick cooking spray. Heat skillet over medium-high heat. Add chicken; cook, stirring occasionally, 6 to 8 minutes or until no longer pink. Remove from skillet; keep warm. Add margarine to skillet; melt. Stir in pepper, onion and curry powder; cook, stirring occasionally, 3 to 5 minutes or until tender. Stir in evaporated milk.

COMBINE cornstarch and small amount of reserved apricot juice in small bowl to make a paste. Stir in remaining reserved juice. Add to skillet; stir well. Bring to a boil over medium heat, stirring constantly. Cook 3 to 4 minutes or until mixture begins to thicken. Add chicken and apricots; stir gently. Heat through. Serve over rice; garnish with almonds, if desired. *Makes 4 servings*

82 CHICKEN LIVERS IN WINE SAUCE

¼ cup CRISCO® Oil
1 medium onion, cut into 8 pieces
½ cup chopped celery
¼ cup snipped fresh parsley
1 clove garlic, minced
⅓ cup all-purpose flour
¾ teaspoon salt
¼ teaspoon black pepper
1 pound chicken livers, drained
½ cup water
½ cup milk
3 tablespoons dry white wine
¾ teaspoon chicken bouillon granules
½ teaspoon dried rosemary
Hot cooked egg noodles

1. Heat Crisco® Oil in large skillet. Add onion, celery, parsley and garlic. Sauté over medium heat until onion is tender. Set aside.

2. Mix flour, salt and pepper in large plastic bag. Add livers. Shake to coat. Add livers and any remaining flour mixture to onion mixture. Brown livers over medium-high heat, stirring occasionally. Stir in water, milk, wine, bouillon granules and rosemary. Heat to boiling, stirring constantly; reduce heat. Cover; simmer, stirring occasionally, 7 to 10 minutes or until livers are no longer pink. Serve with noodles.
Makes 4 to 6 servings

POULTRY PLEASERS

83 TERIYAKI STIR–FRY CHICKEN DINNER

1 package (about 1¾ pounds) PERDUE®
  Fresh Chicken or Oven Stuffer®
  Wingettes (12 to 16)
  Salt and black pepper to taste
2 tablespoons vegetable oil
1 cup broccoli florets
1 can (8 ounces) sliced water chestnuts,
  drained
4 carrots, sliced
4 green onions, thinly sliced
½ cup water
¼ cup soy sauce
¼ cup packed brown sugar
3 tablespoons dry sherry or white vinegar
2 cloves garlic, finely chopped
2 teaspoons grated fresh ginger
2 cups warm cooked rice
  Additional sliced green onions for
  garnish (optional)

Sprinkle wingettes with salt and pepper.

In large nonstick wok or skillet over medium-high heat, heat oil. Stir-fry broccoli 1 minute; add water chestnuts and carrots. Stir-fry 1 minute longer and add 4 sliced onions; stir-fry a few seconds. Remove vegetables and reserve.

Add wingettes to wok and cook until lightly browned on all sides, about 5 minutes. Reduce heat to low; cover and cook 10 minutes, turning occasionally. Remove wingettes to paper towel and pour off drippings. Return wingettes and vegetables to pan; add remaining ingredients except rice and additional onions. Stir until well mixed. Cook, turning frequently, until wingettes are glazed and sauce is thickened, about 3 to 5 minutes. Serve hot over rice, sprinkling with additional green onions , if desired.   *Makes 4 to 6 servings*

84 FRESH ORANGE CHICKEN WITH CARROTS

4 boneless skinless chicken breast halves
  (1 pound)
½ teaspoon dried oregano leaves
¼ teaspoon paprika
¼ teaspoon garlic powder
1 teaspoon vegetable oil
1½ cups thinly sliced carrots (3 medium)
  Grated peel of ½ SUNKIST® orange
1 cup fresh orange juice (3 oranges),
  divided
½ tablespoon cornstarch
1 green onion, sliced diagonally
2 cups hot cooked rice (no salt added)

Rinse chicken breasts and pat dry; remove any excess fat. Combine spices; sprinkle on both sides of chicken. In large nonstick skillet, sprayed with nonstick cooking spray, heat oil. Brown chicken on both sides, over medium-high heat, about 5 minutes. Reduce heat; add carrots, orange peel and ¾ cup orange juice. Cover; simmer 10 to 12 minutes or until chicken is tender. Remove chicken; continue cooking carrots until just tender, about 5 minutes. Combine remaining ¼ cup orange juice and cornstarch; stir into carrot mixture. Cook, stirring until thickened. Return chicken to skillet and add green onion; heat. Serve with rice.

Makes 4 servings

POULTRY PLEASERS

85 CHICKEN CURRY BOMBAY

1 medium onion, cut into wedges
2 cloves garlic, minced
2 teaspoons curry powder
1 tablespoon olive oil
2 half boneless chicken breasts, skinned
 and sliced ¼ inch thick
1 can (14½ ounces) DEL MONTE®
 FreshCut™ Diced Tomatoes, undrained
⅓ cup seedless raisins
1 can (14½ ounces) DEL MONTE®
 FreshCut™ Whole New Potatoes,
 drained and cut into chunks
1 can (14½ ounces) DEL MONTE®
 FreshCut™ Cut Green Beans, drained

1. In large skillet, cook onion, garlic and curry powder in oil until tender, stirring occasionally.

2. Stir in chicken, tomatoes and raisins; bring to a boil. Cover and simmer over medium heat 8 minutes.

3. Add potatoes and green beans. Cook, uncovered, 5 minutes, stirring occasionally. Season with salt and pepper, if desired.

Makes 4 servings

Prep Time: 10 minutes
Cook Time: 18 minutes

Chicken Curry Bombay

POULTRY PLEASERS

86 LEMON CHICKEN WITH WALNUTS

¼ cup **FILIPPO BERIO®** Olive Oil, divided
½ cup chopped walnuts
4 boneless skinless chicken breast halves, pounded thin
2 tablespoons all-purpose flour
1 medium onion, chopped
1 clove garlic, minced
1 cup dry white wine
2 carrots, very thinly sliced
¼ cup lemon juice
½ teaspoon dried thyme leaves
1 zucchini, very thinly sliced
1 yellow squash, very thinly sliced
Chopped fresh parsley

In large skillet, heat 2 tablespoons olive oil over medium-high heat until hot. Add walnuts; cook and stir 2 to 3 minutes or until lightly browned. Remove with slotted spoon; reserve. Lightly coat chicken breasts in flour. Add remaining 2 tablespoons olive oil to skillet; heat over medium-high heat until hot. Add chicken, onion and garlic; cook 5 minutes or until chicken is brown, turning chicken and stirring occasionally. Add wine, carrots, lemon juice and thyme. Cover; reduce heat to low and simmer 8 minutes. Add zucchini and squash; cover and simmer 2 minutes or until vegetables are crisp-tender and chicken is no longer pink in center. Remove chicken and vegetables; keep warm. Boil sauce until slightly thickened. Pour over chicken and vegetables. Top with reserved walnuts and parsley. *Makes 4 servings*

87 KUNG PAO CHICKEN

1 pound boneless skinless chicken breasts, cut into 1-inch pieces
1 tablespoon cornstarch
2 teaspoons **CRISCO®** Vegetable Oil
3 tablespoons chopped green onions with tops
2 cloves garlic, minced
¼ to 1½ teaspoons red pepper flakes
¼ to ½ teaspoon ground ginger
2 tablespoons wine vinegar
2 tablespoons soy sauce
2 teaspoons sugar
⅓ cup unsalted dry roasted peanuts
4 cups hot cooked rice (cooked without salt or fat)

1. Combine chicken and cornstarch in small bowl; toss. Heat Crisco® Oil in large skillet or wok over medium-high heat. Add chicken. Stir-fry 5 to 7 minutes or until no longer pink in center. Remove from skillet. Add onions, garlic, pepper and ginger to skillet. Stir-fry 15 seconds. Remove from heat.

2. Combine vinegar, soy sauce and sugar in small bowl. Stir well. Add to skillet. Return chicken to skillet. Stir until coated. Stir in nuts. Heat thoroughly, stirring occasionally. Serve over hot rice. *Makes 4 servings*

Lemon Chicken with Walnuts

POULTRY PLEASERS

88 LEMON–GINGER CHICKEN WITH PUFFED RICE NOODLES

  Vegetable oil for frying
4 ounces rice noodles, broken in half
1 stalk lemongrass*
3 boneless skinless chicken breast halves
3 cloves garlic, minced
1 teaspoon finely chopped fresh ginger
¼ teaspoon black pepper
¼ teaspoon ground red pepper
¼ cup water
1 tablespoon cornstarch
2 tablespoons peanut oil
6 ounces fresh snow peas, ends trimmed
1 can (8¾ ounces) baby corn, drained,
    rinsed and cut lengthwise into halves
¼ cup chopped cilantro
2 tablespoons packed brown sugar
2 tablespoons fish sauce
1 tablespoon light soy sauce

*Or substitute 1½ teaspoons grated lemon peel.

1. Heat 3 inches vegetable oil in wok or Dutch oven until oil registers 375°F on deep-fry thermometer. Fry noodles in small batches 20 seconds or until puffy, holding down noodles in oil with slotted spoon to fry evenly. Drain on paper towels; set aside.

2. Cut lemongrass into 1-inch pieces, discarding outer leaves and roots.

3. Cut chicken into 2½×1-inch strips.

4. Combine chicken, lemongrass, garlic, ginger, black pepper and red pepper in medium bowl; toss to coat. Combine water and cornstarch in cup; set aside.

5. Heat wok over high heat 1 minute or until hot. Drizzle 2 tablespoons peanut oil into wok and heat 30 seconds. Add chicken mixture; stir-fry 3 minutes or until no longer pink.

6. Add snow peas and baby corn; stir-fry 1 to 2 minutes. Stir cornstarch mixture; add to wok. Cook 1 minute or until thickened.

7. Add cilantro, brown sugar, fish sauce and soy sauce; cook until heated through. Discard lemongrass. Serve over reserved rice noodles. *Makes 4 servings*

89 QUICK CHICKEN STIR–FRY

½ cup MIRACLE WHIP® or MIRACLE WHIP LIGHT® Dressing, divided
4 boneless skinless chicken breast halves (about 1¼ pounds), cut into thin strips
¼ to ½ teaspoon garlic powder
1 package (16 ounces) frozen mixed vegetables *or* 3 cups fresh cut-up vegetables
2 tablespoons soy sauce
2 cups hot cooked MINUTE® Original Rice

HEAT 2 tablespoons dressing in skillet over medium-high heat. Add chicken and garlic powder; stir-fry 3 minutes. Add vegetables; stir-fry 3 minutes or until chicken is cooked through.

REDUCE heat to medium. Stir in remaining dressing and soy sauce; simmer 1 minute. Serve over rice. *Makes 4 servings*

Prep Time: 10 minutes
Cook Time: 7 minutes

*Lemon-Ginger Chicken
with Puffed Rice Noodles*

90 FRENCH PAN–ROASTED HENS

1 package (about 3 pounds) PERDUE®
   Fresh Split Cornish Hens (4 halves)
3 tablespoons olive oil, divided
1 tablespoon herbes de Provence
   Salt and black pepper to taste
3 cloves garlic, peeled, divided
½ cup white wine or water

Rub hens with 1 tablespoon oil and sprinkle with herbes de Provence, salt and pepper. In large deep skillet over medium-high heat, heat remaining 2 tablespoons oil. Add hens and 2 cloves garlic. Brown hens lightly on both sides. Discard cooked garlic and add remaining clove garlic. Reduce heat to low; cover and cook 30 to 40 minutes or until hens are browned and cooked through, turning 2 to 3 times.

Remove hens to warm serving platter; discard garlic. Add wine to skillet; cook 1 minute, stirring to incorporate pan juices. Serve hens with pan sauce.

Makes 2 to 4 servings

91 CHICKEN PECAN DIJON

8 (4-ounce) boneless skinless chicken
   breasts
¼ cup all-purpose flour
¼ cup margarine or butter
2 shallots, chopped
1 clove garlic, minced
⅓ cup sherry cooking wine
1 cup heavy cream*
½ cup seedless grapes, cut into halves
¼ cup GREY POUPON® COUNTRY
   DIJON® Mustard
½ cup PLANTERS® Pecan Pieces
   Additional grapes and mint leaves for
   garnish

Light cream or half-and-half may be substituted for heavy cream.

Coat chicken with flour, shaking off excess; set aside.

In large nonstick skillet, over medium heat, brown chicken in margarine, in batches, 5 to 7 minutes or until done. Remove from skillet and keep warm. In same skillet, over medium-high heat, cook shallots and garlic until tender. Add sherry; cook over high heat, stirring to blend in browned bits on bottom of skillet. Reduce heat; stir in cream, halved grapes and mustard. Cook and stir until sauce thickens. *Do not boil.*

To serve, place chicken breasts on serving platter; top with sauce. Sprinkle with pecan pieces; garnish with additional grapes and mint leaves. *Makes 6 to 8 servings*

French Pan-Roasted Hens

POULTRY PLEASERS

92 ORTEGA® CHICKEN FAJITAS

2 tablespoons vegetable oil
1½ cups (1 medium) quartered sliced onion
1 cup (1 medium) red bell pepper strips
1 cup (1 medium) green bell pepper strips
1 pound (about 4) boneless skinless chicken breasts, cut into ¼-inch strips
2½ cups (24-ounce jar) ORTEGA® Thick & Chunky Salsa, hot, medium or mild, or Garden Style Salsa, medium or mild, divided
2 tablespoons ORTEGA® Diced Jalapeños (optional)
½ cup (6-ounce container) frozen guacamole, thawed
8 soft taco-size (8-inch) flour tortillas, warmed
1 cup (4 ounces) shredded Monterey Jack cheese

HEAT oil in medium skillet over medium-high heat. Add onion and bell peppers; cook, stirring constantly, 3 to 4 minutes or until tender. Remove from skillet. Add chicken to skillet; cook, stirring constantly, 4 to 5 minutes or until no longer pink in center. Add cooked vegetables, 1 cup salsa and jalapeños, if desired; heat through.

SPREAD 1 tablespoon guacamole onto each tortilla. Top with ½ cup chicken mixture and 2 tablespoons cheese; fold into burritos. Serve with remaining 1½ cups salsa.

Makes 8 fajitas

93 CHICKEN THAI STIR–FRY

4 broiler-fryer chicken breast halves, boned, skinned and cut into ½-inch strips
2 tablespoons vegetable oil
2 teaspoons grated fresh ginger
2 cloves garlic, minced
2 cups broccoli florets
1 medium yellow squash, cut into ¼-inch slices
1 medium red bell pepper, cut into 2-inch strips
⅓ cup creamy peanut butter
¼ cup reduced-sodium soy sauce
2 tablespoons white vinegar
2 teaspoons sugar
½ teaspoon red pepper flakes
⅓ cup reduced-sodium chicken broth, fat skimmed
8 ounces uncooked linguine, cooked according to package directions
2 green onions with tops, thinly sliced

In large skillet, heat oil to medium-high. Add chicken, ginger and garlic; cook, stirring, about 5 minutes or until chicken is lightly browned and fork tender. Remove chicken mixture to bowl; set aside. To drippings in same skillet, add broccoli, squash and bell pepper. Cook, stirring, about 5 minutes or until vegetables are crisp-tender. Remove vegetables to bowl with chicken; set aside. To same skillet, add peanut butter, soy sauce, vinegar, sugar and red pepper flakes; stir in chicken broth. Return chicken and vegetables to skillet; heat through. Serve over linguine. Sprinkle with green onions.

Makes 4 servings

*Favorite recipe from **Delmarva Poultry Industry, Inc.***

Ortega® Chicken Fajitas

POULTRY PLEASERS

94 SHANGHAI CHICKEN WITH ASPARAGUS AND HAM

2 cups diagonally cut 1-inch asparagus
   pieces*
1 pound boneless skinless chicken breasts
2 teaspoons vegetable oil
3/4 cup coarsely chopped onion
2 cloves garlic, minced
2 tablespoons teriyaki sauce
1/4 cup diced deli ham
2 cups hot cooked white rice

Or substitute thawed frozen asparagus; omit step 1.

1. To blanch asparagus pieces, cook 3 minutes in enough boiling water to cover. Plunge asparagus into cold water. Drain well.

2. Cut chicken into 1-inch pieces.

3. Heat oil in large nonstick skillet over medium heat. Add onion and garlic; stir-fry 2 minutes. Add chicken; stir-fry 2 minutes. Add asparagus; stir-fry 2 minutes or until chicken is no longer pink.

4. Add teriyaki sauce; mix well. Add ham; stir-fry until heated through. Serve over rice. Garnish with carrot strips and fresh herbs, if desired. *Makes 4 servings*

95 NOUVEAU CHICKEN PAPRIKA

8 teaspoons paprika, divided
2 teaspoons garlic powder
4 boneless skinless chicken breast halves
1 tablespoon butter
1 container (6½ ounces) ALOUETTE®
   Garlic et Herbes Classique
1 tablespoon milk

• Combine 6 teaspoons paprika and garlic powder.

• Coat chicken breasts with paprika mixture.

• Sauté chicken in butter over medium heat about 5 minutes on each side.

• Cover and simmer 15 minutes over low heat.

• Combine Alouette®, milk and remaining 2 teaspoons paprika in small bowl.

• Remove chicken from skillet, reserving liquid.

• Spoon Alouette® mixture into skillet, stirring to mix well with reserved liquid.

• To serve, pour sauce over chicken. Use remaining sauce over rice, pasta or potatoes. *Makes 4 servings*

Shanghai Chicken with Asparagus and Ham

96 CHICKEN WALNUT STIR-FRY

SAUCE
- ²⁄₃ cup chicken broth
- 1½ tablespoons LA CHOY® Soy Sauce
- 1 tablespoon *each:* cornstarch and dry sherry
- ½ teaspoon sugar
- ¼ teaspoon *each:* black pepper and Oriental sesame oil

CHICKEN AND VEGETABLES
- 2 tablespoons cornstarch
- 2 teaspoons LA CHOY® Soy Sauce
- 2 teaspoons dry sherry
- 1 pound boneless skinless chicken breasts, cut into thin 2-inch strips
- 4 tablespoons WESSON® Oil, divided
- 2½ cups fresh broccoli florets
- 1½ teaspoons minced fresh garlic
- 1 teaspoon minced fresh ginger
- 1 (8-ounce) can LA CHOY® Bamboo Shoots, drained
- 1 cup toasted chopped walnuts
- 1 (6-ounce) package frozen snow peas, thawed and drained

In small bowl, combine *sauce* ingredients; set aside. In separate small bowl, combine cornstarch, soy sauce and sherry; mix well. Add chicken; toss gently to coat. In large nonstick skillet or wok, heat *3 tablespoons* Wesson® Oil. Add half of chicken mixture; stir-fry until chicken is no longer pink in center. Remove chicken from skillet; set aside. Repeat with remaining chicken mixture. Heat *remaining 1 tablespoon* Wesson® Oil in same skillet. Add broccoli, garlic and ginger; stir-fry until broccoli is crisp-tender. Return chicken mixture to skillet with remaining ingredients. Heat through; stir occasionally. Stir sauce; add to skillet. Cook, stirring constantly, until sauce is thick and bubbly. Garnish, if desired.
Makes 4 to 6 servings

97 EASY STIR-FRY SAUCE

- ¾ cup HOLLAND HOUSE® Sherry Cooking Wine
- 1 cup reduced-sodium chicken broth
- 2 tablespoons cornstarch
- 1 tablespoon light soy sauce
- 1 tablespoon vegetable oil
- 1 pound thinly sliced boneless chicken
- 1 bunch green onions, thinly sliced
- 2 cloves garlic, minced
- ¼ teaspoon ground ginger
- 4 to 6 cups cut-up fresh vegetables*
- 2 tablespoons toasted sesame seeds (optional)
- Hot cooked rice

Suggested vegetables: Use your favorite combination of snow peas, broccoli florets, thinly sliced carrots or celery, sliced red and green bell peppers, baby corn or mushrooms.

In small bowl, combine cooking wine, chicken broth, cornstarch and soy sauce; set aside. In wok or large skillet, heat oil over high heat. Add chicken, onions, garlic and ginger; stir-fry until chicken is just tender, about 5 minutes. Push chicken to side of skillet and add vegetables. Stir-fry 1 minute; cover and cook 2 minutes or until vegetables are just tender. Stir cooking wine mixture and add to wok. Cook until mixture boils 1 minute, stirring occasionally. Sprinkle with sesame seeds, if desired. Serve over cooked rice. *Makes 4 to 6 servings*

TIP: For a change of pace, substitute steak, pork, shelled shrimp or scallops for the chicken.

POULTRY PLEASERS

98 GARDEN FRESH TURKEY STIR–FRY

1 pound turkey steaks, cutlets or slices, cut into ½-inch strips
1 teaspoon salt, divided
½ teaspoon garlic powder
½ teaspoon paprika
½ teaspoon black pepper
3 tablespoons margarine, divided
1 medium yellow squash, thinly sliced (1½ cups)
1 small green bell pepper, cubed (¾ cup)
¼ pound snow peas
½ teaspoon Italian seasoning
8 to 10 cherry tomatoes

1. Coat turkey strips with ½ teaspoon salt, garlic powder, paprika and black pepper.

2. Over medium-high heat, melt 2 tablespoons margarine in large skillet or wok. Stir-fry turkey strips about 2 to 3 minutes. *Be careful not to overcook.* Remove from skillet; set aside.

3. Melt remaining 1 tablespoon margarine in skillet. Add squash, bell pepper and snow peas. Stir-fry about 1 minute. Sprinkle with remaining ½ teaspoon salt and Italian seasoning. Lower heat and cook until vegetables are crisp-tender.

4. Stir in turkey strips and cherry tomatoes. Heat just until warm. *Makes 6 servings*

*Favorite recipe from **National Turkey Federation***

99 SWEET AND SPICY CHICKEN STIR–FRY

1½ cups uncooked long-grain white rice
1 can (8 ounces) DEL MONTE® *FreshCut*™ Pineapple Chunks In Its Own Juice, undrained
4 boneless chicken breast halves, skinned and cut into bite-size pieces
2 tablespoons vegetable oil
1 large green bell pepper, cut into strips
¾ cup sweet and sour sauce
⅛ to ½ teaspoon red pepper flakes

1. Cook rice according to package directions.

2. Drain pineapple, reserving ⅓ cup juice.

3. In large skillet, stir-fry chicken in hot oil over medium-high heat until no longer pink in center. Add bell pepper and reserved pineapple juice; stir-fry 2 minutes or until crisp-tender.

4. Add sweet and sour sauce, red pepper flakes and pineapple; stir-fry 3 minutes or until heated through.

5. Spoon rice onto serving plate; top with chicken mixture. Garnish, if desired.
Makes 4 servings

Prep Time: 5 minutes
Cook Time: 20 minutes

Light-Style Lemon Chicken (page 91)

100 LAST–MINUTE LEMON CUTLETS

2 tablespoons olive oil
1 package (about ¾ pound) PERDUE®
    Done It! Fresh Chicken Breast Cutlets
¾ cup white wine
2 teaspoons fresh lemon juice
2 teaspoons brown sugar
    Salt and black pepper to taste
1 to 2 tablespoons minced fresh parsley

In large skillet over medium-high heat, heat oil. Add cutlets; sauté 5 minutes or until heated through. Remove to platter and keep warm. Reduce heat to medium. In same skillet, stir wine, lemon juice, brown sugar, salt and pepper. Cook 1 to 2 minutes or until sauce is slightly reduced, stirring constantly. To serve, arrange cutlets on platter; sprinkle with parsley and spoon sauce over all.

Makes 4 servings

101 ITALIAN–STYLE CHICKEN STIR–FRY

1 tablespoon olive oil
1 pound boneless skinless chicken breast
    meat, cut into thin strips
1 cup thinly sliced green bell pepper
1 cup thinly sliced onion
2 cups (1 pound 1 ounce-can)
    CONTADINA® Dalla Casa Buitoni
    Country Italian Cooking Sauce,
    Cacciatore
½ cup sliced ripe olives, drained
3 to 4 pita breads, warmed

HEAT oil in large skillet over high heat. Add chicken, bell pepper and onion; cook, stirring constantly, 5 to 6 minutes or until chicken is no longer pink in center. Add cooking sauce and olives; heat through. Cut pitas in half; stuff mixture into pockets.

Makes 3 to 4 servings

POULTRY PLEASERS

102 LIGHT–STYLE LEMON CHICKEN

2 egg whites, lightly beaten
¾ cup fresh bread crumbs
2 tablespoons sesame seeds (optional)
¾ teaspoon salt
¼ teaspoon black pepper
4 boneless skinless chicken breast halves
2 tablespoons all-purpose flour
¾ cup defatted low-sodium chicken broth
4 teaspoons cornstarch
¼ cup fresh lemon juice
2 tablespoons packed brown sugar
1 tablespoon honey
2 tablespoons vegetable oil
4 cups thinly sliced napa cabbage or romaine lettuce

1. Place egg whites in shallow dish. Combine bread crumbs, sesame seeds, if desired, salt and pepper in another shallow dish.

2. Dust chicken with flour; dip into egg whites. Roll in crumb mixture.

3. Blend chicken broth into cornstarch in small bowl until smooth. Stir in lemon juice, brown sugar and honey.

4. Heat oil in large nonstick skillet over medium heat. Add chicken; cook 5 minutes. Turn chicken over; cook 5 to 6 minutes or until browned and juices run clear. Transfer to cutting board; keep warm.

5. Wipe skillet clean with paper towel. Stir broth mixture and add to skillet. Cook and stir 3 to 4 minutes or until sauce boils and thickens.

6. Place cabbage on serving dish. Cut chicken crosswise into ½-inch slices; place over cabbage. Pour sauce over chicken. Garnish with lemon slices and fresh herbs, if desired. *Makes 4 servings*

103 THAI CHICKEN WITH BASIL

2 tablespoons vegetable oil, divided
1 teaspoon chili paste*
1 pound chicken breast, cut into cubes
¾ cup straw mushrooms
½ cup baby corn
1 cup fresh basil leaves (use holy basil, if available)
3 tablespoons fish sauce
1 tablespoon sugar

If unavailable, substitute crushed dried red chili pepper and 2 tablespoons minced garlic.

Heat wok; add 1 tablespoon oil. Add chili paste and cook over medium heat, stirring until fragrant, about 3 minutes. Add remaining 1 tablespoon oil. Raise heat to high. Add chicken and stir-fry until cooked through. Add mushrooms and baby corn. Mix well. Add basil, fish sauce and sugar. Stir until sugar has dissolved and basil has wilted. Garnish with chilies. Serve on lettuce leaves with side of rice.

Makes 4 servings

Favorite recipe from **The Sugar Association, Inc.**

POULTRY PLEASERS

104 SWEET & SOUR CASHEW CHICKEN

1 can (16 ounces) cling peach slices in
   syrup
1 cup KIKKOMAN® Sweet & Sour Sauce
2 boneless skinless chicken breast halves
1 tablespoon cornstarch
1 tablespoon KIKKOMAN® Soy Sauce
1 tablespoon minced fresh ginger root
½ teaspoon sugar
2 tablespoons vegetable oil, divided
1 onion, chunked
1 green bell pepper, chunked
1 small carrot, cut diagonally into thin
   slices
⅓ cup roasted cashews

Reserving ⅓ cup syrup, drain peaches; cut
slices in half. Blend reserved syrup and
sweet & sour sauce; set aside. Cut chicken
into 1-inch square pieces. Combine
cornstarch, soy sauce, ginger and sugar in
medium bowl; stir in chicken. Heat
1 tablespoon oil in hot wok or large skillet
over high heat. Add chicken and stir-fry
4 minutes; remove. Heat remaining
1 tablespoon oil in same pan. Add onion,
green pepper and carrot; stir-fry 4 minutes.
Stir in chicken and sweet & sour sauce
mixture. Cook and stir until chicken and
vegetables are coated with sauce. Stir in
peaches and cashews; heat through. Serve
immediately.   *Makes 4 servings*

105 QUICK CACCIATORE

1 package (about 1¾ pounds) PERDUE®
   Fresh Skinless Chicken Thighs
Salt and black pepper
2 tablespoons olive oil
1 green bell pepper, cut into strips
1 small onion, chopped
1 clove garlic, minced
1 can (14½ ounces) Italian-style stewed
   tomatoes, undrained
1 tablespoon dried Italian herb seasoning

Sprinkle chicken lightly with salt and black
pepper to taste. In large nonstick skillet over
medium-high heat, heat oil. Add chicken;
cook 3 to 4 minutes on each side or until
browned; remove and set aside. Add bell
pepper, onion and garlic. Sauté 2 to 3
minutes or until slightly softened. Stir in
tomatoes and Italian seasoning. Return
chicken to skillet; reduce heat to medium-
low. Cover and simmer 30 to 40 minutes or
until chicken is fork-tender and cooked
through.

To serve, spoon bell pepper and tomatoes
over chicken.   *Makes 3 to 4 servings*

Sweet & Sour Cashew Chicken

POULTRY PLEASERS

106 BISTRO IN A POT

2 teaspoons olive oil
½ to 1 pound boneless skinless chicken,
    cut into bite-size pieces
½ cup minced shallots
2 large cloves garlic, sliced
2 cups chopped leeks, white and light
    green parts, washed and drained
1½ cups baby carrots, cut into quarters
    lengthwise
1 cup thinly sliced new potatoes
2 tablespoons dried tarragon leaves
3 to 4 teaspoons dried lemon peel
1 cup shredded Jarlsberg Lite cheese
1 cup frozen peas, thawed (optional)
    Minced fresh parsley for garnish

In wok or large skillet with cover, heat oil
over high heat until nearly smoking. Stir-fry
chicken, shallots and garlic. Remove to bowl.
Add leeks to wok and stir-fry 3 minutes. Add
to chicken mixture. Add carrots, potatoes,
tarragon and lemon peel to wok; stir-fry
5 minutes. Add chicken mixture to wok. Add
½ cup water; stir quickly. Cover tightly and
steam 5 minutes. (Add more water if
necessary.)

Remove from heat; add cheese and peas, if
desired. Stir and serve garnished with
parsley. *Makes 4 to 6 servings*

SERVING SUGGESTION: Serve with a green
salad and light sourdough French bread or
crusty rolls.

*Favorite recipe from **Norseland, Inc.***

107 CHICKEN VEGETABLE SAUTÉ

1 tablespoon vegetable oil
4 boneless skinless chicken breast halves
    (about 1½ pounds), cut into strips
1 bag (16 ounces) BIRDS EYE® frozen
    Farm Fresh Mixtures Sugar Snap
    Stir-Fry vegetables
⅔ cup LAWRY'S® Teriyaki Chicken Sauté
    Sauce with Ginger and Sesame
⅓ cup slivered almonds, toasted
    Hot cooked rice (optional)

• In large nonstick skillet, heat oil over
medium heat.

• Add chicken; sauté chicken about 8
minutes or until browned. Remove chicken;
set aside.

• Add vegetables to skillet; sauté about
10 minutes or until crisp-tender.

• Return chicken to skillet; add teriyaki
sauce. Stir to coat. Cook 2 to 3 minutes more
or until heated through.

• Sprinkle with almonds. Serve over rice, if
desired. *Makes 4 servings*

Prep Time: 5 minutes
Cook Time: 20 minutes

Bistro in a Pot

POULTRY PLEASERS

108 GINGER CHICKEN STIR–FRY

1 whole chicken breast, skinned and boned
4 tablespoons KIKKOMAN® Teriyaki Marinade & Sauce, divided
3 teaspoons minced fresh ginger root, divided
1 cup water
2 tablespoons cornstarch
2 tablespoons vegetable oil, divided
2 carrots, cut into julienne strips
1 medium onion, sliced
¾ pound fresh spinach, washed, drained and torn in half

Cut chicken into thin strips. Combine 1 tablespoon teriyaki sauce and 2 teaspoons ginger in small bowl; stir in chicken. Let stand 10 minutes. Meanwhile, combine water, remaining 3 tablespoons teriyaki sauce, cornstarch and 1 teaspoon ginger in small bowl; set aside. Heat 1 tablespoon oil in hot wok or large skillet over high heat. Add chicken and stir-fry 2 minutes; remove. Heat remaining 1 tablespoon oil in same pan. Add carrots and onion; stir-fry 2 minutes. Add chicken and teriyaki sauce mixture; cook and stir until sauce boils and thickens. Stir in spinach; serve immediately.

Makes 4 servings

109 PEPPER AND SWISS CHARD TURKEY STIR–FRY

1 pound turkey cutlets or slices, cut into ¼-inch strips
½ teaspoon salt
¼ teaspoon black pepper
1 tablespoon olive oil, divided
1 red bell pepper, cut into ¼-inch strips
1 yellow bell pepper, cut into ¼-inch strips
1 pound Swiss chard, stalks removed and coarsely chopped
2 tablespoons balsamic vinegar
2 tablespoons sugar

1. In medium bowl, combine turkey, salt and black pepper. In large nonstick skillet, over medium-high heat, sauté turkey in 2 teaspoons oil 4 to 5 minutes or until turkey is no longer pink in center. *Do not overcook.* Remove turkey from pan; set aside.

2. Add remaining 1 teaspoon oil to skillet and sauté bell peppers 2 minutes. Gently fold in Swiss chard.

3. In small bowl, combine vinegar and sugar; stir into vegetable mixture. Reduce heat to medium and stir-fry 2 to 3 minutes or until vegetables are tender. Stir in turkey strips. Serve immediately. *Makes 4 servings*

*Favorite recipe from **National Turkey Federation***

Ginger Chicken Stir-Fry

POULTRY PLEASERS

110 ORIENTAL CHICKEN–PEAR SAUTÉ

2 whole broiler-fryer chicken breasts, cut into halves, boned, skinned and cut into ½-inch strips
2 tablespoons vegetable oil, divided
1 clove garlic, minced
2 carrots, diagonally sliced into ⅛-inch pieces
4 green onions with tops, cut into 1-inch pieces
2 pears, cut into halves, cored and cut into ¼-inch slices
1 package (6 ounces) frozen snow peas, thawed and drained
1 tablespoon cornstarch
1 teaspoon brown sugar
¼ teaspoon ground ginger
3 tablespoons reduced-sodium soy sauce
½ cup reduced-sodium chicken broth
¼ cup unsalted peanuts
   Steamed rice

In large skillet, place 1 tablespoon oil and heat to medium-high. Add chicken and garlic; stir-fry about 5 to 8 minutes or until chicken is lightly browned and fork tender. Remove chicken; set aside. To drippings in skillet, add remaining 1 tablespoon oil and heat to medium-high. Add carrots and onions; stir-fry 3 minutes. Add pears; stir-fry 1 to 2 minutes or until crisp-tender. Add snow peas; stir to mix. In small bowl, mix cornstarch, brown sugar and ginger; stir in soy sauce. Gradually add chicken broth. Return chicken to skillet; add soy sauce mixture and cook, stirring, until thickened. Sprinkle with peanuts. Serve with steamed rice. *Makes 4 servings*

*Favorite recipe from **Delmarva Poultry Industry, Inc.***

111 SWEET SPRING CHICKEN

¼ cup light margarine (stick form)
1 package (about 1¼ pounds) PERDUE® Fresh Skinless Chicken Drumsticks
½ cup orange juice
2 tablespoons honey
2 teaspoons grated peeled fresh ginger
½ teaspoon ground cinnamon

In large nonstick skillet over medium-high heat, melt margarine. Add chicken; cook 6 to 8 minutes or until brown on all sides, turning often. In small bowl, combine orange juice, honey, ginger and cinnamon. Add mixture to skillet; reduce heat to medium-low. Cover and cook 25 to 35 minutes or until chicken is fork-tender, glazed and brown. Serve chicken with pan sauce.

Makes 3 to 4 servings

112 STIR–FRIED CHICKEN

2 tablespoons soy sauce
2 teaspoons cornstarch
2 whole chicken breasts, split, skinned and boned
   Vegetable oil
1 green bell pepper, cut into thin strips
½ small onion, chopped
1 cup diagonally sliced celery
1 medium carrot, diagonally sliced
1 cup sliced mushrooms
1 teaspoon salt
¼ teaspoon ground ginger
1 can (16 ounces) bean sprouts, drained
1 can (5 ounces) water chestnuts, drained and sliced
¼ cup water
3 cups hot cooked rice (1 cup uncooked)
¾ cup peanuts

Stir-Fried Chicken (page 98)

1. Blend soy sauce into cornstarch in cup until smooth; set aside.

2. Slice chicken crosswise across the grain into ¼-inch strips.

3. Place wok or large skillet over high heat. (Test hot pan by adding drop of water to pan; if water sizzles, pan is sufficiently hot.) Add 2 tablespoons oil to wok, swirling to coat side. Heat oil until hot, about 30 seconds.

4. Add chicken to wok; cook and stir 3 to 5 minutes or until chicken is no longer pink in center. Remove chicken from wok; set aside.

5. Reheat wok over high heat. Add 1 tablespoon oil to wok, swirling to coat side. Heat oil until hot, about 30 seconds. Add bell pepper, onion, celery, carrot, mushrooms, salt and ginger to wok; briskly toss and stir vegetables 3 minutes or until vegetables are crisp-tender, adding more oil to wok if needed.

6. Stir chicken into vegetables in wok until well combined; stir in bean sprouts, water chestnuts and water. Push chicken-vegetable mixture to side of wok; add cornstarch mixture. Cook and stir until mixture comes to a boil and thickens.

7. Mound rice onto serving platter; spoon chicken-vegetable mixture over rice. Sprinkle with peanuts. Garnish with celery leaves, if desired.   *Makes 6 servings*

POULTRY PLEASERS

113 PAGODA GARDEN STIR–FRY

1 tablespoon cornstarch
2 tablespoons water, divided
1 tablespoon KIKKOMAN® Soy Sauce
1 clove garlic, minced
½ teaspoon minced fresh ginger root
½ pound boneless skinless chicken, cut into thin strips
3 tablespoons vegetable oil, divided
2 medium zucchini, thinly sliced
2 carrots, cut diagonally into thin slices
1 onion, chunked
¼ pound fresh mushrooms, sliced
⅔ cup KIKKOMAN® Sweet & Sour Sauce

Combine cornstarch, 1 tablespoon water, soy sauce, garlic and ginger in medium bowl; stir in chicken. Let stand 10 minutes. Heat 1 tablespoon oil in hot wok or large skillet over high heat. Add chicken and stir-fry 2 minutes; remove. Heat remaining 2 tablespoons oil in same pan. Add zucchini, carrots and onion; stir-fry 2 minutes. Reduce heat to medium; sprinkle remaining 1 tablespoon water over vegetables. Cover and cook 2 minutes, stirring frequently. Stir in chicken, mushrooms and sweet & sour sauce. Cover and cook 2 minutes longer, stirring occasionally. Serve immediately.

Makes 4 servings

114 PEAR AND APPLE TURKEY STIR–FRY

1 pound turkey cutlets or slices, cut into ¼-inch strips
1 tablespoon raspberry vinegar
1 tablespoon vegetable oil, divided
1 teaspoon minced fresh ginger
1 large clove garlic, minced
½ teaspoon salt
¼ teaspoon black pepper
1 pear, cut into ¼-inch strips
1 Rome Beauty or cooking apple, cut into ¼-inch strips
1 tablespoon lemon juice
½ cup halved green grapes

1. In medium bowl, combine turkey, vinegar, 1 teaspoon oil, ginger, garlic, salt and pepper. Cover and refrigerate while preparing fruit.

2. In medium bowl, combine pear and apple slices with lemon juice.

3. In large nonstick skillet, over medium-high heat, stir-fry pear mixture in 1 teaspoon oil 1 minute. Remove to platter and keep warm.

4. Over medium-high heat, add remaining 1 teaspoon oil to skillet and stir-fry turkey 2½ to 3 minutes or until turkey is no longer pink in center. Gently fold pear mixture and grapes into turkey. Heat until warmed through. Serve immediately.

Makes 4 servings

Favorite recipe from **National Turkey Federation**

Pagoda Garden Stir-Fry

Here's the
Beef (& Lamb)

115 FIVE–SPICE BEEF STIR–FRY

1 pound beef top sirloin, cut into thin strips
2 tablespoons light soy sauce
2 tablespoons plus 1½ teaspoons cornstarch, divided
3 tablespoons walnut or vegetable oil, divided
4 medium carrots, cut into matchstick-size pieces (about 2 cups)
1 red bell pepper, cut into chunks
1 yellow bell pepper, cut into chunks
1 cup chopped onion
¼ to ½ teaspoon red pepper flakes
1 tablespoon plus 1½ teaspoons packed dark brown sugar
2 teaspoons beef bouillon granules
1 teaspoon Chinese five-spice powder
3 cups hot cooked rice
½ cup honey roasted peanuts

1. Place beef in shallow glass baking dish. Combine soy sauce and 2 tablespoons cornstarch in small bowl. Pour soy sauce mixture over beef; toss to coat thoroughly. Set aside.

2. Meanwhile, add 1 tablespoon oil to large nonstick skillet or wok. Heat skillet over high heat 1 minute or until hot. Add carrots. Cook and stir 3 to 4 minutes or until edges begin to brown. Remove carrots and set aside.

3. Reduce heat to medium-high. Add 1 tablespoon oil, bell peppers, onion and red pepper flakes; cook and stir 4 minutes or until onions are translucent. Remove vegetables and set aside separately from carrots.

4. Add remaining 1 tablespoon oil to skillet. Add beef; cook and stir 6 minutes.

5. Meanwhile, in small bowl, combine 1½ cups water with brown sugar, bouillon granules, 5-spice powder and remaining 1½ teaspoons cornstarch. Stir until cornstarch is completely dissolved.

6. Increase heat to high. Add bouillon mixture and reserved bell peppers and onions; bring to a boil. Cook and stir 2 to 3 minutes or until slightly thickened.

7. Toss rice with carrots; place on serving platter. Spoon beef mixture over rice and sprinkle peanuts over beef mixture.

Makes 4 servings

Five-Spice Beef Stir-Fry

116 BEEF & BROCCOLI

¾ **pound boneless tender beef steak (sirloin, rib eye or top loin)**
3 **tablespoons cornstarch, divided**
1 **tablespoon KIKKOMAN® Soy Sauce**
1 **tablespoon dry sherry**
1 **teaspoon minced fresh ginger root**
1 **clove garlic, pressed**
1 **pound fresh broccoli, trimmed**
1 **cup water**
¼ **cup KIKKOMAN® Soy Sauce**
4 **tablespoons vegetable oil, divided**
1 **medium onion, chunked**

Cut beef across grain into thin slices. Combine 1 tablespoon *each* cornstarch, soy sauce and sherry with ginger and garlic in small bowl; stir in beef. Let stand 15 minutes. Meanwhile, remove flowerets from broccoli; cut into bite-size pieces. Peel stalks; cut crosswise into thin slices. Combine water, ¼ cup soy sauce and remaining 2 tablespoons cornstarch; set aside. Heat 2 tablespoons oil in hot wok or large skillet over high heat. Add beef and stir-fry 1 minute; remove. Heat remaining 2 tablespoons oil in same pan. Add broccoli and onion; stir-fry 4 minutes. Add beef and soy sauce mixture; cook and stir until sauce boils and thickens. Serve immediately.

Makes 4 servings

117 LIGHTNING BEEF & MUSHROOMS

4 **tablespoons ST. SUPÉRY® Cabernet Sauvignon**
2 **tablespoons Worcestershire sauce**
1 **tablespoon tomato paste**
1 **teaspoon dried thyme leaves**
¼ **teaspoon TABASCO® pepper sauce**
¼ **teaspoon black pepper**
2 **teaspoons olive oil**
6 **ounces flank steak, cut across grain into ¼-inch slices**
2 **teaspoons minced fresh garlic**
2 **teaspoons grated orange peel**
½ **pound mushrooms, cut into ¼-inch slices**
6 **ounces spaghetti, cooked *al dente* and drained**
2 **medium carrots, grated**
4 **tablespoons chopped parsley**

Combine Cabernet Sauvignon, Worcestershire sauce, tomato paste, thyme, TABASCO® sauce and pepper in small bowl; set aside.

In large skillet or wok, heat oil over medium-high heat. Add beef, garlic and orange peel; stir quickly 30 to 60 seconds or until beef is rare. Remove and set aside. Add mushrooms to skillet; cook 3 to 4 minutes, stirring frequently, or until mushrooms start to release their moisture.

Add spaghetti, carrots, parsley, beef mixture and Cabernet Sauvignon mixture to skillet. Toss together. Serve warm.

Makes 4 servings

Beef & Broccoli

HERE'S THE BEEF (& LAMB)

118 SATAY BEEF

1 pound beef tenderloin, trimmed
1 teaspoon cornstarch
3½ teaspoons soy sauce, divided
1 to 2 teaspoons sesame oil
2 tablespoons vegetable oil
1 medium yellow onion, coarsely chopped
1 clove garlic, minced
1 tablespoon dry sherry
1 tablespoon satay sauce
1 teaspoon curry powder
½ teaspoon sugar
    Fresh chervil and carrot flowers* for
    garnish

*To make carrot garnish, cut carrot crosswise into
thin slices; cut into desired shape with small
decorative cutter or sharp knife.*

1. Cut meat across grain into thin slices;
flatten each slice by pressing with fingers.

2. Combine cornstarch, 3 tablespoons water,
1½ teaspoons soy sauce and sesame oil; mix
well. Add to meat in medium bowl; stir to
coat well. Let stand 20 minutes.

3. Heat vegetable oil in wok or large skillet
over high heat. Add ½ of meat, spreading out
slices so they do not overlap.

4. Cook meat slices on each side just until
lightly browned, 2 to 3 minutes. Remove
from wok; set aside. Repeat with remaining
meat slices.

5. Add onion and garlic to wok; stir-fry until
tender, about 3 minutes.

6. Combine 2 tablespoons water, remaining
2 teaspoons soy sauce, sherry, satay sauce,
curry powder and sugar in small cup. Add to
wok; cook and stir until liquid boils. Return
meat to wok; cook and stir until thoroughly
heated. Garnish, if desired.

Makes 4 servings

119 TERIYAKI CHOP SUEY

SAUCE
⅓ cup beef broth
3 tablespoons LA CHOY® Teriyaki
    Marinade & Sauce
1½ tablespoons *each:* cornstarch and
    packed brown sugar
1 teaspoon garlic powder
¼ teaspoon black pepper

BEEF AND VEGETABLES
1 tablespoon LA CHOY® Teriyaki Marinade
    & Sauce
1 tablespoon cornstarch
1 pound flank or sirloin steak, sliced
    across grain into thin 2-inch strips
3 tablespoons WESSON® Oil
2 cups sliced fresh mushrooms
1 (14-ounce) can LA CHOY® Bean Sprouts,
    drained
1 (14-ounce) can LA CHOY® Chop Suey
    Vegetables, drained
½ cup diagonally-cut ½-inch green onion
    pieces
1 (5-ounce) can LA CHOY® Chow Mein
    Noodles

In small bowl, combine *sauce* ingredients;
set aside. In medium bowl, combine teriyaki
sauce and cornstarch. Add beef; toss gently.
In large nonstick skillet or wok, heat oil. Add
half of beef mixture; stir-fry until lightly
browned. Remove beef from skillet; set
aside. Repeat with remaining beef mixture.
Add mushrooms to skillet; stir-fry 1 minute.
Add bean sprouts and chop suey vegetables;
heat thoroughly, stirring occasionally. Stir
sauce; add to skillet with beef and green
onions. Cook, stirring constantly, until sauce
is thick and bubbly. Garnish, if desired.
Serve over noodles.

Makes 4 to 6 servings

Satay Beef

HERE'S THE BEEF (& LAMB)

120 ITALIAN STIR–FRIED LAMB

12 ounces boneless American lamb, leg or sirloin, thinly bias-sliced into strips about 3-inches long
¾ cup chicken broth
¼ cup dry white wine or water
2 tablespoons pesto
4 teaspoons cornstarch
½ teaspoon dried oregano leaves
1 tablespoon vegetable oil
1 (9-ounce) package frozen Italian-style green beans, thawed
½ cup thinly sliced carrots
1 cup sliced fresh mushrooms
1 cup cherry tomato halves
4 ounces linguine or fettuccine, cooked
2 tablespoons grated Parmesan cheese

In small bowl, stir together chicken broth, wine, pesto, cornstarch and oregano; set aside. Preheat wok or large skillet over high heat; add oil. Stir-fry green beans and carrots 4 minutes. Add mushrooms; stir-fry 1 to 2 minutes or until vegetables are crisp-tender. Remove vegetables from wok; set aside.

Add lamb strips to wok. Stir-fry about 3 minutes or until slightly pink. Remove lamb from wok; add to reserved vegetable mixture. Return vegetable mixture and meat to wok. Stir cornstarch mixture; add to wok. Cook and stir until thickened and bubbly. Stir in tomatoes. Cook 1 minute. Serve over hot cooked pasta; sprinkle with cheese.

Makes 4 servings

Prep Time: 15 minutes
Cook Time: 20 minutes

Favorite recipe from **American Lamb Council**

121 BLACK PEPPER BEEF SHORT RIBS

1 pound short ribs, cut into pieces
¾ cup plus 4 tablespoons LEE KUM KEE® Black Pepper Sauce, divided
Vegetable oil
1 ounce shredded onion
1 ounce shredded green bell pepper
1 ounce shredded red bell pepper

Marinate short ribs in 4 tablespoons Black Pepper Sauce 10 minutes. Heat oil in wok. Pan-fry short ribs until cooked. Remove and drain. Sauté onion until fragrant. Add bell peppers and remaining ¾ cup Black Pepper Sauce. Bring to a boil and add short ribs. Stir well and serve. *Makes 4 to 6 servings*

122 HONEY DIJON BEEF AND VEGETABLE STIR–FRY

⅔ cup HEINZ® Tomato Ketchup
2 tablespoons honey Dijon mustard
1 tablespoon soy sauce
1 pound boneless beef sirloin steak, cut into thin strips
1 red bell pepper, cut into thin strips
1 onion, cut into thin wedges
2 cups broccoli florets
Hot cooked rice

In small bowl, combine ketchup, ⅓ cup water, mustard and soy sauce; set aside. In large preheated nonstick skillet, quickly brown beef; remove. Cook pepper, onion and broccoli, stirring, until crisp-tender, about 4 minutes. Return beef to skillet and stir in reserved ketchup mixture; heat. Serve with rice. *Makes 4 servings*

Italian Stir-Fried Lamb

Beef 'n' Broccoli

123 BEEF 'N' BROCCOLI

½ cup A.1.® Steak Sauce
¼ cup soy sauce
2 cloves garlic, crushed
1 pound top round steak, thinly sliced
1 (16-ounce) bag frozen broccoli, red bell peppers, bamboo shoots and mushrooms, thawed*
Hot cooked rice (optional)

1 (16-ounce) bag frozen broccoli cuts, thawed, may be substituted.

In small bowl, combine steak sauce, soy sauce and garlic. Pour marinade over steak in nonmetal dish. Cover; refrigerate 1 hour, stirring occasionally.

Remove steak from marinade; reserve marinade. In large lightly oiled skillet, over medium-high heat, stir-fry steak 3 to 4 minutes or until steak is no longer pink. Remove steak with slotted spoon; keep warm.

In same skillet, heat vegetables and reserved marinade to a boil; reduce heat to low. Cover; simmer 2 to 3 minutes. Stir in steak. Serve over rice, if desired.

Makes 4 servings

HERE'S THE BEEF (& LAMB)

124 VEAL SCALLOPS WITH ROSEMARY AND BENEDICTINE

2 tablespoons peanut oil
2 tablespoons butter
4 veal scallops, about ⅔ inch thick
    Salt and freshly ground black pepper to
    taste
2 to 3 tablespoons BENEDICTINE Liqueur
1 tablespoon chicken consommé
½ cup dry white wine
2 tablespoons minced shallots
1 tablespoon minced fresh rosemary
    Juice of 1 lemon

Heat oil and butter in large skillet until foamy. Add veal and sauté on both sides until golden. Season with salt and pepper. Add Benedictine and ignite carefully. When flame dies down, add chicken consommé and wine. Simmer 5 minutes. Add shallots, rosemary and lemon juice; simmer 2 minutes. Place veal on serving dish and pour sauce over veal. Serve immediately.
Makes 2 servings

125 TANGY PLUM SHORT RIBS

2 tablespoons vegetable oil
1 teaspoon chopped garlic
¾ pound cooked short ribs, cut into small
    pieces
3 tablespoons LEE KUM KEE® Plum Sauce
1 tablespoon LEE KUM KEE® Oyster
    Flavored Sauce

Heat skillet over medium heat. Add oil. Sauté garlic. Add short ribs and stir-fry until heated through. Add Plum Sauce and Oyster Flavored Sauce. Stir well and serve.
Makes 4 servings

126 UPDATED BEEF STROGANOFF

1 pound beef tenderloin tips
1½ cups uncooked farfalle (bow tie) pasta
    Vegetable cooking spray
    Salt and black pepper (optional)
½ pound mushrooms, cut into ½-inch
    slices
⅓ cup coarsely chopped onion
2 teaspoons vegetable oil
1 to 2 tablespoons all-purpose flour
¾ cup beef broth
1 tablespoon sliced green onion
¼ cup dairy sour half-and-half

1. Cook pasta according to package directions. Keep warm.

2. Meanwhile, trim fat from beef; cut into 1×½-inch pieces. Spray large nonstick skillet with cooking spray. Heat skillet over medium-high heat until hot. Add beef (½ at a time) and stir-fry 1 to 2 minutes or until outside surface is no longer pink. Remove from skillet; keep warm. Season with salt and black pepper, if desired.

3. In same skillet, cook mushrooms and onion in oil 2 minutes or until tender; stir in flour. Gradually add beef broth, stirring until blended. Bring to a boil; cook and stir 2 minutes. Return beef to skillet; heat through.

4. Serve beef mixture over pasta. Sprinkle with green onion; pass sour half-and-half to dollop on top. *Makes 4 servings*

Prep and Cook Time: 25 minutes

*Favorite recipe from **North Dakota Beef Commission***

HERE'S THE BEEF (& LAMB)

127 KUBLAI KHAN'S STIR–FRY WITH FIERY WALNUTS

Fiery Walnuts (recipe follows)
1 pound boneless tender beef steak
    (sirloin, rib eye or top loin) or lamb
    sirloin
2 tablespoons KIKKOMAN® Stir-Fry Sauce
1 teaspoon cornstarch
2 large cloves garlic, minced
2 tablespoons vegetable oil, divided
1 medium onion, cut into ¾-inch chunks
2 large carrots, cut into julienne strips
1 pound fresh spinach, washed and
    drained
½ pound fresh mushrooms, sliced
⅓ cup KIKKOMAN® Stir-Fry Sauce

Prepare Fiery Walnuts. Cut beef across grain into thin slices, then into narrow strips. Combine 2 tablespoons stir-fry sauce, cornstarch and garlic in medium bowl; stir in beef. Heat 1 tablespoon oil in hot wok or large skillet over medium-high heat. Add beef and stir-fry 1½ minutes; remove. Heat remaining 1 tablespoon oil in same pan. Add onion; stir-fry 2 minutes. Add carrots; stir-fry 1 minute. Add spinach and mushrooms; stir-fry 2 minutes, or until spinach is wilted. Add beef and ⅓ cup stir-fry sauce; cook and stir only until beef and vegetables are coated with sauce and heated through. Remove from heat; stir in Fiery Walnuts and serve immediately. *Makes 6 servings*

FIERY WALNUTS: Combine 2 teaspoons vegetable oil, ¼ teaspoon ground red pepper (cayenne) and ⅛ teaspoon salt in small skillet; heat over medium heat until hot. Add ¾ cup walnut halves or large pieces. Cook, stirring, 1 minute, or until walnuts are coated. Turn out onto small baking sheet; spread out in single layer. Bake in 350°F oven 7 minutes or until golden. Cool.

128 QUICK SKILLET SUPPER

½ pound beef sirloin steak
1 tablespoon vegetable oil
2 cups (about 8 ounces) sliced fresh
    mushrooms
1 can (17 ounces) whole kernel corn,
    drained
1 can (14½ ounces) stewed tomatoes,
    undrained
1 clove garlic, minced
1 teaspoon dried oregano leaves
⅛ teaspoon ground black pepper
3 cups hot cooked rice

Partially freeze steak; slice across grain into ⅛-inch strips. Heat oil in large skillet over medium-high heat until hot. Brown meat quickly in oil, about 2 minutes; remove. Add vegetables, garlic, oregano and pepper; stir. Reduce heat to medium; cover and cook 5 minutes. Add meat and cook until heated. Serve over rice. *Makes 6 servings*

Favorite recipe from **USA Rice Federation**

Kublai Khan's Stir-Fry with Fiery Walnuts

HERE'S THE BEEF (& LAMB)

129 HOT GLAZED BEEF ON SAFFRON–ONION RICE

1½ pounds beef sirloin, cut into thin strips
½ cup packed dark brown sugar
½ cup light soy sauce
¼ cup bourbon
½ teaspoon red pepper flakes
1 large package yellow Saffron rice
2 tablespoons vegetable oil, divided
2 cups chopped onions
1 cup chopped red bell pepper
1 can (8 ounces) sliced water chestnuts, drained

1. Place beef in shallow glass baking dish.

2. Combine brown sugar, soy sauce, bourbon and red pepper flakes in small bowl; whisk until sugar has dissolved completely. Pour over beef and marinate 15 minutes, stirring occasionally.

3. Cook rice according to package directions.

4. Meanwhile, add 1 tablespoon oil to large nonstick skillet or wok. Heat over medium-high heat 1 minute. Add onions; cook 15 minutes or until richly browned. Remove from skillet and set aside.

5. Add remaining 1 tablespoon oil and bell pepper to skillet; cook 3 minutes.

6. Toss cooked rice with bell pepper, water chestnuts and onions. Place on serving platter; keep warm.

7. Drain beef; reserve marinade. Increase heat to high, add ½ of beef. Cook and stir 4 minutes or just until all liquid has evaporated. Place beef on top of rice mixture and keep warm. Add remaining beef, repeat cooking procedure and place on serving platter.

8. Reduce heat to medium-high. Add reserved marinade, scraping bottom and sides of skillet. Cook 4 minutes or until liquid is reduced to ⅓ cup.

9. Drizzle cooked marinade over beef and serve immediately.   *Makes 4 servings*

130 DICED BEEF IN CHAR SIU SAUCE

9 ounces diced beef
4 tablespoons LEE KUM KEE® Char Siu Sauce, divided
3 tablespoons vegetable oil, divided
½ teaspoon cornstarch
½ tablespoon LEE KUM KEE® Minced Garlic
6 Chinese mushrooms, soaked and diced
2 ounces diced red bell pepper
2 ounces diced green bell pepper

1. Marinate beef in 1 tablespoon Char Siu Sauce, oil and cornstarch 15 minutes.

2. Heat remaining 2 tablespoons oil in wok. Sauté garlic until aroma comes out. Add beef and stir-fry until cooked. Add mushrooms and bell peppers; stir-fry.

3. Add remaining 3 tablespoons Char Siu Sauce and stir well.   *Makes 4 servings*

Hot Glazed Beef on Saffron-Onion Rice

131 SESAME STEAK

SAUCE
- ¼ cup LA CHOY® Soy Sauce
- ¼ cup chicken broth
- 1½ tablespoons cornstarch
- 1 tablespoon dry sherry
- ¼ teaspoon Oriental sesame oil

STEAK AND VEGETABLES
- 2 tablespoons dry sherry
- 1 tablespoon LA CHOY® Soy Sauce
- 1 tablespoon cornstarch
- 1 pound round steak, sliced into thin 2-inch strips
- 4 tablespoons WESSON® Oil, divided
- 1 teaspoon *each:* minced fresh garlic and ginger
- 1 cup chopped red bell pepper
- 1 cup sliced fresh mushrooms
- 1 (10-ounce) package frozen French-cut green beans, thawed and drained
- 1 (14-ounce) can LA CHOY® Bean Sprouts, drained
- 1 (8-ounce) can LA CHOY® Sliced Water Chestnuts, drained
- ½ cup sliced green onions
- 2 tablespoons toasted sesame seeds

In small bowl, combine *sauce* ingredients; set aside. In medium bowl, combine sherry, soy sauce and cornstarch; mix well. Add steak; toss gently to coat. In large nonstick skillet or wok, heat *3 tablespoons* oil. Add half of steak mixture; stir-fry until lightly browned. Remove steak from skillet; set aside. Repeat with remaining steak mixture. Heat *remaining 1 tablespoon* oil in same skillet. Add garlic and ginger; cook and stir 10 seconds.

Add bell pepper; stir-fry 1 minute. Add mushrooms and green beans; stir-fry 1 minute. Stir sauce; add to skillet with bean sprouts and water chestnuts. Cook, stirring constantly, until sauce is thick and bubbly. Return steak to skillet; heat thoroughly, stirring occasionally. Sprinkle with green onions and sesame seeds. Garnish, if desired. *Makes 4 to 6 servings*

132 WOK SUKIYAKI

- 1 pound beef tenderloin or sirloin
- 1 package (3¾ ounces) bean thread noodles
- 12 fresh shiitake or button mushrooms (about 6 ounces)
- ½ pound firm tofu
- ½ cup beef broth
- ½ cup teriyaki sauce
- ¼ cup sake, rice wine or dry sherry
- 1 tablespoon sugar
- 2 tablespoons vegetable oil, divided
- 6 green onions with tops, diagonally cut into 2-inch pieces
- ½ pound fresh spinach, stemmed, washed and dried
- Hot cooked rice (optional)

1. Trim fat from beef; discard. For ease in slicing, wrap beef in plastic wrap; freeze about 1 hour or until firm but not frozen.

2. Meanwhile, place noodles in bowl; cover with cold water. Let stand 30 minutes or until softened; drain. Cut into 4-inch lengths; set aside.

3. Cut off mushroom stems; discard. Cut out decorative cross in center of each mushroom cap with small paring knife; set aside.

HERE'S THE BEEF (& LAMB)

4. Drain tofu on paper towels. Cut into 1-inch-thick cubes; set aside.

5. Slice beef across grain into ¼-inch-thick strips; set aside.

6. Combine beef broth, teriyaki sauce, sake and sugar in small bowl; mix well. Set aside.

7. Heat wok over high heat 1 minute or until hot. Drizzle 1 tablespoon oil into wok and heat 30 seconds. Add ½ of beef; stir-fry 3 minutes or until browned. Remove from wok to bowl; set aside. Repeat with remaining 1 tablespoon oil and beef.

8. Reduce heat to medium. Add mushrooms to wok; stir-fry 1 minute and move to one side of wok. Add tofu to bottom of wok; fry 1 minute, stirring gently. Move to another side of wok. Add green onions to bottom of wok. Add broth mixture and bring to a boil. Move onions up side of wok.

9. Add noodles and spinach, keeping each in separate piles and stirring gently to soften in teriyaki sauce. Push up side of wok. Add beef and any juices; heat through.

10. Place wok on table over wok ring stand or trivet. Serve with rice, if desired.

Makes 4 servings

Wok Sukiyaki (page 116)

HERE'S THE BEEF (& LAMB)

133 BEEF AND BROCCOLI

1 pound lean beef tenderloin
2 teaspoons minced fresh ginger
2 cloves garlic, minced
½ teaspoon vegetable oil
3 cups broccoli florets
¼ cup water
2 tablespoons teriyaki sauce
2 cups hot cooked white rice

1. Cut beef across grain into ⅛-inch slices; cut each slice into 1½-inch pieces. Toss beef with ginger and garlic in medium bowl.

2. Heat oil in wok or large nonstick skillet over medium heat. Add beef mixture; stir-fry 3 to 4 minutes or until beef is barely pink in center. Remove and reserve.

3. Add broccoli and water to wok; cover and steam 3 to 5 minutes or until broccoli is crisp-tender.

4. Return beef and any accumulated juices to wok. Add teriyaki sauce. Cook until heated through. Serve over rice. Garnish with red pepper strips, if desired.

Makes 4 servings

134 LAMB WITH YOGURT MINT SAUCE

¾ pound boneless lamb or beef, cut into ¼-inch cubes
1 tablespoon olive oil
1 medium onion, cut into wedges
1 can (14½ ounces) DEL MONTE® *FreshCut*™ Diced Tomatoes No Salt Added, undrained
1 to 2 tablespoons chutney
1 teaspoon ground cumin
⅓ cup plain nonfat yogurt
1 tablespoon chopped fresh mint *or* 1 teaspoon dried mint
4 cups hot cooked pasta

1. In large skillet, brown lamb in hot oil over medium-high heat. Stir in onion and cook 3 to 4 minutes or until tender. Add tomatoes, chutney and cumin; cook until thickened.

2. Combine yogurt with mint. Spoon lamb mixture over hot pasta and top with yogurt mixture.   *Makes 4 servings*

Prep Time: 5 minutes
Cook Time: 12 minutes

Beef and Broccoli

HERE'S THE BEEF (& LAMB)

135 BEEF AND GRAVY STIR-FRY

8 ounces uncooked egg noodles
1 tablespoon extra-virgin olive oil, divided
1½ pounds beef sirloin, cut into thin strips, divided
2 cloves garlic, minced
⅓ cup all-purpose flour
2 tablespoons dry red wine
1 tablespoon beef bouillon granules
¾ teaspoon sugar
½ teaspoon dried thyme leaves
½ teaspoon salt
¼ teaspoon black pepper
3 tablespoons chopped parsley

1. Cook noodles according to package directions. Meanwhile, place 1½ teaspoons oil in large nonstick skillet or wok. Heat skillet over medium-high heat 1 minute. Add ½ of beef and cook, stirring, 3 minutes. Place on plate with any accumulated juices and set aside.

2. Add remaining 1½ teaspoons oil to skillet. Add remaining beef and garlic; repeat cooking process. Place on plate with reserved beef and juices.

3. Add flour to skillet; cook and stir 6 to 7 minutes or until aromatic and flour begins to turn golden. Remove from heat; cool slightly by stirring 1 additional minute.

4. Slowly whisk in ½ cup water to make a paste. Slowly whisk in 1½ cups additional water (mixture may be lumpy). Stir in wine, bouillon granules, sugar, thyme, salt and pepper along with reserved beef and any accumulated juices. Return mixture to a boil over medium-high heat. Cook 8 to 10 minutes or until slightly thickened.

5. Place noodles on serving platter. Spoon beef mixture over noodles and top with parsley. *Makes 4 servings*

136 SUNBURST STIR-FRY

1 large red bell pepper, cut into pieces
2 tablespoons vegetable oil, divided
1 onion, cut into wedges
2 cloves garlic, minced
1 small yellow squash, cut into bite-size pieces
1 pound boneless beef sirloin steak, trimmed and cut into thin bite-size strips
2 tablespoons soy sauce
½ to 1 teaspoon red pepper flakes
½ teaspoon black pepper
8 ounces thin egg noodles, cooked

In blender, blend bell pepper until ground. In large skillet, heat 1 tablespoon oil. Stir-fry onion and garlic 2 minutes. Add squash; stir-fry 1 to 2 minutes. Remove from skillet.

Add remaining 1 tablespoon oil to skillet. Stir-fry beef, ½ at a time, 2 to 3 minutes or until no longer pink; return beef to skillet.

Combine soy sauce, red pepper flakes and black pepper. Add to skillet along with squash mixture and bell pepper. Heat through. Serve over egg noodles.

Makes 4 servings

*Favorite recipe from **North Dakota Wheat Commission***

Beef and Gravy Stir-Fry

HERE'S THE BEEF (& LAMB)

137 MONGOLIAN LAMB

SESAME SAUCE
 1 tablespoon sesame seeds
 ¼ cup soy sauce
 1 green onion with tops, finely chopped
 1 tablespoon dry sherry
 1 tablespoon red wine vinegar
 1½ teaspoons sugar
 1 clove garlic, minced
 ½ teaspoon dark sesame oil

LAMB
 1 pound boneless lean lamb* (leg or
    shoulder)
 2 small leeks, trimmed and thoroughly
    cleaned
 4 green onions with tops
 4 tablespoons vegetable oil, divided
 4 slices peeled fresh ginger, divided
    Chili oil (optional)
 2 medium carrots, shredded
 1 medium zucchini, shredded
 1 green bell pepper, cut into matchstick
    pieces
 1 red bell pepper, cut into matchstick
    pieces
 ½ small head napa cabbage, thinly sliced
 1 cup bean sprouts

Or substitute beef flank steak or boneless lean pork for the lamb.

For Sesame Sauce, place sesame seeds in small skillet. Carefully shake or stir over medium heat until seeds begin to pop and turn golden brown, about 2 minutes; cool. Crush seeds with mortar and pestle or place between paper towels and crush with rolling pin. Scrape up sesame paste with knife and transfer to small bowl. Add remaining sauce ingredients; mix well.

Slice meat across grain into 2×¼-inch strips. Cut leeks into 2-inch slivers. Repeat with green onions. Arrange meat and all vegetables on large platter. Have Sesame Sauce, vegetable oil, ginger and chili oil, if desired, near cooking area.

Heat wok or electric griddle to 350°F. Cook one serving at a time. For each serving, heat 1 tablespoon vegetable oil. Add 1 slice ginger; cook and stir 30 seconds. Discard ginger. Add ½ cup meat strips; stir-fry until lightly browned, about 1 minute. Add 2 cups assorted vegetables; stir-fry 1 minute. Drizzle with 2 tablespoons Sesame Sauce; stir-fry 30 seconds. Season with a few drops chili oil, if desired. Repeat with remaining ingredients. *Makes 4 servings*

138 TERIYAKI BEEF

 ¾ pound sirloin tip steak, cut into thin
    strips
 ½ cup teriyaki sauce
 ¼ cup water
 1 tablespoon cornstarch
 1 teaspoon sugar
 1 bag (16 ounces) BIRDS EYE® frozen
    Farm Fresh Mixtures Broccoli, Carrots
    and Water Chestnuts

• Spray large skillet with nonstick cooking spray; cook beef strips over medium-high heat 7 to 8 minutes, stirring occasionally.

• Combine teriyaki sauce, water, cornstarch and sugar; mix well.

• Add teriyaki sauce mixture and vegetables to beef. Bring to a boil; quickly reduce heat to medium.

• Cook 7 to 10 minutes or until broccoli is heated through, stirring occasionally.

Mongolian Lamb

HERE'S THE BEEF (& LAMB)

139 BEEF AND BROCCOLI

SAUCE
¼ cup water
2 tablespoons oyster sauce
1 tablespoon *each:* cornstarch and dry sherry
⅛ teaspoon Oriental sesame oil

BEEF AND VEGETABLES
3 tablespoons LA CHOY® Soy Sauce
1 tablespoon cornstarch
1 pound flank steak, sliced across grain into thin 2-inch strips
4 tablespoons WESSON® Oil, divided
3 cups fresh broccoli florets
1 cup julienne-cut carrots
1 tablespoon *each:* minced fresh garlic and ginger
1 (8-ounce) can LA CHOY® Sliced Water Chestnuts, drained
1 (5-ounce) can LA CHOY® Chow Mein Noodles

In small bowl, combine sauce ingredients; set aside. In large bowl, combine soy sauce and cornstarch; mix well. Add beef; toss gently to coat. Cover and marinate 30 minutes. In large nonstick skillet or wok, heat *2 tablespoons* oil. Add half of beef mixture; stir-fry until lightly browned. Remove beef from skillet; set aside. Repeat with remaining beef mixture. Heat *remaining 2 tablespoons* oil in same skillet. Add broccoli, carrots, garlic and ginger; stir-fry 1 to 2 minutes or until vegetables are crisp-tender. Return beef to skillet. Stir sauce; add to skillet with water chestnuts. Cook, stirring constantly, until sauce is thick and bubbly. Reserve a few noodles; serve beef mixture over remaining noodles. Garnish with reserved noodles.

Makes 4 to 6 servings

140 CURRIED STIR–FRIED AMERICAN LAMB

¾ pound boneless fresh American lamb, sliced into ⅛-inch strips
2 tablespoons vegetable oil, divided
2 cloves garlic, minced
1 small onion, chopped
1 small red apple, unpeeled and diced
½ cup diced green bell pepper
½ cup thinly sliced celery
¼ cup water chestnuts (optional)
6 ounces frozen or fresh snow peas
1 teaspoon minced fresh ginger *or* ¼ teaspoon ground ginger
¼ cup chicken broth
1 tablespoon light soy sauce
1 teaspoon cornstarch
¼ teaspoon curry powder
Hot cooked rice

Heat 1 tablespoon oil in wok; add garlic and sauté briefly. Add onion and lamb; stir-fry 2 to 3 minutes or until lamb is no longer pink. Remove from wok; keep warm. Add remaining 1 tablespoon oil to wok and heat. Add apple, pepper, celery, water chestnuts, if desired, snow peas and ginger. Stir-fry until crisp-tender. Return lamb mixture to wok and cook until mixture is hot and well blended.

In small bowl, combine chicken broth, soy sauce, cornstarch and curry powder. Add to lamb mixture, stirring constantly until thickened and meat and vegetables are glazed. Serve over rice.

Makes 4 servings

Prep Time: 10 minutes
Cook Time: 20 minutes

Favorite recipe from **American Lamb Council**

HERE'S THE BEEF (& LAMB)

141 STIR–FRIED SIRLOIN & SPINACH WITH NOODLES

1 pound boneless beef top sirloin steak, cut 1 inch thick
4 ounces uncooked vermicelli
1 package (10 ounces) fresh spinach leaves, stemmed and thinly sliced
1 cup fresh bean sprouts
¼ cup sliced green onions

MARINADE
¼ cup hoisin sauce
2 tablespoons reduced-sodium soy sauce
1 tablespoon water
2 teaspoons dark sesame oil
2 cloves garlic, crushed
⅛ to ¼ teaspoon red pepper flakes

1. Trim fat from beef steak. Cut steak lengthwise in half and then crosswise into ⅛-inch-thick strips; place in medium bowl. Combine marinade ingredients; pour ½ over beef. Cover and marinate in refrigerator 10 minutes. Reserve remaining marinade.

2. Meanwhile, cook vermicelli according to package directions; set aside.

3. Remove beef from marinade; discard marinade. Heat large nonstick skillet over medium-high heat until hot. Add beef (½ at a time) and stir-fry 1 to 2 minutes or until outside surface is no longer pink. *Do not overcook*. Remove from skillet with slotted spoon; keep warm.

4. In same skillet, combine vermicelli, spinach, bean sprouts, green onions and reserved marinade; cook until spinach is wilted and mixture is heated through, stirring occasionally. Return beef to skillet; mix lightly.   *Makes 4 servings*

Favorite recipe from **North Dakota Beef Commission**

142 UNIVERSAL BEEF STIR–FRY

1 (1-pound) beef flank steak
¼ cup HIRAM WALKER® Creme de Cassis, Sambuca, Anisette or Culinary Liqueur flavor of your choice
1 teaspoon cornstarch
1 teaspoon grated lemon peel
½ teaspoon coriander seeds
¼ teaspoon ground cardamom
1 tablespoon vegetable oil
¾ cup diagonally-sliced carrots
5 green onions, cut into 1-inch pieces
1 medium red bell pepper, cut into julienne strips
1 (10-ounce) package frozen sugar snap peas, thawed
1 tablespoon chopped crystallized ginger
Hot cooked rice

Partially freeze steak. Slice steak diagonally across grain into ¼-inch-wide strips.

Combine liqueur, cornstarch, lemon peel, coriander seeds and cardamom in small bowl. Stir well and set aside.

Preheat wok or large skillet over medium-high heat; add oil. Add steak strips; stir-fry 5 minutes. Remove steak strips; set aside. Add carrots; stir-fry 3 minutes. Add onions, pepper and sugar snap peas; stir-fry 3 minutes. Stir liqueur mixture; add steak strips and liqueur mixture to wok. Cook, stirring constantly, 1 to 2 minutes or until mixture is slightly thickened. Stir in ginger. Serve over hot cooked rice.

Makes 6 servings

HERE'S THE BEEF (& LAMB)

143 BEEF WITH CASHEWS

1 piece fresh ginger (about 1 inch square)
1 pound beef rump steak
4 tablespoons vegetable oil, divided
½ cup water
4 teaspoons cornstarch
4 teaspoons soy sauce
1 teaspoon sesame oil
1 teaspoon oyster sauce
1 teaspoon Chinese chili sauce
8 green onions with tops, cut into 1-inch pieces
2 cloves garlic, minced
⅔ cup unsalted roasted cashews (about 3 ounces)
    Fresh carrot slices and thyme leaves for garnish

1. Peel and finely chop ginger; set aside.

2. Trim fat from meat.

3. Cut meat across grain into thin slices about 2 inches long.

4. Heat 1 tablespoon vegetable oil in wok or large skillet over high heat. Add ½ of meat; stir-fry until browned, 3 to 5 minutes. Remove from wok; set aside. Repeat with 1 tablespoon oil and remaining meat.

5. Combine water, cornstarch, soy sauce, sesame oil, oyster sauce and chili sauce in small bowl; mix well.

6. Heat remaining 2 tablespoons vegetable oil in wok or large skillet over high heat. Add ginger, onions, garlic and cashews; stir-fry 1 minute.

7. Stir cornstarch mixture; add to wok with meat. Cook and stir until liquid boils and thickens. Garnish, if desired.

Makes 4 servings

144 VEAL ESCALLOPS WITH FRUITED WILD RICE STUFFING

3⅓ cups cooked U.S. wild rice
1 cup chopped dried apricots
½ cup butter, softened, divided
½ cup fresh bread crumbs
½ cup chopped nuts, toasted (optional)
2 egg whites
4 tablespoons raisins
    Salt and black pepper to taste
10 boned veal cutlets (3 ounces each), pounded thin
½ pound shiitake mushrooms, sliced
½ cup minced shallots
2 teaspoons minced fresh thyme
    All-purpose flour
2 cups dry white wine

Mix wild rice, apricots, ¼ cup butter, bread crumbs, nuts, if desired, egg whites, raisins, salt and pepper in medium bowl. Spread approximately ½ cup mixture on each cutlet; roll each cutlet and tie with string. Set aside. Sauté mushrooms and shallots in remaining ¼ cup butter 5 minutes in large saucepan. Season with thyme, salt and pepper. Remove mushroom mixture from pan; set aside. Flour rolled cutlets; brown in same pan. Add wine and mushroom mixture; cover and braise 15 minutes over low heat. Slice and serve with mushroom sauce.

Makes 10 servings

*Favorite recipe from **California Wild Rice Association***

Beef with Cashews

145 BEEF TERIYAKI STIR–FRY

1 cup uncooked rice
1 pound beef sirloin, thinly sliced
½ cup teriyaki marinade, divided
2 tablespoons vegetable oil, divided
1 medium onion, cut into halves and sliced
2 cups frozen green beans, rinsed and drained

1. Cook rice according to package directions, omitting salt.

2. Combine beef and ¼ cup marinade in medium bowl; set aside.

3. Heat ½ tablespoon oil in wok or large skillet over medium-high heat until hot. Add onion; stir-fry 3 to 4 minutes or until crisp-tender. Remove from wok to medium bowl.

4. Heat ½ tablespoon oil in wok until hot. Stir-fry beans 3 minutes or until crisp-tender and hot. Drain off excess liquid. Add beans to onion in bowl.

5. Heat remaining 1 tablespoon oil in wok until hot. Drain beef, discarding marinade. Stir-fry beef about 3 minutes or until browned. Stir in vegetables and remaining ¼ cup marinade; cook and stir 1 minute or until heated through. Serve with rice.

Makes 4 servings

Prep and Cook Time: 22 minutes

146 THAI BEEF & PEANUTS

1 pound beef full cut round steak, cut into 2×½×¼-inch strips
2 tablespoons vegetable oil, divided
2 medium onions, cut into half-rings
¼ to ½ teaspoon red pepper flakes
2 red bell peppers, cut into ¼-inch strips
2 medium yellow squash (about 4 ounces), julienned
½ cup Thai peanut sauce*
¼ cup dry roasted peanuts, coarsely chopped
Hot cooked couscous or rice

*Available in larger grocery stores or specialty markets.

1. In large skillet, heat 1 tablespoon oil over medium-high heat until hot. Add beef strips. Cook, stirring frequently, about 4 minutes or until outside surface is no longer pink. Remove beef from skillet.

2. Add remaining 1 tablespoon oil to skillet. Add onions and red pepper flakes, stirring constantly about 3 minutes or until onions begin to soften.

3. Add bell peppers, stirring constantly about 3 minutes or until bell peppers begin to soften.

4. Add squash; cook about 1 minute.

5. Add peanut sauce and return beef to skillet; cook about 3 to 5 minutes or until heated through.

6. Sprinkle peanuts over beef mixture. Serve over cooked couscous.

Makes 4 servings

*Favorite recipe from **North Dakota Beef Commission***

Beef Teriyaki Stir-Fry

HERE'S THE BEEF (& LAMB)

147 ITALIAN BEEF STIR–FRY

1 pound beef round tip steaks,* cut ⅛ to
    ¼ inch thick
2 cloves garlic, crushed
1 tablespoon olive oil
    Salt and black pepper
2 small zucchini, thinly sliced
1 cup cherry tomato halves
¼ cup bottled reduced-calorie Italian salad
    dressing
2 cups hot cooked spaghetti
1 tablespoon grated Parmesan cheese

*Recipe may be prepared using 1 pound beef strips for stir-fry.

Cut beef steaks crosswise into 1-inch-wide strips; cut each strip crosswise in half. Cook and stir garlic in oil in large nonstick skillet over medium-high heat 1 minute. Add beef strips (½ at a time); stir-fry 1 to 1½ minutes. Season with salt and pepper. Remove with slotted spoon; keep warm. Add zucchini to same skillet; stir-fry 2 to 3 minutes or until crisp-tender. Return beef to skillet with tomatoes and dressing; heat through. Serve beef mixture over hot pasta; sprinkle with cheese.   *Makes 4 servings*

SERVING SUGGESTION: Serve with toasted garlic bread.

*Favorite recipe from **North Dakota Beef Commission***

148 SHERRIED BEEF

¾ pound boneless beef top round steak
1 cup water
¼ cup dry sherry
3 tablespoons soy sauce
2 large carrots, cut into diagonal slices
1 large green bell pepper, cut into strips
1 medium onion, cut into chunks
2 tablespoons vegetable oil, divided
1 tablespoon cornstarch
2 cups hot cooked rice

Partially freeze steak; slice across grain into ⅛-inch strips. Combine water, sherry and soy sauce. Pour over beef in small bowl; cover. Marinate 1 hour in refrigerator. Stir-fry vegetables in 1 tablespoon oil in large skillet over medium-high heat. Remove from skillet; set aside. Drain beef, reserving marinade. Brown beef in remaining 1 tablespoon oil. Combine cornstarch with marinade in bowl. Add vegetables and marinade to beef. Cook, stirring, until sauce is thickened; cook 1 minute longer. Serve over rice.   *Makes 4 servings*

*Favorite recipe from **USA Rice Federation***

HERE'S THE BEEF (& LAMB)

149 KNOCKWURST WITH WHITE BEANS AND TOMATOES

1 tablespoon olive oil
1 small onion, chopped
2 cloves garlic, minced
1 can (16 ounces) cannellini or Great Northern beans, drained
1 can (14½ ounces) Italian-style stewed tomatoes, undrained
1 teaspoon dried basil leaves
½ teaspoon dried rosemary
1 package (12 ounces) HEBREW NATIONAL® Beef Knockwurst

Heat oil in large nonstick saucepan over medium-high heat. Add onion and garlic; cook 4 minutes, stirring occasionally. Add beans, tomatoes with liquid, basil and rosemary; bring to a boil. Cut knockwurst crosswise into ½-inch pieces; stir into saucepan. Cover; simmer 10 minutes.

Makes 4 servings

150 BEEF SONOMA & RICE

1 pound lean ground beef (80% lean)
1 clove garlic, minced
1 package (6.8 ounces) RICE-A-RONI® Beef Flavor
½ cup chopped green bell pepper *or* 1 can (4 ounces) chopped green chilies, undrained
¼ cup sliced green onions
1 medium tomato, chopped
2 tablespoons chopped parsley or cilantro

1. In large skillet, brown ground beef and garlic; drain. Remove from skillet; set aside.

2. In same skillet, prepare Rice-A-Roni® mix as package directs, stirring in beef mixture, bell pepper and onions during last 5 minutes of cooking.

3. Sprinkle with tomato and parsley.

Makes 4 servings

HERE'S THE BEEF (& LAMB)

151 BEEF & TOMATO STIR-FRY

½ pound boneless tender beef steak (sirloin, rib eye or top loin)
3 tablespoons cornstarch, divided
4 tablespoons KIKKOMAN® Soy Sauce, divided
1 tablespoon dry sherry
1 clove garlic, minced
2 teaspoons minced fresh ginger root
½ teaspoon sugar
1 cup water
2 tablespoons vegetable oil, divided
2 stalks celery, cut diagonally into ¼-inch-thick slices
1 medium onion, chunked
1 medium-size green bell pepper, chunked
2 medium tomatoes, chunked

Cut beef across grain into thin strips. Combine 1 tablespoon *each* cornstarch, soy sauce and sherry with garlic, ginger and sugar in medium bowl; stir in beef. Let stand 15 minutes. Meanwhile, combine water, remaining 3 tablespoons soy sauce and 2 tablespoons cornstarch in small bowl; set aside. Heat 1 tablespoon oil in hot wok or large skillet over high heat. Add beef and stir-fry 1 minute; remove. Heat remaining 1 tablespoon oil in same pan. Add celery, onion and bell pepper; stir-fry 3 minutes. Add beef, soy sauce mixture and tomatoes; cook and stir until sauce boils and thickens and tomatoes are heated through.

Makes 4 servings

152 SIRLOIN STIR-FRY FETTUCCINE

1 boneless beef top sirloin steak (about 1¼ pounds), cut 1 inch thick
2 tablespoons olive oil
3 cloves garlic, crushed
¾ teaspoon black pepper
1 package (9 ounces) refrigerated uncooked fettuccine
Salt
8 ounces sliced fresh mushrooms
4 pickled hot or mild cherry peppers, seeded and cut into thin strips (optional)
Grated Parmesan cheese
2 tablespoons chopped fresh parsley

1. In medium bowl, combine oil, garlic and black pepper. Reserve 1 tablespoon for pasta. Trim fat from beef steak; cut steak lengthwise in half and then crosswise into ¼-inch-thick strips. Add beef to remaining oil mixture; toss to coat. Set aside.

2. Cook pasta according to package directions. In large bowl, toss pasta and reserved oil mixture; keep warm.

3. Heat large nonstick skillet over medium-high heat until hot. Add beef (½ at a time) and stir-fry 1 to 2 minutes or until outside surface is no longer pink. *Do not overcook.* Remove from skillet with slotted spoon; season with ½ teaspoon salt. In same skillet, add mushrooms; stir-fry 2 to 3 minutes or until tender.

4. Add beef, mushrooms, cherry peppers, 2 tablespoons cheese and parsley to pasta; toss lightly. Season to taste with salt. Sprinkle with additional cheese; garnish as desired. *Makes 4 servings*

Favorite recipe from **North Dakota Beef Commission**

Beef & Tomato Stir-Fry

HERE'S THE BEEF (& LAMB)

153 SKILLET FRANKS AND POTATOES

3 tablespoons vegetable oil, divided
4 HEBREW NATIONAL® Quarter Pound Dinner Beef Franks or Beef Knockwurst
3 cups chopped cooked red potatoes
1 cup chopped onion
1 cup chopped green bell pepper or combination of green and red bell peppers
3 tablespoons chopped fresh parsley (optional)
1 teaspoon dried sage leaves
½ teaspoon salt
¼ teaspoon freshly ground black pepper

Heat 1 tablespoon oil in large nonstick skillet over medium heat. Score franks; add to skillet. Cook franks until browned. Transfer to plate; set aside.

Add remaining 2 tablespoons oil to skillet. Add potatoes, onion and bell pepper; cook and stir about 12 to 14 minutes or until potatoes are golden brown. Stir in parsley, if desired, sage, salt and pepper.

Return franks to skillet; push down into potato mixture. Cook about 5 minutes or until heated through, turning once halfway through cooking time. *Makes 4 servings*

154 BEEFY GREEN BEAN & WALNUT STIR-FRY

1 teaspoon vegetable oil
3 cloves garlic, minced
1 pound lean ground beef or ground turkey
1 bag (16 ounces) BIRDS EYE® frozen Cut Green Beans, thawed
1 teaspoon salt
½ cup California walnut pieces
    Hot cooked egg noodles or rice (optional)

• In large skillet, heat oil and garlic over medium heat about 30 seconds.

• Add beef and beans; sprinkle with salt. Mix well.

• Cook 5 minutes or until beef is well browned, stirring occasionally.

• Stir in walnuts; cook 2 minutes more.

• Serve over noodles, if desired.
    Makes 4 servings

Prep Time: 5 minutes
Cook Time: 7 to 10 minutes

Skillet Franks and Potatoes

HERE'S THE BEEF (& LAMB)

155 HOT AND SPICY ONION BEEF

2 tablespoons soy sauce, divided
1 tablespoon cornstarch, divided
¾ pound flank steak, thinly sliced across grain
2 tablespoons dry sherry
1 teaspoon Oriental sesame oil
1 teaspoon chili paste (optional)
2 tablespoons vegetable oil
1 large onion (12 to 14 ounces), sliced vertically
1 teaspoon minced garlic
Dried whole red chili peppers to taste
1 tablespoon water

Combine 1 tablespoon soy sauce and 1 teaspoon cornstarch in medium bowl. Add beef; stir to coat. Let stand 30 minutes. Combine remaining 1 tablespoon soy sauce, sherry, sesame oil and chili paste, if desired, in small bowl; set aside. Heat wok or large skillet over high heat. Add vegetable oil, swirling to coat side. Add onion, garlic and chili peppers; cook and stir until onion is tender. Add beef; stir-fry 2 minutes or until lightly browned. Add soy sauce mixture; mix well. Combine remaining 2 teaspoons cornstarch and water; mix into onion mixture. Cook and stir until sauce boils and thickens.   *Makes about 4 servings*

Favorite recipe from **National Onion Association**

156 SOUTHWESTERN LAMB STIR-FRY

12 ounces boneless lean American lamb, leg or shoulder, cut into ¼-inch strips
1 tablespoon vegetable oil
1 clove garlic, minced
1 large green bell pepper, cut into strips (about 1 cup)
1 medium onion, sliced and separated into rings (about 1 cup)
2 tablespoons dry taco seasoning mix
1 cup coarsely chopped tomatoes
¼ cup green chili salsa
3 to 4 ounces baby corn ears, drained (optional)
1 cup lettuce, shredded
4 flour tortillas, warmed
Optional toppings: shredded cheese, sliced black olives, sour cream, guacamole

Heat oil and garlic to medium-high in large wok or skillet. Stir in lamb strips, bell pepper, onion rings and taco seasoning. Stir-fry 4 to 6 minutes or until vegetables are crisp-tender and lamb is still slightly pink.

Add tomatoes, salsa and baby corn. Cook 1 to 2 minutes or until thoroughly heated, stirring constantly. Place a layer of shredded lettuce over warm tortilla. Top with lamb mixture and your choice of toppings. Repeat with remaining tortillas.

Makes 4 servings

Favorite recipe from **American Lamb Council**

Grape and Lamb Stir-Fry

157 GRAPE AND LAMB STIR–FRY

1¼ pounds lamb or beef, cut into thin strips
2 tablespoons cornstarch, divided
2 tablespoons soy sauce, divided
1 clove garlic, minced
1 teaspoon grated fresh ginger
1 cup sliced celery
1 cup sliced onion
½ cup chopped green bell pepper
2 tablespoons vegetable oil, divided
2 cups California seedless grapes
¼ cup water
2 tablespoons ketchup
½ teaspoon sugar
¼ teaspoon Worcestershire sauce
Pan-fried noodles or rice

Combine lamb, 1 tablespoon *each* cornstarch and soy sauce, garlic and ginger in large bowl; set aside. In large skillet, stir-fry celery, onion and pepper in 1 tablespoon oil 1 minute. Add grapes and stir-fry 1 minute longer; remove from pan. Heat remaining 1 tablespoon oil over high heat. Cook and stir lamb about 2 minutes or until browned and cooked to desired degree of doneness. Combine water, ketchup, remaining 1 tablespoon *each* cornstarch and soy sauce, sugar and Worcestershire sauce. Stir into lamb in skillet. Cook until mixture bubbles. Add grape mixture; toss lightly to coat. Heat thoroughly. Serve over pan-fried noodles.   *Makes about 6 servings*

*Favorite recipe from **California Table Grape Commission***

HERE'S THE BEEF (& LAMB)

158 SZECHWAN BEEF STIR-FRY

1 pound beef flank steak
2 tablespoons reduced-sodium soy sauce
4 teaspoons dark roasted sesame oil, divided
1½ teaspoons sugar
1 teaspoon cornstarch
2 cloves garlic, crushed
1 tablespoon minced fresh ginger
¼ teaspoon crushed red pepper pods
1 small red bell pepper, cut into 1-inch pieces
1 package (8 ounces) frozen baby corn, thawed
¼ pound snow peas, julienned

Cut beef steak lengthwise into 2 strips; slice across grain into ⅛-inch-thick strips. Combine soy sauce, 2 teaspoons oil, sugar and cornstarch; stir into beef strips in medium bowl. Heat remaining 2 teaspoons oil in large skillet over medium-high heat. Add garlic, ginger and pepper pods; cook 30 seconds. Add bell pepper and corn; stir-fry 1½ minutes. Add snow peas; stir-fry 30 seconds. Remove vegetables. Stir-fry beef strips (½ at a time) 2 to 3 minutes. Return vegetables and beef to skillet and heat through.   *Makes 4 servings*

SERVING SUGGESTION: Serve with hot cooked rice.

*Favorite recipe from **North Dakota Beef Commission***

159 SPICY BEEF AND BROCCOLI STIR–FRY

½ cup HEINZ® Chili Sauce
3 tablespoons water
2 tablespoons soy sauce
1 tablespoon cornstarch
½ teaspoon ground ginger
¼ to ½ teaspoon red pepper flakes
1 pound boneless sirloin steak, cut into ½-inch strips
2 tablespoons vegetable oil, divided
1½ cups broccoli florets
1 small green or red bell pepper, cut into strips
1 small onion, sliced
1 can (8 ounces) sliced water chestnuts, drained
Hot cooked rice

Combine chili sauce, water, soy sauce, cornstarch, ginger and red pepper flakes in small bowl; set aside. In preheated large skillet or wok, stir-fry beef strips in 1 tablespoon oil about 3 minutes or until browned. Remove and set aside. Add remaining 1 tablespoon oil to wok, stir-fry broccoli, bell pepper, onion and water chestnuts 3 to 4 minutes or until vegetables are crisp-tender. Stir in reserved chili sauce mixture; cook until thickened. Stir in browned beef strips and heat 1 to 2 minutes or until hot. Serve over rice.
                Makes 4 servings

HERE'S THE BEEF (& LAMB)

160 SESAME–SOUR CREAM MEATBALLS

¼ cup sesame seeds, divided
1½ pounds ground beef
1 medium onion, finely chopped
½ cup fresh bread crumbs
1 egg
¼ cup milk
½ teaspoon salt
⅛ teaspoon black pepper
⅛ teaspoon ground ginger
4 tablespoons vegetable oil, divided
4 tablespoons butter or margarine, divided
1 cup beef broth, divided
   Sesame-Sour Cream Sauce (recipe follows)
   Fresh Italian parsley sprigs for garnish

1. To toast sesame seeds, spread seeds in large, dry skillet. Shake skillet over medium-low heat until seeds begin to pop and turn golden, about 3 minutes. Set aside 2 tablespoons toasted sesame seeds for Sesame-Sour Cream Sauce.

2. Combine ground beef, onion, bread crumbs, egg, milk, salt, pepper and ginger in large bowl.

3. Place meat mixture on cutting board; pat evenly into 8×6-inch rectangle. Cut meat into 48 (1-inch) squares; shape each square into 1-inch meatball.

4. Heat 2 tablespoons oil and 2 tablespoons butter in large skillet over medium heat. Cook ½ of meatballs until brown on all sides, 8 to 9 minutes. Add ½ cup beef broth. Bring to a boil. Reduce heat to low. Simmer, covered, 5 to 10 minutes. Set cooked meatballs aside. Repeat with remaining meatballs, using remaining 2 tablespoons oil, 2 tablespoons butter and ½ cup broth.

5. Meanwhile, prepare Sesame-Sour Cream Sauce. Place hot meatballs in serving bowl; top with sauce. Sprinkle with remaining 2 tablespoons toasted sesame seeds. Garnish, if desired.   *Makes 4 dozen meatballs*

SESAME–SOUR CREAM SAUCE
2 tablespoons butter or margarine
2 tablespoons all-purpose flour
½ teaspoon ground ginger
¼ teaspoon salt
½ cup beef broth
2 tablespoons toasted sesame seeds
1 tablespoon soy sauce
¾ cup sour cream

1. Melt butter in small saucepan over low heat. Blend in flour, ginger and salt. Cook and stir until bubbly, about 1 minute. Add beef broth. Cook until thickened, stirring constantly, 1 minute. Add sesame seeds and soy sauce.

2. Remove from heat; pour into small bowl. Add sour cream, stirring until smooth.
Makes 1½ cups

161 BROCCOLI BEEF

2 tablespoons vegetable oil
1 teaspoon chopped shallots
10 ounces sliced beef
6 tablespoons LEE KUM KEE® Stir-Fry Sauce or LEE KUM KEE® Spicy Stir-Fry Sauce, divided
1 cup cooked broccoli florets

Heat skillet over medium heat. Add oil. Sauté shallots. Add beef and 2 tablespoons Stir-Fry Sauce; stir-fry. When beef is half done, add broccoli and remaining 4 tablespoons Stir-Fry Sauce. Heat through.
Makes 4 servings

HERE'S THE BEEF (& LAMB)

162 SALTIMBOCCA

4 boneless thin veal slices, cut from the
   leg, or thinly sliced veal cutlets (about
   1¼ pounds)
1 tablespoon FILIPPO BERIO® Olive Oil
1 clove garlic, cut into halves
4 slices prosciutto, cut into halves
8 fresh sage leaves*
½ cup beef broth
5 tablespoons Marsala wine or medium
   sherry
¼ cup half-and-half
   Freshly ground black pepper

*Omit sage if fresh is unavailable. Do not substitute
dried sage leaves.*

Pound veal between 2 pieces waxed paper
with flat side of meat mallet or rolling pin
until very thin. Cut each piece in half to
make 8 small pieces. In large skillet, heat
olive oil with garlic over medium heat until
hot. Add veal; cook until brown, turning
occasionally. Top each piece with slice of
prosciutto and sage leaf. Add beef broth and
Marsala. Cover; reduce heat to low and
simmer 5 minutes or until veal is cooked
through and tender. Transfer veal to warm
serving platter; keep warm. Add half-and-
half to mixture in skillet; simmer 5 to 8
minutes, stirring occasionally, until liquid is
reduced and thickened, scraping bottom of
skillet to loosen browned bits. Remove
garlic. Spoon sauce over veal. Season to
taste with pepper.   *Makes 4 servings*

163 MEAT AND POTATO STIR–FRY

1 tablespoon vegetable oil
1 large baking potato, peeled and cut into
   ½-inch cubes
2 medium carrots, peeled and thinly sliced
1 medium onion, cut into halves and
   sliced
⅔ cup beef broth
1 teaspoon salt, divided
1 pound lean ground round
1 large clove garlic, minced
1 tablespoon dried parsley flakes
1 teaspoon paprika
½ teaspoon ground cinnamon
½ teaspoon ground cumin
¼ teaspoon black pepper

1. Heat oil in wok or large skillet over
medium-high heat until hot. Add potato,
carrots and onion; cook and stir 3 minutes.
Stir in beef broth and ½ teaspoon salt.
Reduce heat to medium. Cover and cook
6 to 7 minutes or until potato is tender,
stirring once or twice. Remove vegetables
from wok; set aside. Wipe out wok with
paper towel.

2. Heat wok over medium-high heat until
hot. Add meat and garlic; stir-fry 3 minutes
or until meat is no longer pink. Add parsley,
paprika, cinnamon, cumin, remaining
½ teaspoon salt and pepper; cook and stir
1 minute. Add vegetables; heat through.
                              Makes 4 servings

Prep and Cook Time: 25 minutes

Saltimbocca

HERE'S THE BEEF (& LAMB)

164 BEEF & BROCCOLI PEPPER STEAK

1 tablespoon margarine or butter
1 pound well-trimmed top round steak, cut into thin strips
1 package (6.8 ounces) RICE-A-RONI® Beef Flavor
2 cups broccoli florets
½ cup red or green bell pepper strips
1 small onion, thinly sliced

1. In large skillet, melt margarine over medium heat. Add steak; sauté just until browned.

2. Remove from skillet; set aside. Keep warm.

3. In same skillet, prepare Rice-A-Roni® mix as package directs; simmer 10 minutes. Add meat and remaining ingredients; simmer 10 minutes more or until most of liquid is absorbed and vegetables are crisp-tender.

Makes 4 servings

165 SALAMI WESTERN

4 eggs
1¼ cups (5 ounces) HEBREW NATIONAL® Beef Salami or Lean Beef Salami Chub, diced
1 teaspoon parve margarine
¼ cup chopped onion
¼ cup chopped green bell pepper
4 soft rolls, split

Beat eggs in medium bowl; stir in salami. Melt margarine in large nonstick skillet over medium heat. Add onion and pepper; cook and stir 5 minutes or until tender. Add egg mixture; cook, stirring frequently, 5 to 7 minutes or until eggs are set. Spoon onto rolls. Serve immediately.

Makes 4 servings

166 BISTRO BURGUNDY STEW

1 pound boneless beef sirloin, cut into 1½-inch pieces
3 tablespoons all-purpose flour
6 slices bacon, cut into 1-inch pieces (about ¼ pound)
2 cloves garlic, crushed
3 carrots, peeled and cut into 1-inch pieces (about 1½ cups)
¾ cup Burgundy or other dry red wine
½ cup GREY POUPON® Dijon Mustard
½ cup beef broth or reduced-sodium beef broth
12 small mushrooms
1½ cups green onions, cut into 1½-inch pieces
Tomato rose and parsley for garnish
Breadsticks (optional)

Coat beef with flour, shaking off excess; set aside.

In large skillet, over medium heat, cook bacon just until done; pour off excess fat. Add beef and garlic; cook until browned. Add carrots, wine, mustard and beef broth. Heat to a boil; reduce heat. Cover; simmer 30 minutes or until carrots are tender, stirring occasionally. Stir in mushrooms and green onions; cook 10 minutes more, stirring occasionally. Garnish with tomato rose and parsley. Serve with breadsticks, if desired.

Makes 4 servings

Beef & Broccoli Pepper Steak

HERE'S THE BEEF (& LAMB)

167 ORANGE FLAVORED BEEF STIR–FRY

1 pound boneless top sirloin, ¾ inch thick
5 tablespoons KIKKOMAN® Stir-Fry Sauce, divided
2 teaspoons minced garlic
¼ teaspoon grated orange peel
1 tablespoon orange juice
½ teaspoon cornstarch
1 pound broccoli
3 tablespoons vegetable oil, divided
1 carrot, cut diagonally into thin slices
1 tablespoon water
¼ cup slivered almonds, toasted

Cut beef into thin strips. Combine 2 tablespoons stir-fry sauce, garlic and orange peel in small bowl; stir in beef. Let stand 20 minutes. Meanwhile, combine remaining 3 tablespoons stir-fry sauce, orange juice and cornstarch; set aside. Remove flowerets from broccoli; cut into bite-size pieces. Peel stalks; cut diagonally into thin slices. Heat 1 tablespoon oil in hot wok or large skillet over high heat. Add half of beef strips and stir-fry 1 minute; remove. Repeat with 1 tablespoon oil and remaining beef strips. Heat remaining 1 tablespoon oil in same pan over medium-high heat. Add broccoli flowerets and stems and carrot; stir-fry 4 minutes. Sprinkle with water. Add beef and stir-fry sauce mixture. Cook and stir until mixture boils and thickens. Sprinkle with almonds; serve immediately with rice, if desired. Garnish as desired.

Makes 4 servings

168 BROCCOLI BEEF STIR–FRY

½ cup beef broth
4 tablespoons HOLLAND HOUSE® Sherry Cooking Wine, divided
1 tablespoon soy sauce
1 tablespoon cornstarch
1 teaspoon sugar
2 tablespoons vegetable oil, divided
2 cups fresh broccoli florets
1 cup fresh snow peas
1 red bell pepper, cut into strips
1 pound boneless top round or sirloin steak, slightly frozen and cut into thin strips
1 clove garlic, minced
Hot cooked rice

To make sauce, in small bowl, combine beef broth, 2 tablespoons cooking wine, soy sauce, cornstarch and sugar; mix well. Set aside. In large skillet or wok, heat 1 tablespoon oil. Stir-fry broccoli, snow peas and bell pepper 1 minute. Add remaining 2 tablespoons cooking wine. Cover; cook 1 to 2 minutes. Remove from pan. Heat remaining 1 tablespoon oil; add meat and garlic. Stir-fry 5 minutes or until meat is browned. Add sauce to meat; cook 2 to 3 minutes or until thickened, stirring frequently. Add vegetables; cook until thoroughly heated. Serve over cooked rice.

Makes 4 servings

Beef with Peppers

169 BEEF WITH PEPPERS

    1 ounce dried mushrooms
    1 teaspoon cornstarch
    1 teaspoon beef bouillon granules
    1 tablespoon soy sauce
    1 teaspoon sesame oil
    1 pound beef tenderloin, trimmed
2½ tablespoons vegetable oil
    1 clove garlic, minced
 ¼ teaspoon Chinese five-spice powder
    2 small yellow onions, cut into wedges
    1 green bell pepper, thinly sliced
    1 red bell pepper, thinly sliced
    8 ounces Chinese-style thin egg noodles,
        cooked and drained (optional)

1. Place mushrooms in bowl; cover with hot water. Let stand 30 minutes; drain.

2. Squeeze excess water from mushrooms. Remove and discard stems. Slice caps into thin strips.

3. Combine cornstarch, bouillon granules, ¼ cup water, soy sauce and sesame oil in small bowl; mix well. Set aside.

4. Cut meat into thin slices 1 inch long.

5. Heat vegetable oil in wok or large skillet over high heat. Add garlic and five-spice powder; stir-fry 15 seconds.

6. Add meat to wok; stir-fry until browned, about 5 minutes. Add onions; stir-fry 2 minutes. Add mushrooms and peppers; stir-fry until peppers are crisp-tender, about 2 minutes.

7. Stir cornstarch mixture; add to wok. Cook and stir until liquid boils and thickens. Serve over hot cooked noodles, if desired.

Makes 4 servings

HERE'S THE BEEF (& LAMB)

170 SWEET AND SOUR BEEF

1 pound lean ground beef
1 small onion, thinly sliced
2 teaspoons minced fresh ginger
1 package (16 ounces) frozen mixed vegetables (snap peas, carrots, water chestnuts, pineapple and red pepper)
6 to 8 tablespoons bottled sweet and sour sauce or sauce from frozen mixed vegetables
Hot cooked rice

1. Place beef, onion and ginger in large skillet; cook over high heat 6 to 8 minutes or until no longer pink, breaking meat apart with wooden spoon. Pour off drippings.

2. Stir in frozen vegetables and sauce. Cook, covered, 6 to 8 minutes, stirring every 2 minutes or until vegetables are heated through. Serve over rice.

Makes 4 servings

Prep and Cook Time: 15 minutes

SERVING SUGGESTION: Serve with sliced Asian apple-pears.

171 SPICY BEEF AND ONION SANDWICHES

Nonstick cooking spray
6 ounces beef sirloin steak, cut 1 inch thick
1 medium onion, thinly sliced
½ cup water
1 tablespoon mustard seeds
1 cup sliced mushrooms
1 tablespoon sugar
1 tablespoon cider vinegar
1 teaspoon olive oil
3 kaiser rolls
3 tablespoons spicy brown mustard

1. Spray large nonstick skillet with cooking spray. Heat skillet over medium heat until hot. Add beef. Partially cover and cook 4 minutes on each side or until cooked through. Remove beef from skillet.

2. Add onion, water and mustard seeds to skillet. Cook over medium-high heat 5 minutes or until water has evaporated. Add mushrooms, sugar, vinegar and oil. Cook 5 minutes or until onions are browned, stirring frequently.

3. Cut rolls crosswise in half. Spread with mustard. Thinly slice meat; layer on rolls. Top with onion mixture.

Makes 3 servings

Sweet and Sour Beef

HERE'S THE BEEF (& LAMB)

172 STIR–FRY TOMATO BEEF

1 cup uncooked long-grain white rice
1 pound flank steak
1 tablespoon cornstarch
1 tablespoon soy sauce
2 cloves garlic, minced
1 teaspoon minced fresh ginger *or*
    ¼ teaspoon ground ginger
1 tablespoon vegetable oil
1 can (14½ ounces) DEL MONTE®
    Original Recipe Stewed Tomatoes

1. Cook rice according to package directions.

2. Meanwhile, cut steak in half lengthwise, then cut crosswise into thin slices.

3. In medium bowl, combine cornstarch, soy sauce, garlic and ginger. Add steak; toss to coat.

4. Heat oil in large skillet over high heat. Add steak; cook, stirring constantly, until browned. Add tomatoes; cook until thickened, about 5 minutes, stirring frequently.

5. Serve steak mixture over hot cooked rice. Garnish, if desired.

Makes 4 to 6 servings

Prep Time: 10 minutes
Cook Time: 20 minutes

173 GRILLED SALAMI SANDWICH

½ cup drained HEBREW NATIONAL®
    Sauerkraut
½ teaspoon caraway seeds
4 slices rye bread
2 tablespoons prepared oil and vinegar-
    based coleslaw dressing, divided
4 ounces HEBREW NATIONAL® Beef
    Salami or Lean Beef Salami Chub,
    thinly sliced
1 tablespoon parve margarine, divided

Combine sauerkraut and caraway seeds in small bowl. Heat medium nonstick skillet over medium heat. For each sandwich, spread 1 bread slice with 1 tablespoon coleslaw dressing. Cover with salami, sauerkraut mixture and second bread slice. Spread outside of sandwich with margarine. Cook in skillet 6 minutes or until lightly browned on each side. Repeat with remaining ingredients.   *Makes 2 servings*

Stir-Fry Tomato Beef

HERE'S THE BEEF (& LAMB)

174 MEXICAN BEEF STIR–FRY

1 pound beef flank steak
2 tablespoons vegetable oil
1 teaspoon ground cumin
1 teaspoon dried oregano leaves
1 clove garlic, crushed
1 red or green bell pepper, cut into thin strips
1 medium onion, cut into thin wedges
1 to 2 jalapeño peppers,* thinly sliced
3 cups thinly sliced lettuce

*Remove interior ribs and seeds if a milder flavor is desired.

Cut beef steak into ⅛-inch-thick strips. Combine oil, cumin, oregano and garlic in small bowl. Heat ½ oil mixture in large nonstick skillet over medium-high heat. Add bell pepper, onion and jalapeño pepper; stir-fry 2 to 3 minutes or until crisp-tender. Remove and reserve. In same skillet, stir-fry beef strips (½ at a time) in remaining oil mixture 1 to 2 minutes. Return vegetables to skillet and heat through. Serve beef mixture over lettuce. *Makes 4 servings*

TIP: Recipe may also be prepared using beef top sirloin or top round steak cut 1 inch thick.

SERVING SUGGESTION: Serve with corn bread twists.

Favorite recipe from **North Dakota Beef Commission**

175 CHINESE TACOS

¾ pound boneless tender beef steak (sirloin, rib eye or top loin)
1 teaspoon cornstarch
2 teaspoons dry sherry
¼ cup KIKKOMAN® Stir-Fry Sauce
1 large clove garlic, pressed
¼ teaspoon crushed red pepper
1 tablespoon vegetable oil
½ cup chopped green onions and tops
10 taco shells
   Taco Fillings: Fresh bean sprouts, shredded napa (Chinese cabbage), red bell pepper strips, cilantro leaves

Cut beef across grain into thin slices, then into thin strips. Blend cornstarch and sherry in medium bowl; add stir-fry sauce, garlic and crushed red pepper, stirring to combine. Stir in beef; let stand 30 minutes. Heat oil in hot wok or large skillet over high heat. Add beef and stir-fry 90 seconds. Add green onions; stir-fry 30 seconds longer. Remove from heat and fill taco shells with desired amount of beef and taco fillings.
Makes 4 to 6 servings

Mexican Beef Stir-Fry

Perfect Pork

176 STIR–FRIED PORK WITH GREEN BEANS AND BABY CORN

¾ **pound pork tenderloin**
 2 **tablespoons soy sauce**
 4 **teaspoons cornstarch, divided**
 1 **tablespoon rice wine or dry sherry**
 1 **teaspoon sugar**
½ **teaspoon sesame oil**
 1 **pound fresh green beans**
 2 **tablespoons peanut oil, divided**
 2 **cloves garlic, minced**
 1 **teaspoon finely chopped fresh ginger**
 1 **tablespoon black bean sauce**
 1 **can (14 ounces) precut baby corn, drained and rinsed *or* 1 can (15 ounces) whole baby corn, drained, rinsed and cut into 1-inch lengths**

1. Slice pork across grain into thin slices; cut slices into ¾-inch strips.

2. Combine soy sauce, 1 teaspoon cornstarch, rice wine, sugar and sesame oil in medium bowl; mix well. Add pork; toss to coat. Set aside to marinate 20 to 30 minutes. Combine remaining 3 teaspoons cornstarch and ⅓ cup water in small cup; set aside.

3. To prepare beans, snap off stem ends from beans, pulling strings down to remove if necessary. Cut beans diagonally into 1½-inch lengths.

4. Heat 1 tablespoon peanut oil in wok or large skillet over high heat. Add beans; stir-fry about 4 minutes. Add 2 tablespoons water; reduce heat to medium-low. Cover and simmer 10 to 12 minutes or until crisp-tender. Remove beans from wok; set aside.

5. Heat remaining 1 tablespoon peanut oil in wok over high heat. Add garlic, ginger and pork mixture; stir fry about 3 minutes or until meat is no longer pink in center. Add black bean sauce; stir-fry 1 minute.

6. Return beans to wok. Stir cornstarch mixture; add to wok. Bring to a boil; cook until sauce thickens. Stir in baby corn; heat through. *Makes 4 servings*

Stir-Fried Pork with Green Beans and Baby Corn

177 STIR–FRIED PORK WITH ORANGES AND SNOW PEAS

1 cup uncooked rice
1 tablespoon vegetable oil
1 pound lean boneless pork, cut into ¼-inch-wide strips
½ pound snow peas, trimmed
½ cup bottled stir-fry sauce
2 tablespoons thawed frozen orange juice concentrate
1 can (11 ounces) mandarin orange sections, drained

1. Cook rice according to package directions.

2. Heat oil in wok or large skillet over high heat until hot. Stir-fry pork 3 minutes or until brown.

3. Add snow peas; stir-fry 2 minutes or until crisp-tender. Add sauce and juice concentrate; stir until well blended. Gently stir in orange sections; heat through. Serve with rice. *Makes 4 servings*

Prep and Cook Time: 20 minutes

178 PORK AND PEANUT STIR–FRY

2 boneless pork chops, cut into stir-fry strips
¼ cup water
4 teaspoons soy sauce
1 tablespoon rice wine vinegar or white wine vinegar
2 teaspoons cornstarch
1 teaspoon chicken bouillon granules
½ teaspoon sugar
1½ teaspoons vegetable oil
1 teaspoon grated fresh ginger
1 clove garlic, crushed
½ teaspoon red pepper flakes
4 green onions, bias-sliced into 1-inch lengths
2 tablespoons coarsely chopped peanuts

For sauce, stir together water, soy sauce, vinegar, cornstarch, bouillon granules and sugar in small bowl. Set aside. In large skillet, heat oil over medium-high heat. Stir-fry ginger, garlic and pepper 30 seconds. Add onions; stir-fry 1 to 2 minutes or until onions are crisp-tender. Remove onion mixture from skillet. Add pork strips to hot skillet. Stir-fry 2 to 3 minutes or until cooked through. Push pork to side of skillet. Add soy sauce mixture to center of skillet; cook and stir until sauce thickens. Return onion mixture to skillet; add peanuts. Stir all ingredients to coat with sauce. Cook and stir 1 minute more or until heated through. *Makes 2 servings*

Prep Time: 25 minutes

Favorite recipe from **National Pork Producers Council**

Stir-Fried Pork with Oranges and Snow Peas

PERFECT PORK

179 SWEET AND SOUR PORK

¾ **pound boneless pork**
1 **teaspoon vegetable oil**
1 **bag (16 ounces) BIRDS EYE® frozen Farm Fresh Mixtures Pepper Stir Fry vegetables**
1 **tablespoon water**
1 **jar (14 ounces) sweet and sour sauce**
1 **can (8 ounces) pineapple chunks, drained**
   Hot cooked rice (optional)

• Cut pork into thin strips.

• In large skillet, heat oil over medium-high heat.

• Add pork; stir-fry until pork is browned.

• Add vegetables and water; cover and cook over medium heat 5 to 7 minutes or until vegetables are crisp-tender.

• Uncover; stir in sweet and sour sauce and pineapple. Cook until heated through. Serve over rice, if desired.   *Makes 4 servings*

Prep Time: 5 minutes
Cook Time: 15 to 18 minutes

180 GERMAN–STYLE BRATWURST & SAUERKRAUT

6 **slices bacon**
1 **small onion, chopped**
1 **clove garlic, minced**
1 **(32-ounce) jar or can sauerkraut, rinsed and well drained**
2 **medium potatoes, peeled and sliced**
½ **cup apple juice or dry white wine**
2 **tablespoons brown sugar**
1 **teaspoon chicken bouillon granules**
1 **teaspoon caraway seeds**
1 **dried bay leaf**
1 **pound BOB EVANS FARMS® Bratwurst (5 links)**
2 **medium apples, cored and sliced**

Cook bacon in large skillet over medium-high heat until crisp. Remove bacon; drain and crumble on paper towel. Set aside. Drain off all but 2 tablespoons drippings in skillet. Add onion and garlic to drippings; cook over medium heat until tender, stirring occasionally. Stir in sauerkraut, potatoes, 1½ cups water, juice, brown sugar, bouillon, caraway and dried bay leaf. Add additional ½ cup water, if necessary, to cover potatoes. Bring to a boil over high heat.

Meanwhile, make 3 or 4 diagonal ¼-inch-deep cuts into one side of each bratwurst. Cook bratwurst in large skillet over medium heat until browned, turning occasionally. Add bratwurst to sauerkraut mixture. Reduce heat to low; simmer, covered, 20 to 30 minutes or until potatoes are just tender, stirring occasionally. Add apples; cook, covered, 5 to 10 minutes or until apples are just tender. Stir in reserved bacon. Remove and discard dried bay leaf. Serve hot. Refrigerate leftovers.   *Makes 5 servings*

Sweet and Sour Pork

PERFECT PORK

181 ORIENTAL PORK STIR–FRY

1½ pounds pork tenderloin
2 teaspoons vegetable oil
1 teaspoon grated fresh ginger
1 clove garlic, minced
2 medium green bell peppers, cut into thin strips
1 (8-ounce) can sliced water chestnuts, drained
3 tablespoons soy sauce
1 tablespoon cornstarch
1½ cups cherry tomato halves

Partially freeze pork; cut pork into 3×½×⅛-inch strips. Preheat nonstick skillet over high heat; add oil. Stir-fry ginger and garlic in hot oil 30 seconds; remove from skillet. Add pork to skillet; stir-fry 5 minutes or until browned. Remove from skillet. Stir-fry remaining pork 5 minutes or until browned; remove from skillet. Add peppers and water chestnuts; stir-fry 3 to 4 minutes. Combine soy sauce and cornstarch; stir into vegetable mixture. Stir in pork; heat through. Add tomato halves, stirring to combine. Serve immediately. *Makes 6 servings*

Prep Time: 20 minutes

*Favorite recipe from **National Pork Producers Council***

182 QUICK CASSOULET

2 slices bacon, cut into ½-inch pieces
¾ pound boneless pork chops, sliced crosswise ¼ inch thick
1 medium onion, chopped
1 clove garlic, minced
1 teaspoon dried thyme leaves
1 can (14½ ounces) DEL MONTE® *FreshCut*™ Diced Tomatoes, undrained
½ cup dry white wine
1 can (15 ounces) white or pinto beans, drained

1. In large skillet, cook bacon over medium-high heat until almost crisp.

2. Stir in pork, onion, garlic and thyme. Season with salt and pepper, if desired.

3. Cook 4 minutes. Add tomatoes and wine; bring to a boil.

4. Cook, uncovered, over medium-high heat 10 minutes or until thickened, adding beans during last 5 minutes. *Makes 4 servings*

Prep and Cook Time: 30 minutes

PERFECT PORK

183 JAMAICAN PORK SKILLET

1 tablespoon vegetable oil
4 well-trimmed center cut pork chops, cut ½ inch thick
¾ teaspoon blackened or Cajun seasoning mix
¼ teaspoon ground allspice
1 cup chunky salsa, divided
1 can (15 ounces) black beans, drained and rinsed
1 can (about 8 ounces) whole kernel corn, drained *or* 1 cup thawed frozen whole kernel corn
1 tablespoon fresh lime juice

1. Heat oil in large deep skillet over medium-high heat until hot. Sprinkle both sides of pork chops with blackened seasoning mix and allspice; cook 2 minutes per side or until browned.

2. Pour ½ cup salsa over pork chops; reduce heat to medium. Cover and simmer about 12 minutes or until pork is no longer pink.

3. While pork chops are simmering, combine beans, corn, remaining ½ cup salsa and lime juice in medium bowl; mix well. Serve bean mixture with pork chops.

Makes 4 servings

Prep and Cook Time: 20 minutes

HINT: For a special touch, add chopped fresh cilantro to the bean mixture.

184 BREAKFAST BURRITOS

6 ounces breakfast sausage
1¾ cups (1-pound can) ORTEGA® Refried Beans
1 tablespoon butter or margarine
8 eggs, lightly beaten
8 soft taco-size (8-inch) flour tortillas, warmed
½ cup (2 ounces) shredded Cheddar cheese
¼ cup chopped tomato
¼ cup chopped green bell pepper
ORTEGA® Thick & Chunky Salsa, mild or Garden Style Salsa, mild

COOK sausage in large skillet over medium-high heat stirring to break into pieces 4 to 5 minutes or until no longer pink in center; drain. Stir in refried beans; heat 3 to 4 minutes. Remove from skillet; keep warm.

MELT butter in medium skillet over medium heat. Add eggs; cook, stirring constantly, 3 to 4 minutes or until eggs are of desired consistency.

PLACE ⅓ cup sausage mixture down center of one tortilla. Top with 2 tablespoons eggs, 1 tablespoon cheese, 1 teaspoon tomato and 1 teaspoon bell pepper; fold into burrito. Repeat with remaining ingredients. Serve with salsa.

Makes 8 servings

PERFECT PORK

185 SPICY PORK STIR-FRY

1 can (about 14 ounces) defatted reduced-
  sodium chicken broth, divided
2 tablespoons reduced-sodium soy sauce
2 tablespoons cornstarch
1 tablespoon grated orange peel
1 pork tenderloin (about 10 ounces)
2 tablespoons peanut oil, divided
1 tablespoon sesame seeds
2 cloves garlic, minced
2 cups broccoli florets
2 cups sliced carrots
1 teaspoon Szechuan seasoning
6 cups hot cooked rice

1. Combine 1½ cups chicken broth, soy sauce, cornstarch and orange peel in medium bowl until smooth. Cut pork lengthwise, then cut crosswise into ¼-inch slices.

2. Heat 1 tablespoon oil in wok or large skillet over high heat until hot. Add pork, sesame seeds and garlic. Stir-fry 3 minutes or until pork is barely pink in center. Remove from wok.

3. Heat remaining 1 tablespoon oil in wok until hot. Add broccoli, carrots, Szechuan seasoning and remaining 2 tablespoons chicken broth. Cook and stir 5 minutes or until vegetables are crisp-tender. Add pork. Stir chicken broth mixture and add to wok. Cook and stir over medium heat until sauce is thickened. Serve over rice.

Makes 6 servings

186 HAM-CHICKEN STIR-FRY

1 (8-ounce) can sliced bamboo shoots,
  undrained
¼ cup soy sauce
¼ cup dry white wine
1 tablespoon sugar
1 tablespoon cornstarch
2 tablespoons vegetable oil
2 partially frozen boneless skinless
  chicken breasts, sliced into thin strips
¾ pound JONES® Ham, sliced into thin
  strips
3 cups diagonally sliced celery
2 green onions with tops, sliced diagonally
⅓ cup slivered almonds, toasted
  Hot cooked rice

Drain bamboo shoots, reserving liquid. Combine soy sauce, wine, sugar, cornstarch and liquid from bamboo shoots in small bowl; set aside.

Heat oil in wok over medium heat 3 minutes. Add chicken and stir-fry 3 to 4 minutes or until opaque. Push to side of wok. Add ham and stir-fry 2 to 3 minutes. Push to side of wok. Add celery and stir-fry 2½ minutes; cover wok and cook for 2½ minutes. Push to side of wok. Add onions and stir-fry 1 minute. Push to side of wok. Add bamboo shoots and stir-fry 1 minute. Push to side of wok. Add soy sauce mixture; when thickened, stir all ingredients together.

Reduce heat to low. Sprinkle with almonds and serve over rice.

Makes 4 to 6 servings

Spicy Pork Stir-Fry

PERFECT PORK

187 NEW SOUTH STIR–FRY

1 teaspoon ground thyme
¼ teaspoon salt
⅛ teaspoon black pepper
1 pound pork tenderloin, trimmed
1 tablespoon vegetable oil
1 clove garlic, minced
1 cup thinly sliced onion
1 cup thinly sliced red bell pepper
1 package (8 ounces) frozen baby corn,
    thawed and drained
1 package (10 ounces) frozen sliced okra,
    cooked and drained
1 tablespoon chopped fresh parsley
1 tablespoon chopped fresh celery heart
    leaves
1 to 2 drops hot pepper sauce
2 cups hot cooked rice

In small bowl, combine thyme, salt and black pepper; blend well. Set aside. Cut pork lengthwise into quarters; cut each quarter into ¼-inch slices. Sprinkle pork slices with thyme mixture. Heat oil in large skillet over medium-high heat. Add pork slices and garlic; stir-fry 3 to 4 minutes or until pork is tender. Add onion, bell pepper and corn; stir-fry 3 to 4 minutes. Stir in okra, parsley, celery leaves and pepper sauce; cook just until mixture is hot, stirring frequently. Serve with rice.   *Makes 4 servings*

Prep Time: 20 minutes

*Favorite recipe from **National Pork Producers Council***

188 STIR–FRY HAM AND LIMA BEANS

1 tablespoon butter or margarine
½ pound cooked ham, cut into 3×¼-inch
    strips
1 medium onion, cut into thin wedges
1 box (10 ounces) BIRDS EYE® frozen
    Deluxe Fordhook Lima Beans
2 tablespoons spicy brown mustard
1 tablespoon honey
¼ teaspoon caraway seeds

• In large skillet, melt butter over medium-high heat.

• Add ham and onion; cook about 8 minutes or until lightly browned, stirring occasionally.

• Stir in lima beans, mustard, honey and caraway; cover and cook 5 minutes.

• Uncover; cook 3 minutes more or until beans are tender, stirring occasionally.
          Makes 4 servings

189 TWO–ONION PORK SHREDS

½ teaspoon Szechuan peppercorns
7½ teaspoons vegetable oil, divided
4 teaspoons soy sauce, divided
4 teaspoons dry sherry, divided
1 teaspoon cornstarch
8 ounces boneless lean pork
2 teaspoons red wine vinegar
½ teaspoon sugar
2 cloves garlic, minced
½ small yellow onion, cut into ¼-inch
    slices
8 green onions with tops, cut into 2-inch
    pieces
½ teaspoon sesame oil

PERFECT PORK

1. For marinade, place peppercorns in small skillet. Cook over medium-low heat, shaking skillet frequently, until fragrant, about 2 minutes. Let cool. Crush peppercorns with mortar and pestle (or place between paper towels and crush with hammer).

2. Transfer peppercorns to medium bowl. Add 1½ teaspoons vegetable oil, 2 teaspoons soy sauce, 2 teaspoons sherry and cornstarch; mix well.

3. Slice pork ⅛-inch thick; cut into 2×½-inch pieces. Add to peppercorn marinade; stir to coat well.

4. Combine remaining 2 teaspoons soy sauce, 2 teaspoons sherry, vinegar and sugar in small bowl; mix well.

5. Heat remaining 6 teaspoons vegetable oil in wok or large skillet over high heat. Stir in garlic. Add pork; stir-fry until no longer pink in center, about 2 minutes. Add yellow onion; stir-fry 1 minute. Add green onions; stir-fry 30 seconds. Add soy-vinegar mixture; cook and stir 30 seconds. Stir in sesame oil.

Makes 2 to 3 servings

Two-Onion Pork Shreds (page 162)

PERFECT PORK

190 TACOS PICADILLOS

¾ pound ground pork
1 medium onion, chopped
½ teaspoon ground cinnamon
½ teaspoon ground cumin
1½ cups DEL MONTE® Traditional Salsa
⅓ cup seedless raisins
⅓ cup toasted chopped almonds
6 flour tortillas

1. In large skillet, brown meat with onion and spices over medium-high heat. Season to taste with salt and pepper, if desired.

2. Stir in salsa and raisins. Cover and cook 10 minutes. Remove cover; cook 5 minutes or until thickened, stirring occasionally.

3. Stir in almonds just before serving. Fill tortillas with meat mixture; roll to enclose. Serve with lettuce, cilantro and sour cream, if desired.   *Makes 6 servings*

Prep Time: 5 minutes
Cook Time: 25 minutes

HELPFUL HINT: If ground pork is not available, boneless pork may be purchased. Cut pork into 1-inch cubes before grinding in food processor.

191 SPICY–SWEET PINEAPPLE PORK

¾ cup LAWRY'S® Hawaiian Marinade with Tropical Fruit Juices
1 tablespoon minced fresh ginger
1 pound pork loin, cut into ½-inch strips or cubes
1 cup salsa
3 tablespoons brown sugar
2 tablespoons cornstarch
2 cans (8 ounces each) pineapple chunks, undrained, divided
2 tablespoons vegetable oil, divided
1 green bell pepper, cut into chunks
3 green onions, diagonally sliced into 1-inch pieces
½ cup whole cashews

In large resealable plastic food storage bag, combine Hawaiian Marinade with Tropical Fruit Juices and ginger. Add pork and marinate in refrigerator 1 hour. In small bowl, combine salsa, brown sugar, cornstarch and juice from 1 can pineapple; set aside. In hot large skillet or wok, heat 1 tablespoon oil. Stir-fry pepper and onions until onions are transparent; remove and set aside. Add remaining 1 tablespoon oil and pork to skillet; stir-fry 5 minutes or until just browned. Return pepper and onions to skillet. Stir salsa mixture; add to skillet. Cook until thickened, stirring constantly. Drain remaining 1 can pineapple. Add pineapple chunks from both cans and cashews; simmer 5 minutes.
                    Makes 6 servings

Taco Picadillo

PERFECT PORK

192 EXOTIC PORK & VEGETABLES

1 large carrot
1 pork tenderloin (about ¾ pound)
2 ounces fresh oyster, shiitake or button mushrooms*
1 baby eggplant
¼ cup water
2 teaspoons cornstarch
4 tablespoons peanut oil, divided
6 whole dried hot red chili peppers
4 cloves garlic, thinly sliced
5 ounces fresh snow peas, ends trimmed
3 tablespoons packed brown sugar
2 tablespoons fish sauce
1 tablespoon sesame oil
  Hot cooked rice

*Or substitute ½ ounce dried Oriental mushrooms, soaked according to package directions.

1. Peel carrot. To make scalloped edges, use citrus stripper or grapefruit spoon to cut groove into carrot, cutting lengthwise from stem end to tip. Continue to cut grooves around carrot about ¼ inch apart until completely around carrot. Cut carrot crosswise into ¼-inch-thick slices.

2. Trim fat from pork; cut pork into thin slices.

3. Wipe mushrooms clean with damp paper towel. Cut thin piece from bottom of stems; discard. Cut large mushrooms into halves.

4. Trim ends from eggplant; discard. Cut into thin slices.

5. Combine water and cornstarch in cup; set aside.

6. Heat wok or large skillet over high heat 1 minute or until hot. Drizzle 2 tablespoons peanut oil into wok and heat 30 seconds. Add peppers and garlic; stir-fry about 1 minute. Add pork; stir-fry 3 to 4 minutes or until no longer pink. Remove pork mixture to bowl and set aside.

7. Add remaining 2 tablespoons peanut oil to wok. Add carrot, mushrooms and eggplant; stir-fry 2 minutes. Add snow peas and pork mixture; stir-fry 1 minute.

8. Stir cornstarch mixture; add to wok. Cook 1 minute or until thickened. Stir in brown sugar, fish sauce and sesame oil; cook until heated through. Serve over rice.

Makes 4 servings

193 SLOPPY JOES

1 pound BOB EVANS FARMS® Italian Roll Sausage
1 medium onion, chopped
½ green bell pepper, chopped
½ cup ketchup
2 tablespoons Dijon mustard
2 tablespoons cider vinegar
1 tablespoon sugar
1 teaspoon minced garlic
8 sandwich buns, split and toasted

Crumble sausage into medium skillet. Add onion and pepper. Cook over medium heat until sausage is browned, stirring occasionally. Drain off any drippings. Stir in remaining ingredients except buns. Bring to a boil. Reduce heat to low; simmer 30 minutes. Serve hot on buns. Refrigerate leftovers. *Makes 8 servings*

Exotic Pork & Vegetables

194 SPICY MUSTARD STIR–FRY

4 tablespoons soy sauce, divided
1 tablespoon cornstarch
5 teaspoons vegetable oil, divided
1 teaspoon hot pepper sauce, divided
1 large pork tenderloin (about ¾ pound),
　　cut into ¼-inch slices
3 tablespoons PLOCHMAN'S® Stone
　　Ground Mustard
6 tablespoons water, divided
3 tablespoons Chinese rice wine or sherry,
　　divided
4 cups cauliflower florets
1½ cups diagonally-cut carrot slices
1 tablespoon minced fresh ginger
2 cloves garlic, minced
4 green onions, cut into ¼-inch pieces
　　Hot cooked rice

1. In small bowl, combine 2 tablespoons soy sauce, cornstarch, 1 teaspoon oil and ½ teaspoon pepper sauce. Add pork, stirring to coat. Let stand at room temperature 15 minutes.

2. In another small bowl, combine mustard, remaining 2 tablespoons soy sauce, 2 tablespoons water, 1 tablespoon rice wine and remaining ½ teaspoon pepper sauce.

3. In large skillet or wok, heat 2 teaspoons oil over medium-high heat. Add cauliflower, carrots, ginger and garlic. Stir-fry 1 minute. Add remaining 2 tablespoons rice wine, then remaining 4 tablespoons water. Cover; cook 3 to 4 minutes or until vegetables are crisp-tender. Remove from skillet; wipe skillet clean.

4. Add remaining 2 teaspoons oil to skillet; heat over high heat. Stir pork mixture to separate slices; add to skillet. Stir-fry until almost done; add green onions. Continue cooking until pork is no longer pink.

5. Return vegetables to skillet; stir in mustard mixture. Heat 1 minute. Serve over rice. *Makes 4 servings*

Prep and Cook Time: 40 minutes

VARIATION: Substitute 1 bag (16 ounces) frozen broccoli, cauliflower and carrot blend for fresh cauliflower and carrots.

195 SPAM™ FAJITAS

　Nonstick cooking spray
1 green bell pepper, cut into julienne
　　strips
½ onion, cut into ¼-inch slices
1 (12-ounce) can SPAM® Luncheon Meat,
　　cut into julienne strips
¾ cup CHI-CHI'S® Salsa
8 (8-inch) flour tortillas, warmed
2 cups shredded lettuce
½ cup (2 ounces) shredded hot pepper
　　Monterey Jack or Cheddar cheese
½ cup nonfat plain yogurt
　　Additional CHI-CHI'S® Salsa (optional)

Spray large nonstick skillet with cooking spray. Heat skillet over medium-high heat. Add bell pepper and onion; sauté 2 minutes. Add SPAM®; sauté 2 minutes. Stir in ¾ cup salsa and heat thoroughly. Spoon about ½ cup SPAM™ mixture onto each tortilla. Top each with ¼ cup lettuce, 1 tablespoon cheese, 1 tablespoon yogurt and additional salsa, if desired. *Makes 8 servings*

SPAM™ Fajita

196 COCO KIWI PORK

1 pound boneless fresh ham (pork leg), sliced for stir-fry
¼ cup soy sauce
¼ cup dry white wine or chicken broth
2 tablespoons honey
1 tablespoon lime juice
1 tablespoon cornstarch
1 teaspoon ground ginger
1 teaspoon vegetable oil
½ onion, thinly sliced
½ cup cashews
½ cup shredded coconut
1 kiwifruit, peeled and sliced

In medium bowl, combine soy sauce, wine, honey, lime juice, cornstarch and ginger. Add pork strips; marinate 20 to 30 minutes. Drain pork, reserving marinade. Heat oil in nonstick skillet over medium-high heat; add pork and stir-fry 3 to 4 minutes. Add onion and stir-fry 1 minute. Add marinade to skillet, cook and stir until sauce thickens. Stir in cashews and coconut; heat through. Serve garnished with kiwifruit slices.

Makes 4 servings

Prep Time: 20 minutes

*Favorite recipe from **National Pork Producers Council***

197 SAUSAGE AND CHICKEN JAMBALAYA STIR–FRY

1 cup uncooked rice
1 teaspoon vegetable oil
¼ pound chicken tenders, cut into 1-inch pieces
½ pound smoked Polish sausage, cut into bite-size pieces
1 large onion, chopped
¾ cup chopped green bell pepper
1 teaspoon bottled minced garlic
1 can (15½ ounces) diced tomatoes, drained
½ cup chicken broth
1 tablespoon dried parsley flakes
½ teaspoon dried thyme leaves
¼ teaspoon salt
¼ teaspoon black pepper
⅛ to ¼ teaspoon ground red pepper

1. Cook rice according to package directions.

2. Heat oil in wok or large skillet over medium-high heat until hot. Stir-fry chicken 2 minutes. Add sausage; stir-fry until sausage and chicken are browned, about 4 minutes. Remove from wok to medium bowl.

3. Add onion and bell pepper to wok; reduce heat to low. Cover and cook 2 to 3 minutes, stirring once or twice. Stir in garlic; cook and stir, uncovered, 1 minute more.

4. Add tomatoes, sausage, chicken, broth, parsley, thyme, salt, black pepper and red pepper. Bring to a boil. Reduce heat to medium-low. Simmer, uncovered, 5 minutes or until most liquid has evaporated. Stir in rice; heat through. *Makes 4 servings*

Prep and Cook Time: 30 minutes

PERFECT PORK

198 PORK TENDERLOIN WITH MANDARIN SALSA

1½ pounds boneless pork loin chops, cut into ¼-inch strips
1 cup orange juice
1 green bell pepper, finely chopped
1 can (10½ ounces) mandarin orange segments, drained and chopped
1⅓ cups chopped red onion, divided
½ cup frozen whole kernel corn, thawed
2 tablespoons olive oil, divided
4 teaspoons bottled minced garlic, divided
1½ teaspoons chili powder, divided
1¼ teaspoons salt, divided
1½ teaspoons cumin
¼ teaspoon ground black pepper

1. Combine pork and orange juice in medium bowl. Set aside.

Pork Tenderloin with Mandarin Salsa

2. To prepare mandarin salsa, combine bell pepper, mandarin oranges, ⅓ cup onion, corn, 1 tablespoon oil, 1 teaspoon garlic, ¼ teaspoon chili powder and ¼ teaspoon salt in another medium bowl. Set aside.

3. Heat remaining 1 tablespoon oil in large nonstick skillet over medium-high heat. Add remaining 1 cup onion and 3 teaspoons garlic. Cook and stir 5 minutes or until onion is softened and starting to brown.

4. Meanwhile, drain pork, reserving orange juice marinade. Toss pork, remaining 1¼ teaspoons chili powder, cumin, remaining 1 teaspoon salt and black pepper in large bowl; add to skillet. Cook and stir 5 minutes or until pork is cooked through and lightly browned. Add ⅓ cup reserved orange juice marinade to skillet; bring to a boil. Reduce heat; simmer 1 to 2 minutes or until liquid thickens slightly. Serve immediately with mandarin salsa.   *Makes 4 servings*

PERFECT PORK

199 STIR–FRIED CAJUN PORK

1 pound boneless pork loin, cut into
   julienne strips
4 tablespoons Cajun-Style Seasoning
   (recipe follows)
1 red bell pepper, diced
1 tart green apple, cored and diced
¼ cup pecan pieces
1 teaspoon vegetable oil

Season pork strips with 2 tablespoons
Cajun-Style Seasoning. Toss pepper, apple
and pecans with 2 tablespoons seasoning;
reserve.

Heat oil in nonstick skillet over medium-high
heat. Stir-fry pork 2 minutes; add reserved
pepper mixture. Cook and stir 2 minutes.
Serve immediately.   *Makes 4 servings*

Prep Time: 10 minutes
Cook Time: 10 minutes

CAJUN–STYLE SEASONING
3 tablespoons paprika
1 tablespoon garlic powder
2 teaspoons dried oregano leaves
2 teaspoons dried thyme leaves
½ teaspoon salt
½ teaspoon white pepper
½ teaspoon ground cumin
½ teaspoon cayenne pepper
¼ teaspoon ground nutmeg

Combine all ingredients in small bowl; mix
well.   *Makes ½ cup*

*Favorite recipe from **National Pork Producers
Council***

200 CHINESE PORK & VEGETABLE STIR–FRY

2 tablespoons vegetable oil, divided
1 pound pork tenderloin or boneless beef
   sirloin, cut into ¼-inch slices
6 cups assorted fresh vegetables*
1 can (8 ounces) sliced water chestnuts,
   drained
1 envelope LIPTON® Recipe Secrets®
   Onion Soup Mix
¾ cup water
½ cup orange juice
1 tablespoon soy sauce
¼ teaspoon garlic powder

*Use any of the following to equal 6 cups: broccoli
florets, snow peas, thinly sliced red or green bell
peppers or thinly sliced carrots.*

In large skillet, heat 1 tablespoon oil over
medium-high heat; brown pork. Remove and
set aside. In same skillet, heat remaining
1 tablespoon oil and cook assorted fresh
vegetables, stirring occasionally, 5 minutes.
Stir in water chestnuts and onion soup mix
blended with water, orange juice, soy sauce
and garlic powder. Bring to a boil over high
heat. Reduce heat to low and simmer,
uncovered, 3 minutes. Return pork to skillet
and cook 1 minute or until heated through.
                  Makes about 4 servings

TIP: Pick up pre-sliced vegetables from your
local salad bar.

PERFECT PORK

201 STIR–FRIED PORK AND VEGGIES

¼ cup GRANDMA'S® Molasses
2 tablespoons HOLLAND HOUSE® Sherry Cooking Wine
2 tablespoons soy sauce
1 tablespoon hoisin sauce
1 pound boneless pork, cut into thin strips
2 tablespoons vegetable oil, divided
1 cup diagonally-cut fresh asparagus or snow peas
1 cup diagonally-sliced carrots (2 medium)
¾ cup beef broth or water
2 tablespoons cornstarch
   Toasted sesame seeds (optional)
   Cooked vermicelli or Oriental noodles

In medium bowl, combine molasses, wine, soy sauce and hoisin sauce; blend well. Add pork; stir to coat. Cover; refrigerate 1 to 2 hours or overnight.

In large skillet, heat 1 tablespoon oil. Stir-fry asparagus and carrots 3 to 5 minutes or until crisp-tender. Remove vegetables from skillet. Add remaining 1 tablespoon oil and pork mixture to skillet. Stir-fry 5 minutes or until brown. In small bowl, combine beef broth and cornstarch; blend well. Stir into pork mixture; cook until mixture thickens, stirring constantly. Return vegetables to skillet; heat through. Sprinkle with sesame seeds, if desired. Serve with vermicelli.

Makes 4 servings

202 SAVORY PORK & APPLE STIR–FRY

1 package (7.2 ounces) RICE-A-RONI® Rice Pilaf
1⅓ cups apple juice or apple cider, divided
1 pound boneless pork loin, pork tenderloin or boneless skinless chicken breast halves
1 teaspoon paprika
1 teaspoon dried thyme leaves
½ teaspoon ground sage or poultry seasoning
½ teaspoon salt (optional)
2 tablespoons margarine or butter
2 medium apples, cored and sliced
1 teaspoon cornstarch
⅓ cup coarsely chopped walnuts

1. Prepare Rice-A-Roni® mix as package directs, substituting 1 cup water and 1 cup apple juice for water in directions.

2. While Rice-A-Roni® is simmering, cut pork into 1½×¼-inch strips. Combine seasonings; toss with pork.

3. In second large skillet, melt margarine over medium heat. Stir-fry pork 3 to 4 minutes or just until pork is no longer pink.

4. Add apples; stir-fry 2 to 3 minutes or until apples are almost tender. Add combined remaining ⅓ cup apple juice and cornstarch. Stir-fry 1 to 2 minutes or until thickened to form glaze.

5. Stir in nuts. Serve rice topped with pork mixture.

Makes 4 servings

Spicy Tomato-Pork Stir-Fry

203 SPICY TOMATO–PORK STIR–FRY

2 cups uncooked instant rice
2/3 cup tomato juice
2 tablespoons soy sauce
1 tablespoon cornstarch
1/4 teaspoon paprika
3 boneless pork chops, cut 3/4 inch thick (about 3/4 pound)
1/4 teaspoon garlic salt
1/8 teaspoon red pepper flakes
2 slices uncooked bacon, chopped
3 medium tomatoes, chopped
2 green onions with tops, sliced diagonally

1. Prepare rice according to package directions. Set aside.

2. Combine tomato juice, soy sauce, cornstarch and paprika in small bowl, stirring until cornstarch dissolves. Set aside.

3. Slice pork across grain into 1/4-inch slices; place in medium bowl. Sprinkle pork with garlic salt and pepper flakes; mix well.

4. Cook bacon in medium skillet over medium-high heat. Remove bacon from skillet using slotted spoon; set aside. Add pork, tomatoes and onions to skillet; cook 3 minutes or until pork is barely pink in center. Stir in tomato juice mixture; cook, stirring constantly, 1 minute or until sauce thickens slightly. Remove from heat; stir in bacon.

5. Serve pork stir-fry over rice.

Makes 4 servings

Prep and Cook Time: 28 minutes

PERFECT PORK

204 GOLDEN PORK STIR–FRY

Sweet and Sour Cooking Sauce (recipe follows)
2 tablespoons vegetable oil, divided
1 clove garlic, crushed or finely chopped
½ pound boneless pork, cut into strips
2 cups broccoli florets
1 red or green bell pepper, thinly sliced
1 Golden Delicious apple, cored and cut into 16 slices
4 cups sliced napa cabbage
Cooked rice or noodles (optional)

1. Prepare Sweet and Sour Cooking Sauce; set aside. In large skillet or wok, heat 1 tablespoon oil over medium-high heat. Add garlic and stir-fry until lightly browned. Remove and discard garlic. Add pork to seasoned oil in skillet and stir-fry until browned; remove pork to bowl and reserve.

2. Add remaining 1 tablespoon oil to skillet. Add broccoli and pepper; stir-fry about 1 minute. Add apple, cabbage and reserved pork; stir-fry 2 minutes longer. Add Sweet and Sour Cooking Sauce; cook, stirring, until sauce thickens. Serve over rice, if desired.

Makes 4 servings

SWEET AND SOUR COOKING SAUCE
2 tablespoons chicken broth or water
1 tablespoon reduced-sodium soy sauce
1 teaspoon cornstarch
1 teaspoon sugar
1 teaspoon grated fresh ginger
1 teaspoon rice wine or cider vinegar
⅛ teaspoon red pepper flakes

In small bowl, combine all ingredients. Stir until well-blended. *Makes about ¼ cup*

Favorite recipe from **Washington Apple Commission**

205 PIQUANT NECTARINE STIR–FRY

1 pound lean pork loin, cut into stir-fry strips
¼ cup soy sauce
¼ cup Dijon mustard
¼ cup peach or nectarine jam
2 tablespoons wine vinegar
1 tablespoon cornstarch
½ teaspoon ground ginger
2 teaspoons vegetable oil, divided
½ cup chopped walnuts
1 small onion, thinly sliced
1 large green bell pepper, sliced into strips
2 nectarines, seeded and cut into thin wedges

Combine soy sauce, mustard, jam, vinegar, cornstarch and ginger in medium bowl. Marinate pork strips in soy sauce mixture 10 minutes. Heat 1 teaspoon oil in nonstick skillet over high heat. Remove pork strips from marinade, reserving marinade; stir-fry pork quickly with walnuts, about 3 minutes. Remove pork and nuts from skillet; set aside. Heat remaining 1 teaspoon oil in skillet; add onion and pepper; stir-fry 2 to 3 minutes. Return pork and nuts to skillet; add nectarines and reserved marinade. Simmer 8 to 10 minutes. *Makes 4 servings*

Prep Time: 20 minutes

Favorite recipe from **National Pork Producers Council**

PERFECT PORK

206 SPAM™ HOT & SPICY STIR–FRY

⅓ cup reduced-sodium teriyaki sauce
⅓ cup water
2 to 3 teaspoons HOUSE OF TSANG® Chinese Hot Oil
½ teaspoon ground ginger
1 (12-ounce) can SPAM® Lite Luncheon Meat, cubed
1 cup broccoli florets
1 cup chopped onion
1 cup snow peas
1 red bell pepper, cut into strips
1 tablespoon plus 1½ teaspoons vegetable oil
1 (14-ounce) can whole baby corn, drained and cut into halves
1 (7-ounce) jar mushrooms, drained
6 cups hot cooked white rice

In small bowl, combine teriyaki sauce, water, Chinese hot oil and ginger; set aside. In wok or large skillet, stir-fry SPAM®, broccoli, onion, snow peas and bell pepper in vegetable oil 2 minutes. Add teriyaki sauce mixture; cook until bubbly. Add baby corn and mushrooms; heat thoroughly. Serve over rice. *Makes 6 servings*

207 PORK AND RED CHILI STIR–FRY

1 pound lean boneless pork loin, cut into thin slices
1 teaspoon vegetable oil
2 cloves garlic, minced
¾ pound fresh green beans, cut into 2-inch lengths *or* 1 (10-ounce) package frozen cut green beans, thawed
2 teaspoons sugar
2 teaspoons soy sauce
2 small red chili peppers, thinly sliced *or* ½ teaspoon red pepper flakes
1 teaspoon shredded fresh ginger *or* ½ teaspoon ground ginger
1 teaspoon sesame oil
1 teaspoon rice vinegar

Heat vegetable oil in nonstick skillet. Add pork and garlic; cook and stir until lightly browned. Add green beans; stir-fry until beans and pork are tender, about 5 minutes. Push meat and beans to one side of skillet. Add sugar, soy sauce, chili peppers and ginger; stir to dissolve sugar. Add sesame oil and vinegar. Stir to coat meat and beans. Serve immediately with cooked rice or shredded lettuce. *Makes 4 servings*

Prep Time: 15 minutes

*Favorite recipe from **National Pork Producers Council***

208 PORK SAUCED WITH MUSTARD AND GRAPES

1 cup seedless or halved seeded Chilean grapes (red, green or combination), divided
6 ounces boneless pork loin, cut into ½-inch slices
1 tablespoon all-purpose flour
2 teaspoons olive oil, divided
¼ cup thinly sliced onion
1 cup reduced-sodium chicken broth
1 tablespoon white wine vinegar
1 tablespoon brown sugar
1 tablespoon mustard
1 teaspoon mustard seeds

Rinse grapes; remove any stems and set aside. Coat pork with flour. Heat 1 teaspoon oil in large nonstick skillet over medium heat. Add pork; cook about 5 minutes, turning once. Remove; set aside. Heat remaining 1 teaspoon oil in skillet over medium-high heat; add onion. Cook and stir until onion is softened. Add ½ cup grapes and remaining ingredients. Bring to a boil; cook until reduced by half, stirring occasionally. Return pork with juices and remaining ½ cup grapes to skillet. Heat until warm. *Makes 2 servings*

*Favorite recipe from **Chilean Fresh Fruit Association***

Gourmet Grits (page 179)

PERFECT PORK

209 GOURMET GRITS

½ pound BOB EVANS FARMS® Italian Roll
  Sausage
3 cups water
1 cup uncooked white grits
½ (10-ounce) package frozen chopped
  spinach, thawed and squeezed dry
¼ cup grated Parmesan cheese
¼ cup chopped sun-dried tomatoes
¼ cup olive oil
1 clove garlic, chopped

Crumble sausage into medium skillet. Cook over medium heat until browned, stirring occasionally. Drain off any drippings; set aside. Bring water to a rapid boil in large saucepan. While stirring, add grits in steady stream until mixture thickens into smooth paste. Reduce heat to low; simmer 5 to 7 minutes, stirring frequently to prevent sticking. Stir in sausage, spinach, cheese and tomatoes. Pour into greased 9×5-inch loaf pan. Refrigerate until cool and firm.

Unmold. Slice into ½-inch-thick slices. Heat oil in large skillet over medium-high heat until hot. Add garlic; cook and stir 30 seconds or until soft. Add grit slices, 4 to 5 at a time, and cook until golden brown on both sides. Repeat until all slices are cooked. Serve hot. Refrigerate leftovers.

Makes 4 to 6 side-dish servings

SERVING SUGGESTIONS: Melt thin slice of mozzarella cheese on top of each browned slice. This also makes a wonderful side dish for chicken, topped with warmed seasoned tomato or spaghetti sauce.

210 SWEET AND SOUR PORK

1 pound boneless pork loin
1 tablespoon vegetable oil
1 medium green bell pepper, cut into
  1-inch pieces
1 medium onion, cut into thin wedges
1 (15¼-ounce) can pineapple chunks in
  juice, undrained
¼ cup packed brown sugar
¼ cup white wine vinegar
2 tablespoons cornstarch
2 tablespoons soy sauce
  Hot cooked rice (optional)

Partially freeze pork. Cut across grain into 2½×2¼-inch strips; set aside. Preheat wok or large skillet over high heat; add oil. Stir-fry pepper and onion in hot oil 2 to 3 minutes or until crisp-tender. Remove from wok. Add more oil, if necessary. Add ½ of pork to wok; stir-fry until browned. Remove pork; stir-fry remaining pork. Return all pork to wok; keep warm.

Drain pineapple, reserving juice. In small saucepan, combine reserved pineapple juice, brown sugar, vinegar, cornstarch and soy sauce. Bring to a boil; cook about 1 minute or until thickened, stirring constantly.

Return pepper and onion to wok. Stir in pineapple and pineapple juice mixture. Cook and stir until heated through. Serve with rice, if desired.   *Makes 4 servings*

Prep Time: 20 minutes

*Favorite recipe from **National Pork Producers Council***

PERFECT PORK

211 HONEY NUT STIR–FRY

1 pound pork steak, pork loin or boneless chicken breast
¾ cup orange juice
⅓ cup honey
3 tablespoons soy sauce
1 tablespoon cornstarch
¼ teaspoon ground ginger
2 tablespoons vegetable oil, divided
2 large carrots, sliced diagonally
2 stalks celery, sliced diagonally
½ cup cashews or peanuts
Hot cooked rice

Cut pork into thin strips; set aside. Combine orange juice, honey, soy sauce, cornstarch and ginger in small bowl; mix well. Heat 1 tablespoon oil in large skillet over medium-high heat. Add carrots and celery; stir-fry about 3 minutes. Remove vegetables; set aside. Pour remaining 1 tablespoon oil into skillet. Add pork; stir-fry about 3 minutes. Return vegetables to skillet; add honey mixture and nuts. Cook and stir over medium-high heat until sauce comes to a boil and thickens. Serve over rice.

Makes 4 to 6 servings

*Favorite recipe from **National Honey Board***

212 GINGER LIME PORK

1 pound pork tenderloin, partially frozen until firm
12 fresh asparagus spears, tough ends removed
4 medium carrots
2 tablespoons vegetable oil, divided
6 tablespoons dry white wine or chicken broth, divided
2 tablespoons lime juice
1 teaspoon finely grated fresh ginger
½ teaspoon finely grated lime peel
⅛ teaspoon salt
⅛ teaspoon black pepper

Cut pork diagonally into ¼-inch-thick pieces. Cut each slice into thin strips; set aside. Slice asparagus diagonally into 1-inch-long pieces. Cut carrots into 2-inch-long julienne pieces. Heat 1 tablespoon oil over medium-high heat in large skillet. Add carrots; cook 5 minutes, stirring often. Add asparagus; cook 1 minute. Lower heat to medium-low. Add 1 tablespoon wine. Cover and cook until vegetables are crisp-tender, about 4 to 5 minutes. Remove. Heat remaining 1 tablespoon oil in skillet over medium heat. Add pork. Cook and stir until no longer pink, about 3 to 4 minutes. Reduce heat to low. Combine remaining 5 tablespoons wine, lime juice, ginger, lime peel, salt and pepper in small bowl; add to skillet. Heat through; return vegetables to skillet. Toss lightly; heat 1 minute. Serve immediately.

Makes 4 servings

Prep Time: 20 minutes

*Favorite recipe from **National Pork Producers Council***

Honey Nut Stir-Fry

Satisfying Seafood

213 SEAFOOD COMBINATION

Fried Noodles (recipe follows)
8 ounces fish fillets, skin removed
1 tablespoon soy sauce
2 teaspoons cornstarch
2 teaspoons dry sherry
1 teaspoon chicken bouillon granules
4 tablespoons vegetable oil, divided
8 green onions with tops, diagonally cut
    into thin slices
3 stalks celery, cut into thin slices
1 can (8 ounces) water chestnuts, drained
    and cut into halves
1 can (8 ounces) sliced bamboo shoots,
    drained
8 ounces fresh or thawed frozen shrimp,
    peeled and deveined
8 ounces sea scallops, cut into quarters

1. Prepare Fried Noodles; set aside. Cut fish fillets into 1½-inch pieces; set aside.

2. Combine ½ cup water, soy sauce, cornstarch, sherry and bouillon granules in small bowl; mix well. Set aside. Heat 2 tablespoons oil in wok or large skillet over high heat. Add onions, celery, water chestnuts and bamboo shoots; stir-fry until crisp-tender, about 2 minutes. Remove; set aside.

3. Heat remaining 2 tablespoons oil in wok over high heat. Add shrimp, fish pieces and scallops; stir-fry until all fish turns opaque and is cooked through, about 3 minutes.

4. Stir cornstarch mixture; add to wok. Cook and stir until liquid boils. Return vegetables to wok; cook and stir 2 minutes. Serve over Fried Noodles. *Makes 6 servings*

FRIED NOODLES
  8 ounces Chinese-style thin egg noodles
  Salt
  Vegetable oil for frying

1. Cook noodles according to package directions until tender but still firm, 2 to 3 minutes; drain. Rinse under cold running water; drain. Spread several layers of paper towels over jelly-roll pans or cookie sheets. Spread noodles over paper towels; let dry 2 to 3 hours.

2. Heat oil in wok or large skillet over medium-high heat to 375°F. Using slotted spoon or tongs, lower small portion of noodles into hot oil. Cook noodles until golden brown, about 30 seconds; drain on paper towels. Repeat with remaining bunches. *Makes 6 servings*

Seafood Combination

SATISFYING SEAFOOD

214 BUTTERFLIED SHRIMP PARMESAN

1½ pounds large shrimp
1 cup (4 ounces) shredded ALPINE LACE®
    Fat Free Pasteurized Process Skim
    Milk Cheese Product—For Parmesan
    Lovers
¼ cup Italian seasoned dry bread crumbs
2 tablespoons unsalted butter substitute
¾ cup chopped red bell pepper
½ cup thinly sliced green onions
1 tablespoon minced garlic
⅛ teaspoon crushed red pepper flakes or
    to taste
⅓ cup minced fresh parsley
6 tablespoons 2% low fat milk

1. Peel the shrimp, leaving the tails on. Then butterfly each shrimp by cutting it along the outer curved edge almost all the way through. Open the shrimp up like a book and remove the dark vein. In a small bowl, toss the cheese with the bread crumbs and set aside.

2. In a large nonstick skillet, melt the butter over medium-high heat. Add the bell pepper, green onions, garlic and red pepper flakes and cook for 5 minutes or until soft. Add the shrimp and sauté for 5 minutes or just until the shrimp turn pink and opaque. Stir in the parsley.

3. In a small saucepan, bring the milk just to a boil, then stir into the shrimp mixture. Stir in the cheese mixture and cook until the cheese is melted. Serve immediately.

Makes 4 servings

215 STIR–FRIED CRAB WITH BLACK BEAN GARLIC SAUCE

SAUCE
¼ cup water
2½ tablespoons LEE KUM KEE® Black Bean
    Garlic Sauce
1 tablespoon LEE KUM KEE® Premium
    Oyster Flavored Sauce
1 tablespoon sugar
½ teaspoon ground white pepper

SEAFOOD AND SEASONINGS
1 pound crabs
1½ tablespoons plus 1 teaspoon cornstarch,
    divided
2 tablespoons vegetable oil
3 green onions, chopped
2 tablespoons LEE KUM KEE® Freshly
    Minced Ginger
½ teaspoon LEE KUM KEE® Freshly Minced
    Garlic

1. Combine sauce ingredients in small bowl; set aside. Dry crabs; dust with 1½ tablespoons cornstarch. Heat oil in wok. Cook crabs halfway through; drain and set aside.

2. Sauté onions, ginger and garlic in wok.

3. Add crabs and sauce; stir-fry 8 minutes.

4. Combine remaining 1 teaspoon cornstarch with 2 tablespoons water. Pour into wok; stir-fry until sauce thickens. Serve immediately. *Makes 4 servings*

Butterflied Shrimp Parmesan

SATISFYING SEAFOOD

216 SCALLOPS WITH VEGETABLES

1 ounce dried mushrooms
4 teaspoons cornstarch
2½ tablespoons dry sherry
4 teaspoons soy sauce
2 teaspoons chicken bouillon granules
2 tablespoons vegetable oil
8 ounces fresh green beans, trimmed and diagonally cut into 1-inch pieces
2 yellow onions, cut into wedges and separated
3 stalks celery, diagonally cut into ½-inch pieces
2 teaspoons minced fresh ginger
1 clove garlic, minced
1 pound fresh or thawed frozen sea scallops, cut into quarters
6 green onions with tops, diagonally cut into thin slices
1 can (15 ounces) baby corn, drained
Whole dried mushroom and celery leaves for garnish

1. Place mushrooms in bowl; cover with hot water. Let stand 30 minutes; drain. Squeeze out as much water as possible from mushrooms. Cut off and discard stems; cut caps into thin slices.

2. Blend cornstarch and 1 cup cold water in small bowl; stir in sherry, soy sauce and bouillon granules. Set aside.

3. Heat oil in wok or large skillet over high heat. Add green beans, yellow onions, celery, ginger and garlic; stir-fry 3 minutes.

4. Stir cornstarch mixture; add to wok. Cook and stir until sauce boils and thickens.

5. Add mushrooms, scallops, green onions and baby corn. Cook and stir until scallops turn opaque, about 4 minutes. Garnish, if desired. *Makes 4 to 6 servings*

217 RAINBOW STIR–FRIED FISH

SAUCE
½ cup chicken broth
2 tablespoons LA CHOY® Soy Sauce
1 tablespoon cornstarch
1 teaspoon sugar
¼ teaspoon red pepper flakes (optional)

FISH AND VEGETABLES
1 pound orange roughy filets,* cut into 1-inch chunks
1 tablespoon LA CHOY® Soy Sauce
3 tablespoons WESSON® Oil
½ cup julienne-cut carrots
1 teaspoon *each:* minced fresh garlic and ginger
2 cups fresh broccoli florets
1 (8-ounce) can LA CHOY® Sliced Water Chestnuts, drained
1 (6-ounce) package frozen snow peas, thawed and drained
½ cup diagonally-sliced green onions

Any firm-fleshed white fish may be substituted.

In small bowl, combine *sauce* ingredients; set aside. In medium bowl, combine fish and soy sauce; toss lightly to coat. In large nonstick skillet or wok, heat oil. Add fish mixture; stir-fry 2 to 3 minutes or until fish flakes easily with fork. Remove fish from skillet; drain. Set aside. Add carrots, garlic and ginger to same skillet; stir-fry 30 seconds. Add broccoli; stir-fry 1 minute. Add water chestnuts and snow peas; heat thoroughly, stirring occasionally. Return fish to skillet. Stir sauce; add to skillet. Heat, stirring gently, until sauce is thick and bubbly. Sprinkle with green onions. Garnish, if desired. *Makes 4 servings*

Scallops with Vegetables

186

218 CAJUN–STYLE CORN WITH CRAYFISH

6 ears corn on the cob
1 tablespoon vegetable oil
1 medium onion, chopped
½ cup chopped green bell pepper
½ cup chopped red bell pepper
1 cup water
1 teaspoon salt
⅛ teaspoon black pepper
⅛ teaspoon ground red pepper
¾ pound crayfish tail meat

1. Cut corn from cobs in two or three layers so that kernels are not left whole. Scrape cobs to remove remaining juice and pulp.

2. Heat oil in large skillet over medium heat. Add onion and bell peppers; cook 5 minutes, stirring occasionally. Add corn, water, salt, black pepper and ground red pepper; bring to a boil. Reduce heat to low; simmer 10 to 15 minutes.

3. Add crayfish; return mixture to a simmer. Cook 3 to 5 minutes or just until crayfish turn opaque. Garnish, if desired.

Makes 6 servings

219 DRUNKEN SHRIMP

1 pound medium-size raw shrimp
2 tablespoons dry sherry
2½ teaspoons cornstarch, divided
1 teaspoon sugar, divided
3 tablespoons KIKKOMAN® Lite Soy Sauce
2 tablespoons water
1 tablespoon distilled white vinegar
2 tablespoons vegetable oil
¼ cup chopped green onions and tops
1 teaspoon minced fresh ginger root
1 clove garlic, minced

Peel shrimp, leaving shells on tails; devein. Combine sherry, 2 teaspoons cornstarch and ½ teaspoon sugar in medium bowl; stir in shrimp until well coated. Cover and refrigerate 30 minutes. Meanwhile, combine lite soy sauce, water, vinegar and remaining ½ teaspoon *each* cornstarch and sugar; set aside. Heat oil in hot wok or large skillet over medium-high heat. Add green onions, ginger and garlic; stir-fry 30 seconds. Add shrimp; stir-fry 3 minutes, or until pink. Pour in lite soy sauce mixture; cook and stir until sauce boils and thickens. Garnish as desired.

Makes 4 servings

Cajun-Style Corn with Crayfish

SATISFYING SEAFOOD

220 STIR–FRIED CRAB LEGS

1½ **pounds frozen Alaska king crab legs, thawed and drained**
 3 **green onions with tops**
 ½ **cup water**
 2 **tablespoons dry sherry**
 2 **tablespoons reduced-sodium soy sauce**
 1 **tablespoon cornstarch**
 1 **teaspoon sugar**
 3 **tablespoons vegetable oil**
 1 **piece fresh ginger (about 1-inch square), sliced**
 2 **cloves garlic, minced**
   Lemon wedges

1. Soak crab legs in water 30 minutes to leach out some of salt brine used for packaging.

2. Meanwhile, cut off roots from green onions; discard. Cut 3-inch piece off bottom of each onion; set aside green tops. Make 3 onion brushes from white pieces for garnish, if desired. (Or, reserve a few 1-inch green onion lengths to make green onion curls.) Cut reserved green tops into 1-inch lengths; set aside.

3. Cut crab legs into 2-inch-long pieces with poultry scissors or cleaver.

4. Combine water, sherry, soy sauce, cornstarch and sugar in small bowl; blend well. Set aside.

5. Heat wok over high heat about 1 minute or until hot. Drizzle oil into wok and heat 15 seconds. Add ginger and stir-fry about 1 minute to flavor oil. Remove and discard ginger with fork. Add crab pieces and garlic. Stir-fry 5 minutes.

6. Stir cornstarch mixture and pour into wok. Add green onion pieces and toss. Cook and stir until sauce boils and thickens. Transfer to serving platter. Garnish with green onion brushes or green onion curls, if desired. Serve with lemon wedges.

Makes 3 to 4 servings

NOTE: To extract meat from legs, snip along each side of shell with scissors and lift out meat with skewer before serving. Reheat meat in wok for a few seconds. Or to save time, serve in the shell with seafood shell crackers. Have guests crack the shells and remove meat with small seafood forks.

221 BLACK BEAN GARLIC FISH

 1 **tablespoon LEE KUM KEE® Black Bean Garlic Sauce**
 1 **teaspoon water**
 ½ **teaspoon sugar**
 2 **tablespoons vegetable oil**
 ½ **medium onion, sliced**
 1 **pound fish fillet, cut into 1-inch pieces**
 ½ **medium green bell pepper, sliced**
 ½ **medium red bell pepper, sliced**
 ½ **tablespoon LEE KUM KEE® Oyster Flavored Sauce**

Combine Black Bean Garlic Sauce, water and sugar in small bowl; set aside. Heat skillet over medium-high heat. Add oil; sauté onion. Add fish and Garlic Sauce mixture. Add bell peppers and Oyster Flavored Sauce. Cook through. *Makes 4 servings*

Stir-Fried Crab Legs

222 GOLDEN SEAFARERS STIR–FRY

1 can (16 ounces) cling peach slices in
   juice or light syrup
⅓ cup KIKKOMAN® Stir-Fry Sauce
1 teaspoon cornstarch
2 tablespoons vegetable oil, divided
⅔ cup large walnut pieces
1 clove garlic, minced
½ teaspoon grated fresh ginger root
½ pound medium-size raw shrimp, peeled
   and deveined
4 ounces fresh snow peas, trimmed
1 cup cherry tomatoes, cut into halves
¼ cup sliced green onions
   Hot cooked rice

Reserving ⅓ cup liquid, drain peaches. Blend liquid with stir-fry sauce and cornstarch in small bowl; set aside. Heat 1 tablespoon oil in hot wok or large skillet over medium heat. Add walnuts, garlic and ginger; stir-fry 1 minute. Remove. Heat remaining 1 tablespoon oil in same pan over high heat. Add shrimp and stir-fry 1 minute; remove. Add snow peas and stir-fry 2 minutes; remove. Pour stir-fry sauce mixture into pan; cook and stir until thickened. Add shrimp, snow peas, peaches, tomatoes and green onions; cook and stir until shrimp and vegetables are coated with sauce and heated through. Stir in reserved walnut mixture. Serve with rice. *Makes 4 to 6 servings*

223 QUICKLY SAUTÉED FISH FILLETS

1 SUNKIST® lemon, cut into 6 wedges
1 pound orange roughy, red snapper or
   catfish fillets, cut into 4 serving-size
   pieces
2 tablespoons all-purpose flour
¼ teaspoon paprika
1 tablespoon olive or vegetable oil
   Salt and black pepper to taste
   Light and Lemony Dill "Butter" (recipe
   follows)

Squeeze juice of 2 lemon wedges (about 1 tablespoon) over both sides of fish fillets. Let stand 5 minutes. Lightly pat dry with paper towel. In pie plate, combine flour and paprika. Dip fish fillets into flour mixture to coat lightly. In large nonstick skillet sprayed with nonstick cooking spray, heat oil. Sauté fish over medium-high heat 3 to 4 minutes on each side or until fish is opaque and just flakes easily with fork. Season with salt and pepper to taste. Garnish each serving with remaining lemon wedges. Serve with Light and Lemony Dill "Butter." *Makes 4 servings*

LIGHT AND LEMONY DILL "BUTTER"
⅓ cup reduced-calorie margarine, softened
1 tablespoon finely chopped green onion
2 teaspoons chopped fresh dill *or*
  ½ teaspoon dried dill weed
  Grated peel of ½ SUNKIST® lemon
⅛ teaspoon white pepper

In small bowl, combine all ingredients. Serve 1 to 2 teaspoons over each serving of sautéed, grilled, broiled or poached fish fillets or steaks. *Makes about ⅓ cup*

Golden Seafarers Stir-Fry

SATISFYING SEAFOOD

224 STIR–FRIED CORKSCREW SHRIMP WITH VEGETABLES

SAUCE
- ¼ cup **LA CHOY® Soy Sauce**
- ¼ cup chicken broth
- 3 tablespoons dry sherry
- 1 tablespoon cornstarch
- 1 teaspoon sugar
- ¼ teaspoon *each:* black pepper and Oriental sesame oil

SHRIMP AND VEGETABLES
- 1 egg white
- 1 tablespoon cornstarch
- 1 pound shrimp, peeled, deveined and cut into halves lengthwise
- 3 tablespoons **WESSON® Oil**, divided
- 1 cup sliced onion
- 1 tablespoon minced fresh garlic
- 1½ teaspoons minced fresh ginger
- 1 cup sliced fresh mushrooms
- ½ cup thinly sliced carrots
- 1 (14-ounce) can **LA CHOY® Bean Sprouts**, well drained
- 1 (8-ounce) can **LA CHOY® Sliced Water Chestnuts**, drained
- 1 (6-ounce) package frozen snow peas, thawed

In small bowl, combine *sauce* ingredients; set aside. In medium bowl, beat together egg white and cornstarch until well blended. Add shrimp; toss gently to coat. In large nonstick skillet or wok, heat *2 tablespoons* oil. Add shrimp mixture; stir-fry until shrimp curl and turn pink. Remove shrimp from skillet; drain.

Heat *remaining 1 tablespoon* oil in same skillet. Add onion, garlic and ginger; stir-fry 30 seconds. Add mushrooms and carrots; stir-fry 1 to 2 minutes or until carrots are crisp-tender. Stir sauce; add to skillet. Cook, stirring constantly, until sauce is thick and bubbly. Return shrimp to skillet with bean sprouts, water chestnuts and snow peas; heat thoroughly, stirring occasionally. Garnish, if desired.

Makes 4 to 6 servings

225 CORNMEAL FRIED CATFISH

- 2 cups all-purpose flour
- 2 eggs
- 2 cups cornmeal
- 2 tablespoons dried thyme leaves
- 2 tablespoons dried oregano leaves
- 2 tablespoons salt
- 1 teaspoon cayenne pepper
- 1 teaspoon dried coriander
- 4 catfish fillets (5 to 6 ounces each)
- 3 tablespoons olive oil

Place flour in pie plate. Whisk eggs in shallow bowl. Combine cornmeal, thyme, oregano, salt, pepper and coriander in another pie plate. Dip each catfish fillet in flour, then eggs, and then cornmeal mixture until well coated. Heat oil in large skillet over medium-high heat until hot. Add fillets; cook about 6 to 7 minutes per side or just until fish is flaky. Serve hot. Refrigerate leftovers. *Makes 4 servings*

Favorite recipe from **Bob Evans Farms®**

SATISFYING SEAFOOD

226 ALBACORE–WALNUT STIR–FRY

½ cup vegetable oil
6 cups sliced celery
6 cups sliced mushrooms
6 cups diced red bell peppers
2 pounds sliced water chestnuts
2 tablespoons minced garlic (about 10 cloves)
2 tablespoons minced fresh ginger
1 teaspoon red pepper flakes
3 cups chicken broth
⅔ cup plum sauce
⅔ cup light soy sauce
½ cup sherry
4 teaspoons cornstarch
1 can (4 pounds 2½ ounces) Albacore tuna in spring water
3 cups chopped walnuts, toasted
6 quarts hot cooked rice

Heat oil in large wok; add celery, mushrooms, bell peppers, water chestnuts, garlic, ginger and pepper flakes. Stir-fry until bell peppers are crisp-tender. Mix together chicken broth, plum sauce, soy sauce, sherry and cornstarch in large bowl; add to wok. Cook until thickened and hot. Gently fold in tuna and walnuts. Serve 1⅛ cup tuna mixture over hot cooked rice. *Makes 24 servings*

Favorite recipe from **Walnut Marketing Board**

227 SCALLOPS ORIENTAL

1 pound fresh or frozen calico or bay scallops
2 tablespoons lemon juice
2 tablespoons soy sauce
½ teaspoon garlic powder
3 tablespoons vegetable oil, divided
1 cup thinly sliced broccoli (florets and stalks)
1 cup thinly sliced cauliflower
1 cup thinly sliced fresh mushrooms
½ cup green onions, cut into 1-inch pieces
¾ cup water
2½ tablespoons cornstarch
1 teaspoon salt
½ teaspoon black pepper
3 cups chow mein noodles

Thaw scallops if frozen. Cut large scallops into halves; place all scallops in large bowl. Combine lemon juice, soy sauce and garlic powder in small bowl. Pour over scallops; let marinate while preparing vegetables. In wok, heat 2 tablespoons oil; add broccoli, cauliflower, mushrooms and onions. Stir-fry 4 minutes. Remove vegetables to platter; keep warm. Add remaining 1 tablespoon oil to wok. Drain scallops, reserving marinade. Add scallops to wok. Stir-fry 1 to 2 minutes or until scallops are opaque. Add reserved vegetables to wok. In small bowl, combine water, cornstarch, salt, pepper and reserved marinade; mix well. Add to wok; stir only until sauce is thickened. Serve over chow mein noodles. *Makes 4 to 6 servings*

Favorite recipe from **Florida Department of Agriculture and Consumer Services, Bureau of Seafood and Aquaculture**

SATISFYING SEAFOOD

228 SKILLET SHRIMP WITH ROTELLE

3 tablespoons FILIPPO BERIO® Olive Oil
1 medium onion, chopped
2 cloves garlic, minced
2 cups uncooked rotelle or other curly pasta
3 cups chicken broth
1 cup asparagus tips
¾ pound raw medium shrimp, peeled and deveined
¾ cup halved cherry tomatoes
¼ cup pitted ripe olives
1 teaspoon dried oregano leaves
1 teaspoon dried basil leaves
   Salt and freshly ground black pepper

In large skillet, heat olive oil over medium heat until hot. Add onion and garlic; cook and stir 4 to 6 minutes or until onion is softened but not brown. Add pasta; stir to coat pasta with oil. Increase heat to high; pour in chicken broth. Bring to a boil. Reduce heat to medium-high; cook, stirring occasionally, 12 to 14 minutes or until pasta is *al dente* (tender but still firm). Add asparagus. Cook, stirring frequently, 2 to 3 minutes or until asparagus is crisp-tender. Add shrimp, tomatoes, olives, oregano and basil. Cook, stirring frequently, 3 minutes or until liquid is almost completely absorbed and shrimp are opaque *(do not overcook shrimp)*. Season to taste with salt and pepper.   *Makes 4 to 6 servings*

229 SHRIMP TAPAS IN SHERRY SAUCE

1 slice thick-cut bacon, cut into ¼-inch strips (optional)
2 tablespoons olive oil
2 ounces cremini or button mushrooms, cut into quarters
½ pound raw large shrimp (about 14 shrimp), peeled (last tail segment attached) and deveined
2 cloves garlic, thinly sliced
2 tablespoons medium dry sherry
1 tablespoon fresh lemon juice
¼ teaspoon red pepper flakes
   Fresh parsley for garnish
   Lemon wedges for garnish

1. Cook bacon, if desired, in large skillet over medium heat until brown and crispy. Remove from skillet with slotted spoon and drain on paper towels. Set aside.

2. Add oil to bacon drippings in skillet. Add mushrooms; cook and stir 2 minutes.

3. Add shrimp and garlic; cook and stir 3 minutes or until shrimp turn pink and opaque. Stir in sherry, lemon juice and pepper.

4. Remove shrimp to serving bowl with slotted spoon. Cook sauce 1 minute or until reduced and thickened. Pour over shrimp. Sprinkle with reserved bacon. Garnish, if desired.   *Makes 2 servings*

Skillet Shrimp with Rotelle

SATISFYING SEAFOOD

230 SOUTHERN BREADED CATFISH

⅓ cup pecan halves
¼ cup cornmeal
2 tablespoons all-purpose flour
1 teaspoon paprika
¼ teaspoon ground red pepper
2 egg whites
4 catfish fillets (about 1 pound)
4 cups hot cooked rice

1. Place pecans in food processor or blender; process until finely chopped. Combine pecans, cornmeal, flour, paprika and pepper in shallow bowl.

2. Beat egg whites in small bowl with wire whisk until foamy. Dip catfish fillets in pecan mixture, then in egg whites, then again in pecan mixture. Place fillets on plate; cover and refrigerate at least 15 minutes.

3. Spray large nonstick skillet with nonstick cooking spray; heat over medium-high heat. Place catfish fillets in single layer in skillet.

4. Cook fillets 2 minutes per side or until golden brown. Serve over rice. Serve with vegetables and garnish, if desired.

Makes 4 servings

231 NEW ENGLAND FISHERMAN'S SKILLET

4 small red potatoes, diced
1 medium onion, chopped
1 tablespoon olive oil
2 stalks celery, chopped
2 cloves garlic, minced
½ teaspoon dried thyme leaves
1 can (14½ ounces) DEL MONTE®
  FreshCut™ Diced Tomatoes with
  Green Pepper and Onion, undrained
1 pound firm white fish (such as halibut, snapper or cod)

In large skillet, brown potatoes and onion in oil over medium-high heat, stirring occasionally. Season with herb seasoning mix, if desired. Stir in celery, garlic and thyme; cook 4 minutes. Add tomatoes; bring to a boil. Cook 4 minutes or until thickened. Add fish; cover and cook over medium heat 5 to 8 minutes or until fish flakes easily with fork. Garnish with lemon wedges and chopped parsley, if desired.

Makes 4 servings

Prep Time: 10 minutes
Cook Time: 25 minutes

Southern Breaded Catfish

232 VEGGIE AND SCALLOP STIR–FRY

1 tablespoon vegetable oil
1 bag (16 ounces) BIRDS EYE® frozen
    Farm Fresh Mixtures Pepper Stir Fry
    vegetables
½ pound small sea scallops
1 small onion, chopped *or* 3 green onions,
    sliced
1 tablespoon light soy sauce
1 tablespoon Oriental salad dressing
⅛ teaspoon ground ginger
    Garlic powder
    Hot cooked rice (optional)

• In wok or large skillet, heat oil over medium heat.

• Add vegetables; cover and cook 3 to 5 minutes or until crisp-tender.

• Uncover; add scallops and onion. Stir-fry 2 minutes.

• Stir in soy sauce and Oriental salad dressing.

• Reduce heat to low; simmer 3 to 5 minutes or until some of liquid absorbs.

• Stir in ginger, garlic powder, salt and pepper to taste; increase heat to medium-high. Stir-fry until all liquid is absorbed and scallops turn opaque and begin to brown.

• Serve over rice, if desired.

Makes 4 servings

Prep Time: 3 minutes
Cook Time: 10 to 12 minutes

233 ZESTY STIR–FRY SHRIMP AND VEGETABLES

¾ cup reduced-sodium chicken broth
1 tablespoon cornstarch
    Grated peel and juice of ½ SUNKIST®
    lemon
1 teaspoon light soy sauce
2 teaspoons vegetable oil, divided
1 teaspoon sesame oil
¾ pound raw medium shrimp, peeled and
    deveined
1 medium clove garlic, minced
16 small button mushrooms
¾ cup red bell pepper cut into ½-inch
    squares
1 small onion, sliced
½ cup frozen peas, thawed
    Cooked Chinese-style noodles or
    linguine

Combine chicken broth, cornstarch, lemon juice and soy sauce in small bowl; set aside. In large nonstick skillet sprayed with nonstick cooking spray, heat 1 teaspoon vegetable oil and sesame oil. Stir-fry shrimp and garlic until shrimp just turn pink, about 2½ to 3 minutes. Remove shrimp with slotted spoon. Add remaining 1 teaspoon vegetable oil to skillet and stir-fry mushrooms, pepper and onion with lemon peel until vegetables are just tender, about 2½ to 3 minutes. Stir in chicken broth mixture. Cook over medium heat, stirring, until sauce thickens. Add shrimp and peas; heat through. Serve over noodles.

Makes 4 servings

Scallops & Snow Peas

234 SCALLOPS & SNOW PEAS

¾ **pound fresh or thawed bay scallops**
¾ **cup water**
2 **tablespoons KIKKOMAN® Soy Sauce**
2 **tablespoons dry white wine**
4 **teaspoons cornstarch**
½ **teaspoon sugar**
3 **small dried whole red chili peppers**
1 **tablespoon vegetable oil**
1 **medium onion, cut into 1-inch pieces**
2 **teaspoons slivered fresh ginger root**
½ **pound fresh snow peas, trimmed and cut diagonally in half**
1½ **teaspoons Oriental sesame oil**

Cook scallops in small amount of boiling water 30 seconds; drain. Combine ¾ cup water, soy sauce, wine, cornstarch and sugar in small bowl; set aside. Cut each chili pepper open lengthwise, being careful not to cut all the way through; set aside. Heat vegetable oil in hot wok or large skillet over medium heat; add chilies and stir-fry 30 seconds. Remove chilies; increase heat to high. Add onion and ginger; stir-fry 1 minute. Add snow peas; stir-fry 2 minutes longer. Add scallops, chilies and soy sauce mixture; cook and stir until sauce boils and thickens. Remove from heat and stir in sesame oil. Serve immediately. *Makes 4 servings*

SATISFYING SEAFOOD

235 BRAISED SHRIMP WITH VEGETABLES

½ cup chicken broth
1 teaspoon cornstarch
1 teaspoon oyster sauce
½ teaspoon minced fresh ginger
¼ teaspoon sugar
⅛ teaspoon black pepper
8 ounces fresh broccoli
1 tablespoon vegetable oil
1 pound raw large shrimp, peeled and deveined
2 cans (4 ounces each) whole button mushrooms, drained
1 can (8 ounces) sliced bamboo shoots, drained

1. Combine chicken broth, cornstarch, oyster sauce, ginger, sugar and pepper in small bowl; mix well. Set aside.

2. Remove woody stems from broccoli; discard.

3. Coarsely chop head of broccoli and remaining stems; set aside.

4. Heat oil in wok or large skillet over high heat. Add shrimp; stir-fry until shrimp turn pink, about 3 minutes.

5. Add broccoli to wok; stir-fry 1 minute. Add mushrooms and bamboo shoots; stir-fry 1 minute.

6. Stir cornstarch mixture; add to wok. Cook and stir until sauce boils and thickens, about 2 minutes. *Makes 4 servings*

236 SCAMPI ALLA "FIREMAN CHEF"

6 tablespoons butter
4 tablespoons minced garlic
1½ pounds raw large prawns, peeled and deveined
6 green onions, thinly sliced
¼ cup dry white wine
Juice of 1 lemon (about 2 tablespoons)
8 large sprigs parsley, finely chopped
Salt and black pepper to taste
Lemon slices and fresh parsley sprigs for garnish

1. To clarify butter, melt butter in small saucepan over low heat. *Do not stir.* Skim off white foam that forms on top. Strain clarified butter through cheesecloth into glass measuring cup to yield ⅓ cup. Discard milky residue at bottom of pan.

2. Heat clarified butter in large skillet over medium heat. Add garlic; cook and stir 1 to 2 minutes or until softened but not brown.

3. Add prawns, green onions, wine and lemon juice; cook and stir until prawns turn pink and are firm and opaque, 1 to 2 minutes on each side. *Do not overcook.*

4. Just before serving, add chopped parsley and season with salt and pepper. Serve on individual shell-shaped or small gratin dishes. Garnish, if desired.

Makes 4 main-dish or 8 appetizer servings

Braised Shrimp with Vegetables

SATISFYING SEAFOOD

237 MEXICAN SHRIMP WITH HOT CHILI PEPPER BUTTER

2 tablespoons extra-virgin olive oil, divided
2 cloves garlic, minced, divided
1 cup chopped onions, divided
2 pounds large shrimp, peeled and deveined, divided
⅓ cup chili powder, divided
¼ teaspoon ground red pepper
½ cup butter or margarine
¼ cup fresh lime juice (about 2 limes)
¾ teaspoon salt
3 cups hot cooked white rice or yellow Spanish rice
Lime wedges

1. Heat large nonstick skillet or wok over medium-high heat; add 1 tablespoon oil and heat 1 minute. Add 1 clove garlic; cook 15 seconds. Add ½ cup onions and half of the shrimp. Sprinkle with half of the chili powder and pepper; cook 5 minutes or until shrimp are opaque. Place in large bowl; set aside.

2. Repeat with remaining oil, garlic, onion, shrimp, chili powder and pepper.

3. Return reserved shrimp mixture to skillet; add butter, lime juice and salt. Cook until butter melts completely.

4. Place rice on serving platter. Spoon shrimp mixture on top of rice and serve with lime wedges. *Makes 4 servings*

238 SHRIMP WITH CHILE CILANTRO RICE

4 cups cooked long-grain white rice
1 cup Green Chile-Cilantro Pesto (recipe follows)
½ cup chicken broth
4 slices (about 4 ounces) bacon
1 pound raw large or medium shrimp, peeled and deveined
½ cup (6) chopped green onions
2 cloves garlic, finely chopped
ORTEGA® Thick & Chunky Salsa, mild

COMBINE rice, Green Chile-Cilantro Pesto and chicken broth in medium saucepan; cook over medium heat until heated through. Keep warm.

COOK bacon in large skillet over medium-high heat until crisp. Crumble bacon; set aside. Discard all but 2 tablespoons drippings from skillet. Add shrimp, green onions and garlic; cook, stirring frequently, 3 to 5 minutes or until shrimp turn pink.

PLACE rice mixture on platter; top with shrimp mixture, salsa and bacon.
Makes 6 to 8 servings

GREEN CHILE–CILANTRO PESTO:
COMBINE 2 cups fresh cilantro sprigs, 1 cup (7-ounce can) ORTEGA® Diced Green Chiles, 1 cup (4 ounces) grated Parmesan cheese, ¾ cup toasted pine nuts, 4 large cloves peeled garlic and 1 tablespoon lime juice in food processor or blender. Process until well chopped. Process, while slowly adding ½ cup corn oil, for additional 20 to 30 seconds or until mixture is almost smooth.

Mexican Shrimp with Hot Chili Pepper Butter

SATISFYING SEAFOOD

239 SEARED SALMON TERIYAKI

¼ cup soy sauce
¼ cup sake
2 tablespoons sugar
1½ pounds red salmon fillet with skin
     (1¼ inches thick)
2 tablespoons vegetable oil, divided
2 medium zucchini (12 ounces), cut into
    strips
2 medium yellow squash (12 ounces), cut
    into strips
1 tablespoon butter
¼ teaspoon salt
¼ teaspoon black pepper
1 tablespoon toasted sesame seeds
    Lemon slices (optional)

1. Combine soy sauce, sake and sugar in cup; stir until sugar dissolves. Set aside.

2. Rinse and dry salmon. Run fingers over cut surface of salmon; remove any bones that remain. Cut crosswise into 4 pieces.

3. Heat wok over high heat until hot. Add 1 tablespoon oil; heat 30 seconds. Add zucchini, yellow squash and butter. Cook and stir 4 to 5 minutes or until lightly browned and tender. Sprinkle squash mixture with salt and pepper. Transfer to serving platter. Sprinkle with sesame seeds; cover and keep warm.

4. Add remaining 1 tablespoon oil to wok and heat over high heat until sizzling hot. Carefully place fish in wok, skin sides up. Cook 4 minutes or until browned. Reduce heat to medium-high. Turn fish over using 2 pancake turners or flat spatulas. Cook, skin sides down, 8 to 10 minutes or until fish flakes easily when tested with fork, loosening fish on bottom occasionally. Place fish over squash mixture on platter. Cover and keep warm.

5. Pour off fat from wok. Stir soy sauce mixture and pour into wok. Boil until mixture is reduced by half and slightly thickened. Spoon sauce over fish. Serve with lemon, if desired. *Makes 4 servings*

240 SEA BASS FOR TWO IN LEMON APPLE SAUCE

¾ cup plus 2 tablespoons apple juice,
    divided
    Grated peel and juice of ½ SUNKIST®
    lemon
½ pound sea bass fillets
¼ teaspoon dried dill weed
1 small green apple, unpeeled and diced
½ tablespoon reduced-fat margarine
½ tablespoon honey
½ teaspoon Dijon mustard
1 tablespoon cornstarch
2 tablespoons sliced green onions
1 cup hot cooked rice (cooked without
    salt)

In large nonstick skillet, combine ¾ cup apple juice, lemon peel and lemon juice. Add fish fillets and sprinkle with dill. Bring to a boil. Reduce heat; cover and simmer 10 to 12 minutes or until fish flakes easily with fork. Remove fish. Add apple, margarine, honey and mustard to skillet, stirring until margarine melts. Combine cornstarch and remaining 2 tablespoons apple juice in small bowl; add to apple mixture. Cook, stirring until thickened. Return fish to skillet and add green onions; heat through. Serve fish with rice and sauce. *Makes 2 servings*

Seared Salmon Teriyaki

241 HOISIN–FLAVORED MUSHROOMS AND SHRIMP

2 tablespoons vegetable oil
1 pound fresh white mushrooms, sliced (about 5 cups)
1 tablespoon minced fresh ginger
1 teaspoon minced garlic
1⅓ cups uncooked orzo pasta
2 cans (about 14 ounces each) chicken broth
¼ cup hoisin sauce
   Pinch ground red pepper
12 ounces cooked cleaned deveined shrimp
½ cup green onions, cut into 1-inch pieces

In large saucepan, heat oil until hot; add mushrooms, ginger and garlic. Cook until mushrooms release their liquid, about 5 minutes. Stir in pasta, chicken broth, hoisin sauce and pepper; bring to a boil. Simmer, covered, stirring occasionally until pasta is firm-tender and some liquid remains, about 10 minutes. Stir in shrimp and onions; cook until shrimp are heated through, 1 to 2 minutes. *Makes 4 servings*

Favorite recipe from **Mushroom Council**

242 DAREN'S SEAFOOD SAUTÉ

2 tablespoons olive oil
3 cloves CHRISTOPHER RANCH Garlic, chopped
2 tablespoons CHRISTOPHER RANCH Pesto Sauce
¼ pound scallops
¼ pound small prawns, peeled and deveined
¼ pound calamari rings
1 tablespoon cajun seasoning or cayenne pepper
   Salt and black pepper to taste
1 pound hot cooked pasta (optional)
   Parmesan cheese

Add oil and garlic to skillet or wok and sauté over medium heat until garlic is lightly browned. Blend in pesto, then add seafood and seasoning. Sauté until done, about 5 minutes. Serve alone or toss with pasta, if desired. Sprinkle with cheese before serving.

Makes 4 servings

243 STIR–FRY FISH HASH

2 pounds fresh or frozen thawed mullet
   fillets or other fish fillets, skin
   removed
2 tablespoons soy sauce
2 tablespoons dry sherry
1/4 teaspoon sugar
1/4 teaspoon ground red pepper
1/8 teaspoon ground ginger
1/2 cup vegetable oil
1 cup cashews
4 cups sliced unpeeled zucchini
4 cups sliced fresh mushrooms
4 cups diagonally-sliced Chinese cabbage
2 cups green onions, cut into 3-inch
   pieces
1/2 teaspoon salt

Cut fish into 2-inch cubes. Combine soy
sauce, sherry, sugar, pepper and ginger in
medium bowl. Mix well; add fish and stir.
Marinate fish in refrigerator 15 minutes. In
large skillet or wok, heat oil over medium-
high heat. Add cashews; cook about 3
minutes or until lightly browned, stirring
constantly. Remove cashews with slotted
spoon; drain on paper towel. Add zucchini,
mushrooms, cabbage, onions and salt to
skillet; cook until crisp-tender, about 5
minutes. Remove vegetables from pan with
slotted spoon; set aside. Add fish to skillet;
reduce heat and cover. Cook fish over low
heat 8 to 10 minutes or until fish flakes easily
when tested with fork. Add cashews and
cooked vegetables to skillet; stir carefully.
Heat 1 to 2 minutes before serving. Serve
immediately.   *Makes 6 servings*

*Favorite recipe from **Florida Department of
Agriculture and Consumer Services, Bureau of
Seafood and Aquaculture***

244 TARRAGON SCALLOPS & ZUCCHINI

1 1/4 pounds sea scallops
6 tablespoons butter or margarine
2 small zucchini, thinly sliced
1/4 teaspoon onion powder
2 cups instant white rice
3 large green onions with tops, chopped
3 tablespoons chopped fresh tarragon *or*
   3/4 teaspoon dried tarragon leaves
1/4 teaspoon salt
2 tablespoons lemon juice
2 teaspoons cornstarch

1. Rinse scallops; pat dry with paper towels.
Cut large scallops into halves.

2. Melt butter in large nonstick skillet over
medium heat. Stir in scallops, zucchini and
onion powder; cook and stir 2 minutes.
Cover; reduce heat. Cook 7 minutes.

3. Meanwhile, prepare rice according to
package directions. Combine green onions,
tarragon and salt in small bowl. Blend lemon
juice and cornstarch in another small bowl,
stirring until cornstarch dissolves; set aside.

4. Stir green onion and cornstarch mixtures
into skillet. Increase heat to medium; cook
and stir 1 minute or until sauce thickens and
scallops are opaque. Serve over rice.
                    Makes 4 servings

Prep and Cook Time: 20 minutes

SATISFYING SEAFOOD

245 EASY SEAFOOD STIR–FRY

1 package (1 ounce) dried black Chinese mushrooms*
½ cup defatted low-sodium chicken broth
2 tablespoons dry sherry
1 tablespoon low-sodium soy sauce
4½ teaspoons cornstarch
1 teaspoon vegetable oil, divided
½ pound bay scallops or halved sea scallops
¼ pound raw medium shrimp, peeled and deveined
2 cloves garlic, minced
6 ounces (2 cups) fresh snow peas, cut diagonally into halves
2 cups hot cooked rice
¼ cup thinly sliced green onions

*Or substitute 1½ cups sliced fresh mushrooms. Omit step 1.

1. Place mushrooms in small bowl; cover with warm water. Soak 20 minutes to soften. Drain; squeeze out excess water. Discard stems; slice caps.

2. Blend chicken broth, sherry and soy sauce into cornstarch in another small bowl until smooth.

3. Heat ½ teaspoon oil in wok or large nonstick skillet over medium heat. Add scallops, shrimp and garlic; stir-fry 3 minutes or until seafood is opaque. Remove and reserve. Add remaining ½ teaspoon oil to wok. Add mushrooms and snow peas; stir-fry 3 minutes or until snow peas are crisp-tender. Stir broth mixture and add to wok. Heat 2 minutes or until sauce boils and thickens.

4. Return seafood and any accumulated juices to wok; heat through. Serve over rice. Top with onions. *Makes 4 servings*

246 CRYSTAL SHRIMP WITH SWEET & SOUR SAUCE

½ cup KIKKOMAN® Sweet & Sour Sauce
1 tablespoon water
2 teaspoons cornstarch
½ pound medium-size raw shrimp, peeled and deveined
1 egg white, beaten
2 tablespoons vegetable oil, divided
1 clove garlic, minced
2 carrots, cut diagonally into thin slices
1 medium-size green bell pepper, chunked
1 medium onion, chunked
1 tablespoon sesame seed, toasted

Blend sweet & sour sauce and water; set aside. Measure cornstarch into large plastic food storage bag. Coat shrimp with egg white; drain off excess egg. Add shrimp to cornstarch in bag; shake bag to coat shrimp. Heat 1 tablespoon oil in hot wok or large skillet over medium-high heat. Add garlic; stir-fry 10 seconds, or until fragrant. Add shrimp and stir-fry 2 minutes, or until pink; remove. Heat remaining 1 tablespoon oil in same pan over high heat. Add carrots, green pepper and onion; stir-fry 4 minutes. Add shrimp and sweet & sour sauce mixture. Cook and stir until shrimp and vegetables are coated with sauce. Remove from heat; stir in sesame seed. Serve immediately.
Makes 4 servings

Easy Seafood Stir-Fry

SATISFYING SEAFOOD

247 ORANGE ALMOND SCALLOPS

3 tablespoons orange juice
1 tablespoon low-sodium soy sauce
1 clove garlic, minced
1 pound bay scallops or halved sea
    scallops
1 tablespoon cornstarch
1 teaspoon vegetable oil, divided
1 green bell pepper, cut into short, thin
    strips
1 can (8 ounces) sliced water chestnuts,
    drained and rinsed
3 tablespoons toasted blanched almonds
3 cups hot cooked rice
½ teaspoon finely grated orange peel

1. Combine orange juice, soy sauce and garlic in medium bowl. Add scallops; toss to coat. Marinate at room temperature 15 minutes or cover and refrigerate up to 1 hour.

2. Drain scallops; reserve marinade. Blend marinade into cornstarch in small bowl until smooth.

3. Heat ½ teaspoon oil in wok or large nonstick skillet over medium heat. Add scallops; stir-fry 2 minutes or until scallops are opaque. Remove and reserve.

4. Add remaining ½ teaspoon oil to wok. Add bell pepper and water chestnuts. Stir-fry 3 minutes.

5. Return scallops along with any accumulated juices to wok. Stir marinade mixture and add to wok. Stir-fry 1 minute or until sauce boils and thickens. Stir in almonds. Serve over rice. Sprinkle with orange peel. Garnish with orange peel and fresh herbs, if desired.

Makes 4 servings

248 STIR–FRY SHRIMP AND CHICKEN

1 can (8 ounces) pineapple chunks,
    undrained
⅓ cup HEINZ® Chili Sauce
2 teaspoons cornstarch
2 teaspoons soy sauce
2 cups snow peas (about 6 ounces)
1 cup diagonally-sliced celery
8 to 10 green onions, cut into 1-inch
    pieces
1 teaspoon minced fresh ginger
2 tablespoons vegetable oil, divided
2 boneless skinless chicken breast halves,
    cut into 1½-inch chunks
½ to ¾ pound deveined peeled raw large
    shrimp*

One package (12 ounces) peeled deveined frozen shrimp, thawed, may be substituted.

Drain pineapple, reserving juice; set pineapple aside. Combine reserved juice with chili sauce, cornstarch and soy sauce in small bowl; set aside. In preheated wok or large skillet, stir-fry snow peas, celery, onions and ginger in 1 tablespoon oil 2 minutes or until crisp-tender; remove. Stir-fry chicken in remaining 1 tablespoon oil 2 minutes; add shrimp and stir-fry 2 to 3 minutes longer. Return vegetables to wok; stir in reserved pineapple, then chili sauce mixture. Cook until sauce is thickened.

Makes 4 servings

SATISFYING SEAFOOD

249 ALBACORE STIR–FRY

3 tablespoons vegetable oil
½ cup sliced onion
1 clove garlic, minced or pressed
1 bag (16 ounces) frozen Oriental
    vegetables, thawed and drained*
1 can (12 ounces) STARKIST® Solid White
    Tuna, drained and chunked
3 tablespoons soy sauce
1 tablespoon lemon juice
1 tablespoon water
1 teaspoon sugar
2 cups hot cooked rice

*May use 4 cups fresh vegetables such as carrots, snow peas, broccoli, bell peppers, mushrooms, celery and bean sprouts.

In wok or large skillet, heat oil over medium-high heat; cook and stir onion and garlic until onion is soft. Add thawed frozen vegetables; cook about 3 to 4 minutes or until crisp-tender. Add tuna, soy sauce, lemon juice, water and sugar. Cook 1 more minute; serve over rice.

Makes 4 servings

Albacore Stir-Fry

250 SHRIMP AND VEGETABLES WITH LO MEIN NOODLES

2 tablespoons vegetable oil
1 pound raw medium shrimp, peeled
2 packages (21 ounces each) frozen
    lo mein stir-fry mix with sauce
¼ cup peanuts
    Fresh cilantro
1 small wedge cabbage

1. Heat oil in wok or large skillet over medium-high heat until hot. Add shrimp; stir-fry 3 minutes or until shrimp are pink and opaque. Remove from wok to medium bowl. Set aside.

2. Remove sauce packet from stir-fry mix. Add frozen vegetables and noodles to wok; stir in sauce. Cover and cook 7 to 8 minutes, stirring frequently.

3. While vegetable mixture is cooking, chop peanuts and enough cilantro to measure 2 tablespoons. Shred cabbage.

4. Stir shrimp, peanuts and cilantro into vegetable mixture; heat through. Serve immediately with cabbage.

Makes 6 servings

Prep and Cook Time: 19 minutes

251 SAUCY STIR–FRIED FISH

SAUCE
½ cup chicken broth
3 tablespoons dry sherry
1 tablespoon LA CHOY® Soy Sauce
1½ teaspoons cornstarch

FISH AND VEGETABLES
1 tablespoon cornstarch
1 tablespoon vodka or chicken broth
1 teaspoon LA CHOY® Soy Sauce
1 pound firm-fleshed white fish, cut into
    1-inch chunks
2 tablespoons WESSON® Oil
½ teaspoon minced fresh garlic
¼ teaspoon minced fresh ginger
1 (8-ounce) can LA CHOY® Bamboo
    Shoots, drained
½ cup chopped carrots
1 (5-ounce) can LA CHOY® Chow Mein
    Noodles

In small bowl, combine *sauce* ingredients; set aside. In medium glass or plastic bowl, combine cornstarch, vodka and soy sauce; mix well. Add fish; toss gently to coat. Cover and marinate 10 to 15 minutes. In large nonstick skillet or wok, heat oil. Add garlic and ginger; cook and stir 30 seconds. Add fish; gently stir-fry until fish flakes easily with fork, about 3 to 4 minutes. Remove fish from skillet; set aside. Add bamboo shoots and carrots to same skillet; stir-fry 1 to 2 minutes or until carrots are crisp-tender. Stir sauce; add to skillet. Cook, stirring constantly, until sauce is thick and bubbly. Return fish to skillet; heat thoroughly, stirring occasionally. Serve over noodles.

Makes 4 to 6 servings

Shrimp and Vegetables with Lo Mein Noodles

SATISFYING SEAFOOD

252 SHRIMP IN CHILI SAUCE

1 pound large shrimp (about 23 shrimp), peeled (last tail segment attached) and deveined
1 tablespoon rice wine or dry sherry
4 cloves garlic, chopped
1 teaspoon paprika
1/4 teaspoon ground red pepper
1 or 2 fresh green jalapeño chilies*
2 tablespoons water
2 tablespoons ketchup
1 teaspoon cornstarch
1/2 teaspoon sugar
1/4 teaspoon salt
2 tablespoons vegetable oil
  Edible flowers, such as violets, and zucchini "leaves" for garnish

Chili peppers can sting and irritate the skin; wear rubber gloves when handling peppers and do not touch eyes.

1. Combine shrimp, wine, garlic, paprika and red pepper in medium bowl; mix well. Cover and refrigerate 1 to 4 hours to marinate.

2. Cut chilies lengthwise into halves. Scrape out and discard stems, seeds and veins. Cut halves crosswise into 1/8-inch slices.

3. Combine water, ketchup, cornstarch, sugar and salt in small bowl; mix well. Set aside.

4. Heat wok over high heat about 1 minute or until hot. Drizzle oil into wok and heat 30 seconds. Add shrimp mixture and chilies; stir-fry about 3 minutes or until shrimp turn pink and opaque.

5. Stir cornstarch mixture; add to wok. Cook and stir about 2 minutes or until sauce coats shrimp and thickens. Transfer shrimp to serving dish or individual serving plates. Garnish, if desired. Serve immediately.
Makes 4 servings

253 STIR–FRIED FISH WITH CHILI GARLIC SAUCE

4 tablespoons vegetable oil, divided
1/2 teaspoon ground white pepper
1/2 teaspoon cornstarch
14 ounces fish fillet, cut into 1-inch pieces
2 1/2 ounces sliced celery
2 ounces sliced carrot
3 tablespoons LEE KUM KEE® Chili Garlic Sauce
1 tablespoon water
1 green onion, chopped

1. Combine 1 tablespoon oil, pepper and cornstarch in medium bowl; add fish. Marinate fish 10 minutes. Cook celery and carrot in boiling water 1 minute; drain and set aside. Combine Chili Garlic Sauce and water in small bowl; set aside.

2. Heat 2 tablespoons oil in wok. Stir-fry fish until golden brown; remove and set aside.

3. Heat remaining 1 tablespoon oil in wok; stir-fry onion, celery, carrot and fish. Add Chili Garlic Sauce mixture; cook 2 minutes.
Makes 4 servings

Shrimp in Chili Sauce

SATISFYING SEAFOOD

254 COMBINATION CHOP SUEY

2 whole chicken breasts
4 cups chicken broth
1 cup water
4 teaspoons soy sauce
2 teaspoons cornstarch
1 teaspoon chicken bouillon granules
3 tablespoons vegetable oil
8 ounces boneless lean pork, finely chopped
½ head bok choy or napa cabbage (about 8 ounces), finely chopped
4 ounces fresh green beans, trimmed and cut into 1-inch pieces
3 stalks celery, diagonally cut into ½-inch pieces
2 yellow onions, chopped
1 large carrot, chopped
8 ounces medium shrimp, peeled and deveined
1 can (8 ounces) sliced bamboo shoots, drained
Hot cooked rice (optional)
Carrot curls* and fresh thyme leaves for garnish

*To make carrot curls, cut thin lengthwise slice from whole peeled carrot with vegetable peeler. Roll up slice tightly, starting at short end; secure with wooden pick. Add to bowl of ice water; let stand several hours or overnight. Remove wooden pick.

1. Combine chicken and chicken broth in large saucepan. Bring to a boil over medium-high heat. Reduce heat to low; cover. Simmer 20 to 30 minutes or until chicken is no longer pink in center. Remove from heat. Let stand until chicken is cool.

2. Remove skin and bones from chicken. Coarsely chop chicken.

3. Combine water, soy sauce, cornstarch and bouillon granules; set aside.

4. Heat oil in wok or large skillet over high heat. Add pork; stir-fry until no longer pink in center, about 5 minutes. Remove from wok; set aside.

5. Add cabbage, beans, celery, onions and carrot to wok; stir-fry until crisp-tender, about 3 minutes. Stir soy sauce mixture; add to wok. Cook and stir until liquid boils and thickens, about 3 minutes. Add chicken, shrimp, pork and bamboo shoots. Cook and stir until shrimp turn pink and are cooked through, about 3 minutes. Serve over hot cooked rice and garnish, if desired.

Makes 4 to 6 servings

255 SPICY FISH FILLETS WITH LEMON

Grated peel of ½ SUNKIST® lemon
1 teaspoon toasted sesame seeds
¼ teaspoon onion salt
⅛ teaspoon ground white pepper
⅛ teaspoon ground cumin
⅛ teaspoon paprika
⅛ teaspoon red pepper flakes (optional)
4 talapia or sole fillets (about ¾ pound)
1 tablespoon vegetable oil
Fresh lemon wedges

In small bowl, combine lemon peel, sesame seeds, onion salt and spices. Sprinkle over and rub onto both sides of fish fillets. Heat oil in large nonstick skillet sprayed with nonstick cooking spray. Sauté fish over medium-high heat 3 minutes; turn fish and cook 2 to 3 minutes longer or until fish is opaque and flakes easily with fork. Serve with lemon wedges and garnish with parsley sprigs, if desired. *Makes 2 to 4 servings*

SATISFYING SEAFOOD

256 SHRIMP WITH SNOW PEAS

1 pound raw shrimp
½ cup chicken broth
¼ cup soy sauce
3 tablespoons dry sherry or white wine
2 tablespoons cornstarch
2 teaspoons minced fresh ginger
¼ cup vegetable oil
1 (6-ounce) package frozen snow peas, thawed and patted dry, *or* ½ pound fresh snow peas
3 green onions, cut into 1-inch pieces
½ can (8 ounces) sliced water chestnuts
Hot cooked rice

Peel shrimp and, if large, cut into halves lengthwise. Combine chicken broth, soy sauce, sherry, cornstarch and ginger in small bowl; set aside. In wok or large skillet, heat oil until hot. Add shrimp. Cook, stirring rapidly, 3 to 4 minutes or until pink; remove. Add snow peas; stir-fry 3 to 4 minutes or until soft. Remove from wok; set aside. Repeat procedure with onions and water chestnuts. Add shrimp, snow peas, onions and water chestnuts to wok. Add chicken broth mixture and cook until sauce thickens slightly, about 2 to 3 minutes. Serve over rice. *Makes 4 servings*

Favorite recipe from **Florida Department of Agriculture and Consumer Services, Bureau of Seafood and Aquaculture**

Combination Chop Suey (page 218)

SATISFYING SEAFOOD

257 PHOENIX & DRAGON STIR–FRY

1 chicken breast, sliced
3 tablespoons vegetable oil, divided
2 tablespoons plus 1 teaspoon cornstarch, divided
$\frac{1}{3}$ teaspoon plus $\frac{1}{4}$ teaspoon salt, divided
$\frac{1}{4}$ teaspoon white pepper, divided
1 cup sliced button mushrooms
$\frac{1}{4}$ cup sliced onion
$\frac{1}{4}$ cup sliced celery
$\frac{1}{4}$ cup sliced carrot
2 cloves garlic, chopped
3 ounces chopped clams with juice ($\frac{1}{2}$ small can), undrained
1 cup heavy cream
$\frac{1}{4}$ cup wine
1 teaspoon fresh thyme *or* $\frac{1}{2}$ teaspoon dried thyme leaves
1 whole California spiny lobster, cleaned and meat cut into 1-inch chunks (shell reserved)
1 tablespoon oyster sauce
1 tablespoon sherry
1 tablespoon lemon juice
1 avocado, peeled and cut into chunks
Toasted pine nuts for garnish

Combine chicken slices with 1 tablespoon oil, 1 teaspoon cornstarch, $\frac{1}{4}$ teaspoon salt and $\frac{1}{8}$ teaspoon white pepper in medium bowl; marinate 30 minutes.

Heat wok until hot; add remaining 2 tablespoons oil. Stir-fry chicken about 1 minute or until lightly browned. Add mushrooms, onion, celery and carrot; stir-fry 30 seconds. Add garlic; stir-fry 15 seconds or until garlic is aromatic. Add clams with juice, cream, wine and thyme; simmer, covered, 1½ minutes. Add lobster meat and main lobster shell. Cook until shell turns red. Cover; simmer 1 minute.

Remove lobster shell; reserve. Add oyster sauce, sherry, lemon juice and remaining $\frac{1}{3}$ teaspoon salt and $\frac{1}{8}$ teaspoon white pepper. Mix remaining 2 tablespoons cornstarch with 3 tablespoons cold water in small bowl. Thicken sauce using cornstarch mixture as needed. Turn off heat and adjust seasoning.

Mix in avocado and ladle onto platter. Top with pine nuts and arrange lobster shell around stir-fry for garnish.

Makes 4 to 6 servings

*Favorite recipe from **California Seafood Council***

258 SQUID AND ONION HOT POT WITH CHILI GARLIC SAUCE

14 ounces squid
2 tablespoons vegetable oil
2 tablespoons LEE KUM KEE® Chili Garlic Sauce
$\frac{1}{2}$ teaspoon salt
Dash white pepper
1 onion, shredded
2 ounces shredded carrot
1 stalk celery, shredded
4 fresh black mushrooms, shredded
4 tablespoons white wine or chicken broth

1. Clean squid and cross-cut into rings. Blanch 1 minute and refresh with cold water. Drain.

2. Heat oil in wok. Add Chili Garlic Sauce, salt and pepper. Cook until aromatic. Add onion and carrot. Stir-fry 1 minute.

3. Add celery, mushrooms and squid. Mix well and add wine. Cook, covered, 3 minutes or until done. *Makes 4 servings*

SATISFYING SEAFOOD

259 LOUISIANA STIR–FRY

2 tablespoons vegetable oil
1 pound raw medium shrimp, peeled and deveined *or* ½ pound sea scallops
1 bag (16 ounces) BIRDS EYE® frozen Farm Fresh Mixtures Broccoli, Corn & Red Peppers
½ green bell pepper, chopped
2 teaspoons water
1 can (14½ ounces) stewed tomatoes, drained
¼ teaspoon hot pepper sauce (optional)
Hot cooked rice (optional)

• In wok or large skillet; heat oil over medium-high heat.

• Add shrimp; stir-fry 2 to 3 minutes or until shrimp turn pink and opaque. Remove to serving plate.

• In wok, add vegetables, bell pepper and water; cover and cook 4 to 6 minutes.

• Uncover; stir in tomatoes and pepper sauce, if desired. Cook 3 to 4 minutes or until heated through and slightly thickened.

• Return shrimp to wok; cook and stir about 1 minute or until heated through.

• Serve over rice, if desired.

Makes 4 servings

Prep Time: 15 minutes
Cook Time: 12 to 15 minutes

VARIATIONS: Substitute 1 package (16 ounces) frozen fully cooked shrimp or 1 pound imitation crab legs. Add to cooked vegetables and cook until heated through.

260 SWEET AND SOUR FISH

⅓ cup GRANDMA'S® Molasses
¼ cup cider vinegar
¼ cup plus 2 tablespoons cornstarch
2 tablespoons pineapple juice, reserved from chunks
2 tablespoons ketchup
2 tablespoons soy sauce
1 pound swordfish or red snapper, cut into 1-inch cubes
3 tablespoons vegetable oil, divided
1 green, red or yellow bell pepper, cut into strips
2 green onions, chopped
1 (8-ounce) can pineapple chunks in its own juice, drained, reserving 2 tablespoons juice for sauce
Cherry tomatoes, cut into halves
Hot cooked rice or noodles

In medium bowl, combine molasses, vinegar, 2 tablespoons cornstarch, pineapple juice, ketchup and soy sauce; blend well. Set aside. Coat swordfish with remaining ¼ cup cornstarch. In large skillet, heat 2 tablespoons oil. Stir-fry 5 minutes or until fish flakes easily with fork. Remove from skillet. Heat remaining 1 tablespoon oil in skillet. Stir-fry bell pepper and onions 2 minutes or until crisp-tender. Add molasses mixture; cook until thickened. Add fish, pineapple and tomatoes; cook until heated through. Serve with rice.

Makes 4 servings

261 PHOENIX & DRAGON

1 boneless, skinless chicken breast half
1 teaspoon cornstarch
2 teaspoons KIKKOMAN® Soy Sauce
½ teaspoon minced fresh ginger root
¼ teaspoon sugar
⅔ cup bottled clam broth
1 tablespoon cornstarch
2 tablespoons KIKKOMAN® Soy Sauce
4 teaspoons water
1 teaspoon distilled white vinegar
2 tablespoons vegetable oil, divided
½ pound medium-size raw shrimp, peeled
    and deveined
1 large carrot, thinly sliced
1 medium-size green bell pepper, cut into
    ¾-inch squares
6 ounces fresh mushrooms, sliced
2 large stalks celery, cut diagonally into
    thin slices

Cut chicken into 1-inch square pieces. Combine 1 teaspoon cornstarch, 2 teaspoons soy sauce, ginger and sugar in small bowl; stir in chicken. Let stand 15 minutes. Meanwhile, combine clam broth, 1 tablespoon cornstarch, 2 tablespoons soy sauce, water and vinegar in small bowl; set aside. Heat 1 tablespoon oil in hot wok or large skillet over high heat. Add chicken; stir-fry 2 minutes. Add shrimp and stir-fry 2 minutes longer; remove chicken and shrimp. Heat remaining 1 tablespoon oil in same pan. Add carrot and green pepper; stir-fry 2 minutes. Add mushrooms and celery; stir-fry 2 minutes longer. Stir in chicken, shrimp and soy sauce mixture; cook and stir until sauce boils and thickens. Serve immediately.   *Makes 4 servings*

262 HALIBUT WITH CILANTRO AND LIME

1 pound halibut, tuna or swordfish steaks
2 tablespoons fresh lime juice
¼ cup low-sodium soy sauce
1 teaspoon cornstarch
½ teaspoon minced fresh ginger
½ teaspoon vegetable oil
½ cup slivered red or yellow onion
2 cloves garlic, minced
¼ cup coarsely chopped cilantro

1. Cut halibut into 1-inch pieces; sprinkle with lime juice.

2. Blend soy sauce into cornstarch in cup until smooth. Stir in ginger.

3. Heat oil in wok or large nonstick skillet over medium heat. Add onion and garlic; stir-fry 2 minutes. Add halibut; stir-fry 2 minutes or until halibut is opaque.

4. Stir soy sauce mixture; add to wok. Stir-fry 30 seconds or until sauce boils and thickens. Sprinkle with cilantro. Garnish with lime wedges, if desired.
    Makes 4 servings

Phoenix & Dragon

Garden
Delights

263 GREEN BEANS AND SHIITAKE MUSHROOMS

   10 to 12 dried shiitake mushrooms (about
       1 ounce)
    3 tablespoons oyster sauce
    1 tablespoon cornstarch
    4 cloves garlic, minced
   ⅛ teaspoon red pepper flakes
    1 tablespoon vegetable oil
   ¾ to 1 pound fresh green beans, ends
       trimmed
   ⅓ cup julienned fresh basil
   ⅓ cup roasted peanuts (optional)
    2 green onions, diagonally cut into thin
       slices (optional)

1. Place mushrooms in bowl; cover with hot water. Let stand 30 minutes or until caps are soft. Drain mushrooms; squeeze out excess water. Remove and discard stems. Slice caps into thin strips.

2. Combine ¼ cup water, oyster sauce, cornstarch, garlic and pepper flakes in small bowl; mix well. Set aside.

3. Heat wok or medium skillet over medium-high heat. Add oil and swirl to coat surface. Add mushrooms, beans and ½ cup water; cook and stir until water boils.

4. Reduce heat to medium-low; cover and cook 8 to 10 minutes or until beans are crisp-tender, stirring occasionally.

5. Stir cornstarch mixture; add to wok. Cook and stir until sauce thickens and coats beans. (If cooking water has evaporated, add enough water to form thick sauce.)

6. Stir in basil, peanuts and green onions, if desired; mix well. Transfer to serving platter.
Makes 4 to 6 servings

Green Beans and Shiitake Mushrooms

GARDEN DELIGHTS

264 SZECHUAN VEGETABLE STIR–FRY

8 ounces firm tofu, cut into cubes
1 cup vegetable broth, divided
½ cup orange juice
⅓ cup soy sauce
1 to 2 teaspoons hot chili oil
½ teaspoon fennel seeds
½ teaspoon ground black pepper
2 tablespoons cornstarch
3 tablespoons vegetable oil
3 medium carrots, diagonally sliced
1 cup sliced green onions with tops
3 cloves garlic, minced
2 teaspoons minced fresh ginger
¼ pound button mushrooms, sliced
1 red bell pepper, cut into 1-inch squares
¼ pound fresh snow peas, trimmed and cut
      diagonally into halves
8 ounces broccoli florets, steamed
½ cup peanuts
4 to 6 cups hot cooked rice

1. Place tofu in square glass baking dish. Combine ½ cup vegetable broth, orange juice, soy sauce, chili oil, fennel seeds and black pepper in small bowl; pour over tofu. Let stand 15 to 60 minutes. Drain; reserve marinade.

2. Combine cornstarch and remaining ½ cup vegetable broth in medium bowl. Add reserved marinade; set aside.

3. Heat vegetable oil in wok or large skillet over high heat until hot. Add carrots, onions, garlic and ginger; stir-fry 3 minutes. Add tofu, mushrooms, bell pepper and snow peas; stir-fry 2 to 3 minutes or until vegetables are crisp-tender. Add broccoli; stir-fry 1 minute or until heated through. Stir cornstarch mixture. Add to wok and cook 1 to 2 minutes or until bubbly. Stir in peanuts. Serve over rice.

Makes 4 to 6 servings

265 VEGETABLES SAMFAINA

3 tablespoons FILIPPO BERIO® Olive Oil,
      divided
1 cup diced peeled eggplant
1 cup diced onion
1 cup diced red bell pepper
1 cup diced green bell pepper
1 cup diced zucchini
1½ teaspoons fresh oregano *or* ¾ teaspoon
      dried oregano leaves
1 clove garlic, minced
½ teaspoon salt
½ teaspoon freshly ground black pepper
      Lemon slices (optional)
      Chopped fresh parsley (optional)

In large nonstick skillet, heat 1 tablespoon olive oil over medium heat until hot. Add eggplant; cook and stir 2 minutes or just until eggplant starts to brown. Remove with slotted spoon; reserve. Add remaining 2 tablespoons olive oil to skillet. Add onion and bell peppers; cook and stir 1½ minutes. Add zucchini; cook and stir 1½ minutes. Add oregano, garlic, salt and black pepper; cook and stir 1 minute. Add reserved eggplant; cook until heated through. Garnish with lemon slices and parsley, if desired.

Makes 4 servings

Szechuan Vegetable Stir-Fry

GARDEN DELIGHTS

266 FRESH VEGETABLE BASIL MEDLEY

3 small zucchini
3 small yellow squash
2 medium carrots
4 teaspoons vegetable oil
2 teaspoons dried basil leaves
    Fresh basil leaves (optional)

Cut vegetables into julienne strips. Heat oil in large skillet over medium-high heat. Add carrots; cook 1 minute. Add zucchini, squash and dried basil; cook and stir until vegetables are crisp-tender. Garnish with fresh basil, if desired. Serve hot. Refrigerate leftovers.

Makes 4 to 6 side-dish servings

Favorite recipe from **Bob Evans Farms**®

267 SAVORY LEMON POTATO WEDGES

1½ pounds potatoes (about 4 medium), unpeeled and cut lengthwise into 6 wedges each
    Juice of 1 SUNKIST® lemon (3 tablespoons), divided
1 medium clove garlic, minced
¼ cup sliced green onions
2 tablespoons reduced-calorie margarine
    Grated peel of ½ lemon
½ teaspoon dried dill weed

In covered nonstick skillet, cook potatoes in gently boiling water with 2 tablespoons lemon juice and garlic 17 to 20 minutes or until tender *(do not overcook)*; remove potato mixture and drain well. In same skillet, sauté green onions in margarine with lemon peel and dill. Add potatoes and remaining 1 tablespoon lemon juice; heat.

Makes 4 servings

268 SPINACH AND TOMATO TOFU TOSS

    Nonstick cooking spray
¾ cup chopped onion
1 teaspoon chopped garlic
1 package (10 ounces) extra-firm tofu, drained and cut into ½-inch cubes
2 teaspoons soy sauce
¼ teaspoon black pepper
¼ pound washed spinach leaves, divided
4 whole wheat pitas, cut into halves
2 large ripe tomatoes, chopped
¾ cup chopped red bell pepper

1. Spray large nonstick skillet with cooking spray; heat over medium heat until hot. Add onion and garlic. Cook and stir 2 minutes or until onion is crisp-tender.

2. Add tofu, soy sauce and black pepper to skillet; toss until well combined. Cook over medium heat 3 to 4 minutes or until heated through. Remove from heat and cool slightly.

3. Set aside 8 whole spinach leaves; tear remaining leaves into bite-size pieces. Line pita halves with whole spinach leaves. Add tomatoes, torn spinach and bell peppers to tofu mixture; toss to combine. Fill pita halves with tofu mixture. Serve immediately.

Makes 4 servings

Fresh Vegetable Basil Medley

GARDEN DELIGHTS

269 MA PO BEAN CURD

1 tablespoon Szechuan peppercorns*
   (optional)
¾ cup chicken broth
1 tablespoon soy sauce
1 tablespoon dry sherry
1½ tablespoons cornstarch
2 tablespoons vegetable oil
4 ounces lean ground pork
2 teaspoons minced fresh ginger
2 cloves garlic, minced
1 tablespoon hot bean sauce
12 to 14 ounces bean curd, drained and cut
   into ½-inch cubes
2 green onions with tops, thinly sliced
1 teaspoon sesame oil
   Fresh chives for garnish

Szechuan peppercorns are deceptively potent. Wear rubber or plastic gloves when crushing them and do not touch eyes or lips when handling.

1. Place peppercorns in small dry skillet. Cook and stir over medium-low heat until fragrant, about 2 minutes; let cool. Place peppercorns between paper towels; crush with hammer.

2. Combine chicken broth, soy sauce and sherry in small bowl; set aside. Combine cornstarch and 3 tablespoons water in small cup; mix well. Set aside.

3. Heat vegetable oil in wok or large skillet over high heat. Add pork; stir-fry until no longer pink, about 2 minutes. Add ginger, garlic and hot bean sauce. Stir-fry 1 minute.

4. Add chicken broth mixture and bean curd; simmer, uncovered, 5 minutes. Stir in onions. Stir cornstarch mixture; add to wok. Cook until sauce boils and thickens slightly, stirring constantly. Stir in sesame oil. Sprinkle with ground peppercorns and garnish. *Makes 3 to 4 servings*

270 INDIAN VEGETABLE CURRY

2 to 3 teaspoons curry powder
1 can (16 ounces) sliced potatoes, drained
1 bag (16 ounces) BIRDS EYE® frozen
   Farm Fresh Mixtures Broccoli,
   Cauliflower and Carrots
1 can (15 ounces) chick-peas, drained
1 can (14½ ounces) stewed tomatoes,
   undrained
1 can (about 14 ounces) vegetable or
   chicken broth
2 tablespoons cornstarch

• Stir curry powder in large skillet over high heat until fragrant, about 30 seconds.

• Stir in potatoes, vegetables, chick-peas and tomatoes; bring to a boil. Reduce heat to medium-high; cover and cook 8 minutes.

• Blend vegetable broth with cornstarch; stir into vegetables. Cook until thickened.
                        Makes about 6 servings

Prep Time: 5 minutes
Cook Time: 15 minutes

SERVING SUGGESTION: Serve with white or brown rice.

Ma Po Bean Curd

271 ZUCCHINI SHANGHAI STYLE

4 dried Chinese black mushrooms
½ cup defatted low-sodium chicken broth
2 tablespoons ketchup
2 teaspoons dry sherry
1 teaspoon low-sodium soy sauce
1 teaspoon red wine vinegar
¼ teaspoon sugar
1½ teaspoons vegetable oil, divided
1 teaspoon minced fresh ginger
1 clove garlic, minced
1 tomato, peeled, seeded and chopped
1 green onion, finely chopped
1 teaspoon cornstarch
1 pound zucchini (about 3 medium), diagonally cut into 1-inch pieces
½ small yellow onion, cut into wedges and separated

1. Soak mushrooms in warm water 20 minutes. Drain, reserving ¼ cup liquid. Squeeze out excess water. Discard stems; slice caps. Combine reserved mushroom liquid, chicken broth, ketchup, sherry, soy sauce, vinegar and sugar in small bowl.

2. Heat 1 teaspoon oil in large saucepan over medium heat. Add ginger and garlic; stir-fry 10 seconds. Add mushrooms, tomato and green onion; stir-fry 1 minute. Add chicken broth mixture; bring to a boil over high heat. Reduce heat to medium; simmer 10 minutes.

3. Combine 1 tablespoon water and cornstarch in small bowl. Heat remaining ½ teaspoon oil in large nonstick skillet over medium heat. Add zucchini and yellow onion; stir-fry 30 seconds. Add 3 tablespoons water. Cover and cook 3 to 4 minutes or until vegetables are crisp-tender, stirring occasionally. Add tomato mixture to skillet. Stir cornstarch mixture and add to skillet. Cook until sauce boils and thickens.

Makes 4 side-dish servings

272 SAUTÉED GARLIC POTATOES

2 pounds boiling potatoes, peeled and cut into 1-inch pieces
3 tablespoons FILIPPO BERIO® Olive Oil
6 cloves garlic, skins on
1 tablespoon lemon juice
1 tablespoon chopped fresh chives
1 tablespoon chopped fresh parsley
Salt and freshly ground black pepper

Place potatoes in large colander; rinse under cold running water. Drain well; pat dry. In large nonstick skillet, heat olive oil over medium heat until hot. Add potatoes in single layer. Cook, stirring and turning frequently, 10 minutes or until golden brown. Add garlic. Cover; reduce heat to low and cook very gently, shaking pan and stirring mixture occasionally, 15 to 20 minutes or until potatoes are tender when pierced with fork. Remove garlic; discard skins. In small bowl, crush garlic; stir in lemon juice. Add to potatoes; mix well. Cook 1 to 2 minutes or until heated through. Transfer to serving dish; sprinkle with chives and parsley. Season to taste with salt and pepper.

Makes 4 servings

Zucchini Shanghai Style

GARDEN DELIGHTS

273 TOMATO, POTATO & BASIL SKILLET

1 tablespoon olive oil, divided
3 cups sliced potatoes, divided
⅓ cup minced fresh basil
2 eggs
2 egg whites
2 tablespoons skim milk
1 tablespoon Dijon mustard
1 teaspoon dry mustard
½ teaspoon salt
¼ teaspoon freshly ground black pepper
2 cups sliced plum tomatoes
    Fresh basil leaves for garnish

1. Heat 1½ teaspoons oil in medium skillet over medium heat until hot. Layer half of potato slices in skillet. Cover and cook 3 minutes or until lightly browned. Turn potatoes and cook, covered, 3 minutes or until lightly browned. Remove potatoes from skillet. Repeat with remaining 1½ teaspoons oil and potatoes.

2. Arrange all potatoes in skillet. Sprinkle with minced basil. Whisk together eggs, egg whites, milk, mustards, salt and pepper in small bowl. Pour over potatoes. Arrange tomatoes over potato mixture. Reduce heat to low. Cover and cook 10 minutes or until eggs are set. Garnish with additional fresh basil, if desired.   *Makes 4 servings*

274 SWEET 'N SOUR STIR–FRY

2 tablespoons vegetable oil
1 cup thinly sliced carrots
1 cup snow peas
1 small green bell pepper, cut into chunks
1 medium tomato, cut into wedges
1 cup sliced water chestnuts
½ cup sliced cucumber, cut into halves
¾ cup WISH-BONE® Sweet 'n Spicy French Dressing*
2 tablespoons packed brown sugar
2 teaspoons soy sauce
    Sesame seeds (optional)

*Also terrific with WISH-BONE® Russian Dressing.

In medium skillet, heat oil over medium heat; cook carrots, snow peas and bell pepper, stirring frequently, 5 minutes or until crisp-tender. Add tomato, water chestnuts, cucumber and Sweet 'n Spicy French Dressing blended with brown sugar and soy sauce. Simmer 5 minutes or until vegetables are tender. Top with sesame seeds, if desired.   *Makes about 6 servings*

Tomato, Potato & Basil Skillet

GARDEN DELIGHTS

275 VEGETARIAN STIR–FRY

1 bag (16 ounces) BIRDS EYE® frozen
    Mixed Vegetables*
2 tablespoons water
1 can (14 ounces) kidney beans, drained
1 jar (14 ounces) spaghetti sauce
½ teaspoon garlic powder
½ cup grated Parmesan cheese

*Or substitute your favorite BIRDS EYE® frozen
vegetable combination.

• In large skillet, place vegetables and water.

• Cover; cook 7 to 10 minutes over medium
heat. Uncover; stir in beans, spaghetti sauce
and garlic powder; cook until heated
through.

• Sprinkle with cheese.

Makes 4 servings

Prep Time: 2 minutes
Cook Time: 12 to 15 minutes

SERVING SUGGESTION: Serve over hot
cooked rice or pasta.

276 STEWED MUSHROOMS ON ASPARAGUS WITH VEGETARIAN OYSTER SAUCE

7 ounces asparagus, trimmed
  Salt
  Vegetable oil
2 slices ginger
4 ounces fresh black mushrooms
4 ounces baby corn
3 tablespoons LEE KUM KEE® Vegetarian
    Oyster Flavored Sauce
¼ teaspoon sugar
1 teaspoon cornstarch mixed with
    1 tablespoon water
¼ teaspoon LEE KUM KEE® Sesame Oil

1. Cook asparagus in boiling water with salt
and vegetable oil 3 minutes. Remove and
arrange on plate.

2. Heat 2 tablespoons vegetable oil in wok.
Sauté ginger until fragrant. Add mushrooms
and baby corn. Stir-fry 1 minute.

3. Combine Vegetarian Oyster Flavored
Sauce, ⅔ cup water and sugar in small bowl;
add to wok. Simmer 5 minutes. Add
cornstarch mixture; simmer until thickened.
Place mixture over asparagus and sprinkle
with Sesame Oil.   *Makes 4 to 6 servings*

Vegetarian Stir-Fry

GARDEN DELIGHTS

277 ROSEMARY HASH POTATOES

2 tablespoons olive oil
1 clove garlic, minced
2 teaspoons snipped fresh rosemary
1½ pounds red skin potatoes, unpeeled and cut into ½-inch cubes
½ teaspoon salt
½ teaspoon black pepper
    Fresh rosemary sprig and tomato wedges (optional)

Heat oil in large skillet over medium heat until hot. Add garlic and snipped rosemary; cook and stir 2 minutes. Add potatoes, salt and pepper. Cook 5 minutes, stirring occasionally. Reduce heat to medium-low; cook, uncovered, about 20 minutes or until potatoes are golden brown and crisp, turning occasionally. Garnish with rosemary sprig and tomato, if desired. Serve hot. Refrigerate leftovers.

Makes 4 to 6 side-dish servings

Favorite recipe from **Bob Evans Farms®**

278 SAUTÉED GARLIC CLOVES

1 tablespoon olive oil
40 cloves CHRISTOPHER RANCH Whole Peeled Garlic
    Dash dried Italian seasoning
    Dash LAWRY'S® Lemon Pepper
¼ cup water, white wine or chicken broth, or combination
    French bread baguettes or crackers

Pour olive oil in heated electric wok or skillet. Add garlic, Italian seasoning and lemon pepper; sauté until lightly browned *(be careful not to burn garlic)*. Add liquid; stir and bring to a boil. Cover and simmer, stirring occasionally, until garlic cloves are soft and easy to mash, about 7 minutes. Spread warm cloves on bread and serve.

Makes 6 to 8 servings

Rosemary Hash Potatoes

GARDEN DELIGHTS

279 HOT AND SPICY SPINACH

1 red bell pepper, cut into 1-inch pieces
1 clove garlic, minced
1 pound fresh spinach, rinsed and
    chopped
1 tablespoon mustard
1 teaspoon lemon juice
¼ teaspoon red pepper flakes

1. Spray large skillet with nonstick cooking spray; heat over medium heat. Add bell pepper and garlic; cook and stir 3 minutes.

2. Add spinach; cook and stir 3 minutes or just until spinach begins to wilt.

3. Stir in mustard, lemon juice and red pepper flakes. Serve immediately.

Makes 4 servings

280 CHICK–PEA PATTIES

1 can (15 ounces) chick-peas, rinsed and
    drained
1 cup shredded carrots
⅓ cup seasoned dry bread crumbs
2 tablespoons creamy Italian salad
    dressing
1 egg
2 tablespoons vegetable oil

1. Mash chick-peas coarsely in medium bowl with hand potato masher, leaving some larger pieces. Stir in carrots, bread crumbs, salad dressing and egg.

2. Shape chick-pea mixture into 4 patties.

3. Heat oil in large nonstick skillet over medium-high heat. Add patties; cook 3 minutes per side or until well-browned.

4. Remove from skillet using spatula; drain on paper towels. Serve immediately.

Makes 4 servings

Prep and Cook Time: 18 minutes

Hot and Spicy Spinach

GARDEN DELIGHTS

281 BROCCOLI & RED PEPPER SAUTÉ

2 tablespoons olive or vegetable oil
4 cups small broccoli florets
1 large red bell pepper, cut into thin strips
1 medium onion, sliced
1 clove garlic, finely chopped
1 envelope LIPTON® Recipe Secrets®
   Golden Herb with Lemon Soup Mix*
1 cup water
¼ cup sliced almonds, toasted (optional)

Also terrific with LIPTON® Recipe Secrets® Savory Herb with Garlic Soup Mix.

In large skillet, heat oil over medium heat and cook broccoli, bell pepper, onion and garlic, stirring occasionally, 5 minutes or until onion is tender. Add Golden Herb with Lemon Soup Mix blended with water. Simmer, covered, 5 minutes or until broccoli is tender. Sprinkle with almonds, if desired.

Makes about 6 servings

282 HOLLAND HOUSE® STIR-FRY SAUCE

1 teaspoon vegetable oil
1 bunch green onions, thinly sliced
2 cloves garlic, minced
¼ teaspoon ground ginger
¾ cup HOLLAND HOUSE® Sherry
   Cooking Wine
1 tablespoon reduced-sodium or regular
   soy sauce
1 cup reduced-sodium chicken broth
2 tablespoons cornstarch
1 to 2 tablespoons toasted sesame seeds
   (optional)

In medium saucepan, heat oil and cook onions, garlic and ginger until onions are just tender, about 4 minutes. Stir in Holland House® Cooking Wine, soy sauce and chicken broth blended with cornstarch. Bring to a boil and stir 1 minute.

Serve as sauce for grilled or broiled vegetables, steamed vegetables or with your favorite stir-fry recipe. Sprinkle with toasted sesame seeds, if desired.

Makes about 2 cups

Broccoli & Red Pepper Sauté

GARDEN DELIGHTS

283 COUNTRY GARDEN STIR–FRY WITH HERBED BUTTER

½ **pound whole green beans, stemmed**
4 **carrots, diagonally sliced ⅛ inch thick**
2 **cups fresh cauliflower florets**
¼ **cup butter or margarine, softened**
1 **tablespoon fresh lemon juice**
1 **tablespoon finely chopped parsley**
½ **teaspoon salt**

1. Place ⅓ cup water in large nonstick skillet or wok. Add beans, carrots and cauliflower. Bring to a boil. Reduce heat, cover tightly and simmer 8 to 10 minutes or until crisp-tender.

2. Meanwhile, in small bowl, whisk together butter, lemon juice, parsley and salt; set aside.

3. When vegetables are crisp-tender, uncover, increase heat to high and cook, stirring gently, until all liquid has evaporated. *Be careful not to burn vegetables.*

4. Remove from heat; toss gently with butter mixture. *Makes 4 side-dish servings*

284 VEGETABLE SAUTÉ

2 **tablespoons olive oil**
6 **cups assorted cut-up vegetables, such as bell peppers, broccoli, green beans, cauliflower, sugar snap peas, carrots, mushrooms, yellow squash, onions and zucchini**
1 **envelope GOOD SEASONS® Italian Salad Dressing Mix**
2 **tablespoons red wine vinegar**

HEAT oil in large skillet over medium-high heat. Add vegetables; cook and stir until crisp-tender.

STIR in salad dressing mix and vinegar; cook and stir until thoroughly heated. Garnish with chopped fresh parsley, if desired. *Makes 4 to 6 servings*

Country Garden Stir-Fry with Herbed Butter

GARDEN DELIGHTS

285 HUEVOS RANCHEROS ORTEGA® STYLE

2 tablespoons vegetable oil
1 cup (1 small) sliced quartered onion
1 cup (1 small) sliced green or red bell pepper
2 cloves garlic, finely chopped
1¾ cups (16-ounce jar) ORTEGA® Garden Style Salsa, medium or mild
½ cup (4-ounce can) ORTEGA® Diced Green Chiles
¼ teaspoon ground oregano
1 package (10) ORTEGA® Tostada Shells, warmed
10 fried or poached eggs
1 cup (4 ounces) shredded Cheddar or Monterey Jack cheese
Sliced green onions (optional)

HEAT oil in large skillet over medium-high heat. Add onion, bell pepper and garlic; cook, stirring occasionally, 3 to 4 minutes or until vegetables are tender and onions are slightly golden.

ADD salsa, chiles and oregano. Bring to a boil. Remove from heat.

TOP each tostada shell with ⅓ cup sauce, 1 egg, cheese and green onions.

Makes 10 servings

TIP: This traditional Mexican morning meal is usually served with refried beans on the side. Huevos Rancheros Ortega® Style are best when served warm from the skillet.

286 VEGETABLE STIR–FRY

2 cups broccoli florets
1 cup snow peas
1 cup thinly sliced carrots
1 cup sliced fresh mushrooms
1 medium red bell pepper, cut into strips
1 tablespoon vegetable oil
1 jar (12 ounces) HEINZ® HomeStyle Mushroom or Brown with Onions Gravy
¼ cup frozen orange juice concentrate, thawed
2 tablespoons reduced-sodium soy sauce
1 tablespoon brown sugar
Hot cooked rice

In preheated wok or large skillet, stir-fry vegetables in oil until crisp-tender, about 2 minutes. Stir in gravy, orange juice concentrate, soy sauce and brown sugar; heat. Serve over rice. *Makes 4 servings*

Huevos Rancheros Ortega® Style

GARDEN DELIGHTS

287 STIR–FRIED TOFU AND VEGETABLES

½ pound firm tofu
1 cup vegetable oil
1 yellow onion, peeled and cut into
    8 wedges
1 zucchini, trimmed and cut crosswise
    into 1-inch-thick slices
1 yellow squash, trimmed and cut
    crosswise into 1-inch-thick slices
8 button mushrooms, cut into thick slices
1 red bell pepper, cut into ¼-inch-wide
    strips
4 ounces fresh snow peas, trimmed
¼ cup water
1 tablespoon soy sauce
1 tablespoon tomato paste
¼ teaspoon salt
⅛ teaspoon black pepper

1. Drain tofu on paper towels. Cut crosswise into ¼-inch-thick slices. Set aside.

2. Heat oil in wok over medium-high heat about 4 minutes or until hot. Add tofu and fry about 3 minutes per side or until golden brown, turning once. Remove tofu with slotted spatula to baking sheet or large plate lined with paper towels; drain. Drain oil from wok, reserving 2 tablespoons.

3. Return reserved oil to wok. Heat over medium heat 30 seconds or until hot. Add onion and stir-fry 1 minute. Add zucchini, yellow squash and mushrooms; cook 7 to 8 minutes or until zucchini and yellow squash are crisp-tender, stirring occasionally.

4. Add bell pepper, snow peas and water. Stir-fry 2 to 3 minutes or until crisp-tender. Stir in soy sauce, tomato paste, salt and black pepper until well mixed. Add fried tofu; stir-fry until heated through and coated with sauce. Transfer to serving platter. Serve immediately.   *Makes 4 servings*

288 PEAS FLORENTINE STYLE

2 (10-ounce) packages frozen peas
¼ cup FILIPPO BERIO® Olive Oil
4 ounces Canadian bacon, cubed
1 clove garlic, minced
1 tablespoon chopped fresh Italian parsley
1 teaspoon sugar
    Salt to taste

Place peas in large colander or strainer; run under hot water until slightly thawed. Drain well. In medium skillet, heat olive oil over medium heat until hot. Add bacon and garlic; cook and stir 2 to 3 minutes or until garlic turns golden. Add peas and parsley; cook and stir over high heat 5 to 7 minutes or until heated through. Drain well. Stir in sugar; season with salt.

Makes 5 servings

Stir-Fried Tofu and Vegetables

GARDEN DELIGHTS

289 INDIAN–STYLE VEGETABLE STIR–FRY

1 teaspoon canola oil
1 teaspoon curry powder
1 teaspoon ground cumin
⅛ teaspoon red pepper flakes
1½ teaspoons finely chopped seeded
     jalapeño pepper
2 cloves garlic, minced
¾ cup chopped red bell pepper
¾ cup thinly sliced carrots
3 cups cauliflower florets
½ teaspoon salt
2 teaspoons finely chopped cilantro
     (optional)

1. Heat oil in large nonstick skillet over medium-high heat. Add curry powder, cumin and red pepper flakes; cook and stir about 30 seconds.

2. Stir in jalapeño and garlic. Add bell pepper and carrots; mix well to coat with spices. Add cauliflower; reduce heat to medium.

3. Stir in ¼ cup water; cook and stir until water evaporates. Add ¼ cup water; cover and cook about 8 to 10 minutes or until vegetables are crisp-tender, stirring occasionally.

4. Add salt; mix well. Sprinkle with cilantro and garnish with mizuma and additional red bell pepper, if desired. Serve immediately.

Makes 6 servings

290 GARLIC STIR–FRY

¼ cup vegetable or peanut oil
3 small slices fresh ginger
4 cloves CHRISTOPHER RANCH Whole
     Peeled Garlic, crushed
  Fresh vegetables cut into bite-size
     pieces, including zucchini,
     cauliflower, broccoli, onions, bell
     peppers, carrots, celery, snow peas
     and water chestnuts
½ cup white wine
1 teaspoon salt
½ teaspoon black pepper
  Dash dried oregano leaves
  Dash dried parsley leaves
½ fresh lemon

Heat oil in wok. Sauté ginger with garlic being careful not to burn garlic. Remove ginger when golden brown; discard. Add vegetables, stirring immediately to coat with oil. Add wine, salt and black pepper. Stir vegetables and cook approximately 2 to 3 minutes. Add oregano, parsley and a squeeze of lemon. Cook about 1 minute; serve.   *Makes 4 to 6 servings*

Indian-Style Vegetable Stir-Fry

GARDEN DELIGHTS

291 CHINESE VEGETABLES

1 pound fresh broccoli
1½ teaspoons vegetable oil
2 medium yellow onions, cut into wedges
 and separated
2 cloves garlic, minced
1½ tablespoons minced fresh ginger
8 ounces fresh spinach, coarsely chopped
4 ribs celery, diagonally cut into ½-inch
 pieces
8 ounces fresh snow peas *or* 1 package
 (6 ounces) thawed frozen snow peas,
 trimmed and strings removed
4 medium carrots, sliced
8 green onions, diagonally cut into thin
 slices
¾ cup defatted low-sodium chicken broth
1 tablespoon low-sodium soy sauce

1. Cut broccoli tops into florets. Cut stalks into 2×¼-inch strips.

2. Heat oil in wok or large nonstick skillet over high heat. Add broccoli stalks, yellow onions, garlic and ginger; stir-fry 1 minute. Add broccoli florets, spinach, celery, snow peas, carrots and green onions; toss lightly.

3. Add chicken broth and soy sauce to vegetables; toss to coat. Bring to a boil; cover and cook 2 to 3 minutes or until vegetables are crisp-tender.

Makes 4 side-dish servings

292 ALMOND BROCCOLI STIR–FRY

1 bunch (about 1 pound) broccoli
¾ cup BLUE DIAMOND® Chopped Natural
 Almonds
3 tablespoons vegetable oil
3 cloves garlic, thinly sliced
2 tablespoons soy sauce
1 tablespoon sugar
1 teaspoon grated fresh ginger *or*
 ¼ teaspoon ground ginger
1 teaspoon lemon juice

Cut broccoli into florets. Trim and peel stalks; cut on diagonal into thin slices and reserve. In large skillet or wok, cook and stir almonds in oil 1 minute. Add broccoli and stir-fry until barely tender, about 2 minutes. Add garlic; stir-fry until just tender, about 1 minute. Stir in soy sauce, sugar and ginger. Continue stir-frying until sugar dissolves, about 1 minute. Add lemon juice.

Makes 4 servings

Chinese Vegetables

GARDEN DELIGHTS

293 SOUTHERN–STYLE SUCCOTASH

2 tablespoons margarine
1 cup chopped onion
1 package (10 ounces) frozen lima beans, thawed
1 cup frozen corn, thawed
½ cup chopped red bell pepper
1 can (15 to 16 ounces) hominy, drained
⅓ cup fat-free reduced-sodium chicken broth
½ teaspoon salt
¼ teaspoon hot pepper sauce
¼ cup chopped green onion tops or chives

1. Melt margarine in large nonstick skillet over medium heat. Add onion; cook and stir 5 minutes. Add lima beans, corn and bell pepper. Cook and stir 5 minutes.

2. Add hominy, chicken broth, salt and pepper sauce; simmer 5 minutes or until most of liquid has evaporated. Remove from heat; stir in green onions.

Makes 6 servings

SERVING SUGGESTION: Serve with cornmeal biscuits.

294 STIR–FRY VEGETABLES

¼ cup GRANDMA'S® Robust Flavor Molasses
¼ cup chicken broth
2 tablespoons soy sauce
4 teaspoons cornstarch
1 tablespoon minced garlic
1 tablespoon minced fresh ginger
⅛ teaspoon ground red pepper
1 tablespoon canola oil
2 pounds fresh vegetables sliced into bite-size pieces (celery, zucchini, onion, bell peppers, Chinese cabbage and snow peas)

Combine Grandma's® Molasses, chicken broth, soy sauce, cornstarch, garlic, ginger and ground red pepper in small bowl; set aside. Heat oil in wok or large heavy skillet. Add vegetables and stir-fry 2 to 3 minutes or until crisp-tender. Mix in molasses mixture. Cook just until sauce thickens and coats vegetables.

Makes 4 to 6 servings

Southern-Style Succotash

GARDEN DELIGHTS

295 POTATO–ZUCCHINI PANCAKES WITH WARM CORN SALSA

Warm Corn Salsa (recipe follows)
2 cups frozen hash brown potatoes, thawed
1½ cups shredded zucchini, drained
½ cup cholesterol-free egg substitute
¼ cup all-purpose flour
2 tablespoons chopped onion
2 tablespoons chopped green bell pepper
¼ teaspoon salt
⅛ teaspoon ground black pepper
Nonstick cooking spray

1. Prepare Warm Corn Salsa. Keep warm.

2. Combine potatoes, zucchini, egg substitute, flour, onion, bell pepper, salt and black pepper in medium bowl until well blended.

3. Spray large nonstick skillet with cooking spray; heat over medium-high heat until hot. Drop potato mixture by ¼ cupfuls into skillet. Cook pancakes, 4 or 6 at a time, about 3 minutes on each side or until golden brown. Place 2 pancakes onto serving plate; top with ½ cup Warm Corn Salsa. Garnish as desired. *Makes 6 servings*

WARM CORN SALSA
Nonstick cooking spray
2 tablespoons chopped onion
2 tablespoons finely chopped green bell pepper
1 package (9 ounces) frozen corn, thawed
1 cup chunky salsa
2 teaspoons chopped cilantro

1. Spray small nonstick skillet with cooking spray; heat over medium heat until hot. Add onion and bell pepper. Cook and stir 3 minutes or until crisp-tender. Add corn, salsa and cilantro. Reduce heat to medium-low. Cook 5 minutes or until heated through. *Makes 3 cups*

296 VEGETARIAN STIR–FRY

2 tablespoons vegetable oil
5 ounces sliced carrots
3 ounces sliced onion
3 ounces baby corn
5 tablespoons LEE KUM KEE® Vegetarian Stir-Fry Sauce, divided
6 ounces snow peas
3 ounces sliced mushrooms
2 tablespoons pine nuts

Heat skillet over medium heat. Add oil. Sauté carrots, onion and baby corn in 2 tablespoons Vegetarian Stir-Fry Sauce until tender. Add snow peas, mushrooms and remaining 3 tablespoons sauce. Stir-fry until heated through. Sprinkle with pine nuts and serve. *Makes 4 servings*

Potato-Zucchini Pancakes with Warm Corn Salsa

297 BRAISED EGGPLANT IN GARLIC SAUCE

1 medium eggplant (1¼ pounds)
1 teaspoon salt
2 tablespoons light soy sauce
1 tablespoon sesame oil
1 tablespoon rice wine or dry sherry
1 tablespoon rice vinegar or distilled
   white vinegar
2 teaspoons cornstarch
2 teaspoons sugar
2 tablespoons vegetable oil
2 cloves garlic, minced
¼ cup chicken broth
1 small red bell pepper, cut into ½-inch-
   wide strips
1 green onion with tops, cut into 1-inch
   lengths
   Lemon balm for garnish

1. To prepare eggplant, trim off cap and stem end; cut lengthwise in half, then into 1-inch-thick spears. To roll-cut eggplant, hold one end of an eggplant spear firmly and cut 1¼-inch-long diagonal slice at other end. Roll spear away from you to next side and cut another diagonal slice. Continue rolling and cutting until spear is completely cut. Repeat with remaining spears.

2. Place eggplant in large colander over bowl; sprinkle with salt. Let stand 30 minutes to extract moisture.

3. Combine soy sauce, sesame oil, rice wine, vinegar, cornstarch and sugar in cup; mix well. Set aside.

4. Rinse eggplant with cold water; pat dry with paper towels. Heat wok over high heat about 1 minute or until hot. Drizzle vegetable oil into wok and heat 15 seconds. Add eggplant and stir-fry about 5 minutes or until lightly browned. Add garlic and stir-fry 15 seconds.

5. Add chicken broth to wok; cover and reduce heat to medium. Cook eggplant 3 minutes.

6. Uncover wok. Increase heat to medium-high. Add bell pepper and onion; stir-fry 2 minutes. Stir reserved cornstarch mixture; add to wok. Cook and stir until liquid boils and thickens. Transfer to warm serving dish. Garnish, if desired. Serve immediately.

Makes 6 servings

298 GLAZED STIR–FRY HOLIDAY VEGETABLES

3 tablespoons fresh lemon juice
2 tablespoons sugar
1 tablespoon low-sodium soy sauce
2 teaspoons cornstarch
½ teaspoon grated lemon peel
4 teaspoons vegetable oil
3 cups fresh broccoli florets
1 medium red bell pepper, cut into 1-inch
   pieces
1 cup julienne-cut peeled jicama
   Lemon peel, cut into slivers

In small bowl, combine lemon juice, sugar, soy sauce, cornstarch and grated lemon peel. Stir in ½ cup water; set aside. Heat oil in large nonstick skillet. Add broccoli and pepper; stir-fry over high heat 2 minutes. (Add additional oil, if necessary.) Add jicama; continue cooking 1 to 2 minutes or until vegetables are crisp-tender. Pour sugar mixture over vegetables; continue cooking just until glaze thickens. Toss vegetables to coat thoroughly with glaze. Garnish with lemon peel slivers. *Makes 6 servings*

*Favorite recipe from **The Sugar Association, Inc.***

Braised Eggplant in Garlic Sauce

GARDEN DELIGHTS

299 SESAME BROCCOLI

1½ pounds fresh broccoli, trimmed
    Boiling water
¼ cup KIKKOMAN® Stir-Fry Sauce
¾ teaspoon Oriental sesame oil
2 tablespoons vegetable oil
1 tablespoon slivered fresh ginger root
2 teaspoons sesame seed, toasted

Remove flowerets from broccoli; cut into bite-size pieces. Peel stalks; cut crosswise into ¼-inch slices. Place in medium bowl; pour in enough boiling water to cover and let stand 2 minutes. Drain; cool on several layers of paper towels. Combine stir-fry sauce and sesame oil; set aside. Heat vegetable oil in hot wok or large skillet over medium-high heat. Add broccoli and ginger; stir-fry 3 minutes. Add stir-fry sauce mixture; cook and stir until broccoli is coated with sauce. Transfer to serving platter and sprinkle sesame seed evenly over broccoli.

Makes 6 servings

300 GRAPE AND NAPA CABBAGE STIR–FRY

1 cup sliced onion
1 tablespoon olive oil
4 cups napa cabbage cut into ½-inch slices
2 cups halved California seedless grapes
4 dried shiitake mushrooms, rehydrated and cut into ½-inch slices
2 tablespoons chopped fresh basil *or* 2 teaspoons dried basil leaves
    Salt and black pepper to taste
¼ cup water
1 teaspoon cornstarch

Sauté onion in oil in wok or large skillet until tender. Add cabbage, grapes, mushrooms, basil, salt and pepper; stir-fry until cabbage is crisp-tender. Combine water and cornstarch in small bowl; mix well and add to grape mixture. Stir-fry about 1 minute or until sauce thickens.   *Makes 4 servings*

*Favorite recipe from **California Table Grape Commission***

Top to bottom: Golden Coins (page 270)
and Sesame Broccoli

GARDEN DELIGHTS

301 VEGETABLE SAUTÉ

2 tablespoons FILIPPO BERIO® Olive Oil
2 yellow squash, trimmed and cut into
  1-inch chunks
1 medium onion, sliced
4 baby eggplants, trimmed and cut into
  halves lengthwise
1 medium yellow bell pepper, cut into
  ¼-inch strips
8 baby carrots, peeled and trimmed
8 cherry tomatoes, cut into halves
1 tablespoon chopped garlic
1 tablespoon chopped fresh thyme*
½ cup coarsely chopped fresh basil*
  Salt and freshly ground black pepper
  Fresh thyme sprig (optional)

*Omit herbs if fresh are unavailable. Do not
substitute dried herb leaves.*

In large heavy skillet, heat olive oil over
medium-high heat until hot. Add squash,
onion, eggplants, bell pepper and carrots.
Cook, stirring constantly, 5 minutes. Add
tomatoes, garlic and chopped thyme. Cook,
stirring constantly, 3 minutes or until
vegetables are crisp-tender. Stir in basil.
Season to taste with salt and black pepper.
Garnish with thyme sprig, if desired.

Makes 6 servings

302 BUDDHA'S DELIGHTFUL VEGETABLES

1½ cups chicken broth
3 tablespoons low-sodium soy sauce
2 tablespoons plus 1 teaspoon sesame oil,
  divided
1½ tablespoons rice wine or sake
1 tablespoon sugar
1 tablespoon cornstarch
3 dried red chili peppers
½ cup sliced green onions
1 tablespoon minced garlic
2 carrots, thinly sliced into coins
2 cups small broccoli florets
1 red bell pepper, cut into thin strips
2 cups shredded napa cabbage
1 cup baby corn
1 (8-ounce) can sliced water chestnuts
  Hot cooked rice

Combine chicken broth, soy sauce, 1
teaspoon oil, rice wine, sugar and cornstarch
in small bowl; blend well and set aside.

Heat wok. Add remaining 2 tablespoons oil;
heat until very hot. Add chilies; stir-fry until
darkened. Add onions and garlic; stir-fry 1
minute. Add carrots; stir-fry 4 minutes. Add
broccoli and bell pepper; stir-fry 1 minute.
Add cabbage; stir-fry 1 minute. Add baby
corn and water chestnuts; stir-fry 30
seconds. Add reserved chicken broth
mixture to wok and mix well. Cover wok;
cook until vegetables are crisp-tender. Serve
over rice.   *Makes 8 servings*

*Favorite recipe from **The Sugar Association, Inc.***

Vegetable Sauté

GARDEN DELIGHTS

303 PORTOBELLO STIR–FRY WITH BLUE CHEESE

8 ounces uncooked fusilli pasta or any corkscrew-style pasta
1 pound stemmed portobello mushrooms, cleaned and cut into ½-inch slices
½ cup extra-virgin olive oil
3 tablespoons fresh lemon juice
2 cloves garlic, minced
¾ teaspoon salt
½ teaspoon dry mustard
¼ teaspoon black pepper
¼ cup crumbled blue cheese

1. Cook pasta according to package directions.

2. Meanwhile, place mushrooms in 13×9-inch glass baking dish in single layer.

3. In small bowl, whisk together oil, lemon juice, garlic, salt, mustard and pepper. Pour over mushrooms; marinate 10 minutes.

4. Heat large nonstick skillet over medium-high heat. Add half of the mushrooms in single layer. Cook 4 minutes; turn mushrooms and cook 4 minutes or until mushrooms begin to brown.

5. Place pasta on serving platter. Top with mushrooms; cover with foil and keep warm. Repeat cooking procedure with remaining mushrooms.

6. Place mushrooms on pasta; top with blue cheese and serve immediately.

Makes 4 servings

NOTE: It's important not to marinate the mushrooms for more than 15 minutes because the meaty texture of the mushrooms will begin to break down.

304 VEGETABLE OAT PILAF

½ cup chopped mushrooms
½ cup chopped green bell pepper
½ cup sliced green onions
1 tablespoon vegetable oil
1¾ cups uncooked QUAKER® Oats (quick or old fashioned)
2 egg whites *or* ¼ cup egg substitute
¾ cup low-sodium chicken broth
1 medium tomato, seeded and chopped

In large saucepan, cook and stir mushrooms, pepper and onions in oil over medium heat 2 to 3 minutes. In small bowl, mix oats and egg whites until oats are evenly coated. Add oats to vegetable mixture in saucepan; cook and stir over medium heat until oats are dry and separated, about 5 to 6 minutes. Add chicken broth; continue cooking and stirring 2 to 3 minutes or until liquid is absorbed. Stir in tomato. Serve immediately.

Makes 8 servings

Portobello Stir-Fry with Blue Cheese

GARDEN DELIGHTS

305 CARROT–ARTICHOKE SAUTÉ

1 tablespoon butter
2 small carrots, diagonally cut into thin
   slices
1 clove garlic, minced
½ teaspoon dried basil leaves, dill weed or
   tarragon leaves
1 small red bell pepper, cut into thin strips
1 medium yellow squash, cut into
   matchsticks
4 jarred artichoke hearts, drained, rinsed
   and cut into quarters
1½ teaspoons lemon juice
   Salt and black pepper to taste

1. Melt butter in large skillet over medium heat. Add carrots, garlic and basil; cook and stir 2 minutes. Add bell pepper; cook and stir 2 minutes. Add yellow squash and artichokes; cook and stir 3 minutes.

2. Add lemon juice; cook and stir 1 minute. Add salt and black pepper to taste.

Makes 2 servings

Prep and Cook Time: 20 minutes

306 VEGETARIAN TOFU STIR–FRY

1 block tofu
2 tablespoons vegetable oil
1 teaspoon minced fresh ginger root
1 medium onion, chunked
⅛ teaspoon salt
6 ounces fresh snow peas, trimmed and
   cut diagonally in half
⅓ cup KIKKOMAN® Stir-Fry Sauce
2 medium-size fresh tomatoes, chunked
¼ cup slivered blanched almonds, toasted

Cut tofu into ½-inch cubes; drain well on several layers of paper towels. Heat oil in hot wok or large skillet over high heat. Add ginger; stir-fry 30 seconds, or until fragrant. Add onion and salt; stir-fry 2 minutes. Add snow peas; stir-fry 1 minute. Add stir-fry sauce, tomatoes and tofu. Gently stir to coat tofu and vegetables with sauce. Reduce heat and cook only until tomatoes and tofu are heated through. Sprinkle with almonds; serve immediately. *Makes 4 servings*

Carrot-Artichoke Sauté

307 SPINACH AND MUSHROOM STIR–FRY

2 tablespoons peanut oil
2 cloves garlic, minced
1 teaspoon finely chopped fresh ginger
¼ to ½ teaspoon red pepper flakes
1 red bell pepper, cut into 1-inch triangles
2 ounces fresh shiitake or button mushrooms,* sliced
10 ounces fresh spinach, washed, stemmed and coarsely chopped
1 teaspoon fish sauce

Or substitute ½ ounce dried Oriental mushrooms, soaked according to package directions.

Heat wok over high heat 1 minute or until hot. Drizzle oil into wok; heat 30 seconds. Add garlic, ginger and red pepper flakes; stir-fry 30 seconds. Add bell pepper and mushrooms; stir-fry 2 minutes. Add spinach and fish sauce; stir-fry 1 to 2 minutes or until spinach is wilted.   *Makes 4 servings*

308 STUFFED HAIRY GOURD VEGETARIAN STYLE

15 ounces hairy gourd
2 tablespoons vegetable oil
2 ounces diced carrot
5 Chinese dry mushrooms, rehydrated and diced
2 ounces diced baby corn
2 ounces diced celery
2 ounces diced dried bean curd
1 ounce dried black fungus, soaked
4 tablespoons LEE KUM KEE® Vegetarian Oyster Flavored Sauce
½ teaspoon sugar
1 teaspoon cornstarch mixed with 1 tablespoon water

1. Peel hairy gourd and cut into halves; scrape away pith. Cook in boiling water 3 minutes. Rinse and drain.

2. Heat oil in wok. Add carrot, mushrooms, baby corn, celery, bean curd and black fungus; stir-fry until fragrant. Combine 1 cup water, Vegetarian Oyster Flavored Sauce and sugar in small bowl; add to wok with hairy gourd. Stir until mixture comes to a boil. Lower heat and simmer 5 minutes or until hairy gourd softens.

3. Remove hairy gourd and arrange on plate. Add cornstarch mixture to wok; cook until thickened. Divide mixture over hairy gourd halves and serve.   *Makes 4 to 6 servings*

NOTE: You may substitute cucumbers for hairy gourd.

Spinach and Mushroom Stir-Fry

GARDEN DELIGHTS

309 STIR-FRIED EGGPLANT AND TOFU

1 green onion
4 ounces lean ground pork
2 cloves garlic, minced
1 teaspoon finely chopped fresh ginger
½ teaspoon sesame oil
4 ounces firm tofu
½ cup chicken broth
½ teaspoon cornstarch
1 pound Asian eggplant
2 tablespoons peanut oil
1 tablespoon soy sauce
1 teaspoon Chinese chili sauce
½ teaspoon sugar
   Kale for garnish

1. Reserve green part of green onion. Cut white part lengthwise into halves. Cut halves lengthwise into thin slivers. Cut slivers crosswise until onion is in uniform fine pieces.

2. Cut green part of onion diagonally into 1½-inch lengths; set aside for garnish.

3. Combine pork, chopped green onion, garlic, ginger and sesame oil in small bowl.

4. Drain tofu on paper towels. Cut into ½-inch cubes.

5. Combine chicken broth and cornstarch in small bowl; set aside.

6. To prepare eggplant, trim off cap and stem end; cut lengthwise into halves, then into 1-inch-thick spears. To roll-cut eggplant, hold one end of an eggplant spear firmly and cut 1¼-inch-long diagonal slice at other end. Roll spear away from you to next side and cut another diagonal slice. Continue rolling and cutting until spear is completely cut. Repeat with remaining spears.

7. Heat peanut oil in wok or large skillet over high heat. Add eggplant; stir-fry 5 to 6 minutes or until tender. Add tofu; stir-fry 1 minute. Remove eggplant and tofu from wok; set aside.

8. Add pork mixture to wok; stir fry about 2 minutes or until browned. Add soy sauce, chili sauce and sugar; cook and stir until heated through.

9. Return eggplant and tofu to wok. Stir cornstarch mixture; add to wok. Cook and stir until sauce is clear and thickened. Garnish, if desired.   *Makes 4 servings*

310 GOLDEN COINS (SESAME STIR-FRIED CARROTS)

⅓ cup KIKKOMAN® Stir-Fry Sauce
2 tablespoons water
2 tablespoons vegetable oil
1½ pounds carrots, peeled and cut crosswise into ⅛-inch slices
1 tablespoon minced fresh ginger root
1 tablespoon sesame seed, toasted
1½ teaspoons Oriental sesame oil

Blend stir-fry sauce and water; set aside. Heat vegetable oil in hot wok or large skillet over high heat. Add carrots and ginger; reduce heat to medium-high and stir-fry 5 minutes. Add stir-fry sauce mixture. Cook, stirring, until carrots are coated with sauce. Remove from heat; stir in sesame seed and sesame oil. Serve immediately.

Makes 6 servings

Stir-Fried Eggplant and Tofu

GARDEN DELIGHTS

311 RISOTTO–STYLE PRIMAVERA

1 tablespoon FILIPPO BERIO® Olive Oil
1 small zucchini, sliced
1 medium onion, sliced
½ red bell pepper, cut into thin strips
3 mushrooms, sliced
½ cup uncooked long-grain rice
¼ cup dry white wine
1 cup chicken broth
1¾ cups water, divided
2 tablespoons grated Parmesan cheese
    Salt and freshly ground black pepper

In large saucepan or skillet, heat olive oil over medium heat until hot. Add zucchini, onion, bell pepper and mushrooms. Cook and stir 5 to 7 minutes or until zucchini is crisp-tender. Remove vegetables; set aside. Add rice and wine; stir until wine is absorbed. Add chicken broth. Cook, uncovered, stirring frequently, until absorbed. Add 1 cup water. Cook, uncovered, stirring frequently, until absorbed. Add remaining ¾ cup water. Cook, uncovered, stirring frequently, until absorbed. (Total cooking time will be about 25 minutes or until rice is tender and mixture is creamy.) Stir in vegetables and Parmesan cheese. Season to taste with salt and black pepper.   *Makes 4 servings*

312 CHEESY VEGETARIAN STIR–FRY

2 teaspoons olive oil
1 cup thinly sliced onion
3 cloves garlic, minced
4 cups small zucchini cut lengthwise into
    quarters then into 1½-inch pieces
1 to 2 teaspoons dried Italian herbs
1 (9-ounce) package frozen artichoke
    hearts, thawed, cooked and drained
    (optional)
½ cup marinara sauce
½ cup shredded JARLSBERG LITE™ Cheese

Heat oil in wok over high heat; stir-fry onion and garlic 3 minutes or until lightly browned. Add zucchini and herbs; stir-fry 3 minutes or until crisp-tender. Remove from heat and stir in artichoke hearts, marinara sauce and Jarlsberg Lite™.   *Makes 4 to 6 servings*

TIP: Serve with cannellini beans or over pasta such as orrechiette or linguine.

Risotto-Style Primavera

GARDEN DELIGHTS

313 BROCCOLI–TOFU STIR–FRY

2 cups uncooked rice
1 can (about 14 ounces) vegetable broth, divided
3 tablespoons cornstarch
1 tablespoon reduced-sodium soy sauce
½ teaspoon sugar
¼ teaspoon sesame oil
1 package (16 ounces) extra-firm tofu
1 teaspoon peanut oil
1 tablespoon minced fresh ginger
3 cloves garlic, minced
3 cups broccoli florets
2 cups sliced mushrooms
1 large red bell pepper, cut into strips
½ cup chopped green onions
    Prepared Szechuan sauce (optional)

1. Cook rice according to package directions. Combine ¼ cup vegetable broth, cornstarch, soy sauce, sugar and sesame oil in small bowl until well blended. Drain tofu; cut into 1-inch cubes.

2. Heat peanut oil in large nonstick wok or skillet over medium heat until hot. Add ginger and garlic. Cook and stir 5 minutes. Add remaining vegetable broth, broccoli, mushrooms, bell pepper and green onions. Cook and stir over medium-high heat 5 minutes or until vegetables are crisp-tender. Add tofu; cook 2 minutes, stirring occasionally. Stir cornstarch mixture; add to vegetable mixture. Cook and stir until sauce thickens. Serve over rice with Szechuan sauce, if desired. Garnish as desired.

Makes 6 servings

314 COUNTRY SKILLET HASH

2 tablespoons butter or margarine
4 pork chops (¾ inch thick), diced
¼ teaspoon black pepper
¼ teaspoon cayenne pepper (optional)
1 medium onion, chopped
2 cloves garlic, minced
1 can (14½ ounces) DEL MONTE®
    FreshCut™ Whole New Potatoes, drained and diced
1 can (14½ ounces) DEL MONTE®
    FreshCut™ Diced Tomatoes with Green Pepper & Onion, undrained
1 medium green bell pepper, chopped
½ teaspoon dried thyme leaves

1. In large skillet, melt butter over medium heat. Add pork; cook, stirring occasionally, until no longer pink in center. Season with black pepper and cayenne pepper, if desired.

2. Add onion and garlic; cook until tender. Stir in potatoes, tomatoes, bell pepper and thyme. Cook 5 minutes, stirring frequently. Season with salt, if desired.

Makes 4 servings

Prep Time: 10 minutes
Cook Time: 15 minutes

TIP: The hash may be topped with a poached or fried egg.

Broccoli-Tofu Stir-Fry

GARDEN DELIGHTS

315 SPICY SOUTHWESTERN VEGETABLE SAUTÉ

1 bag (16 ounces) frozen green beans
2 tablespoons water
1 tablespoon olive oil
1 red bell pepper, chopped
1 medium yellow summer squash or zucchini, chopped
1 jalapeño pepper, seeded and chopped*
½ teaspoon garlic powder
½ teaspoon ground cumin
½ teaspoon chili powder
¼ cup sliced green onions
2 tablespoons chopped fresh cilantro (optional)
1 tablespoon brown sugar

Jalapeño peppers can sting and irritate the skin; wear rubber gloves when handling peppers and do not touch eyes.

1. Heat large skillet over medium heat; add green beans, water and oil. Cover; cook 4 minutes, stirring occasionally.

2. Add bell pepper, squash, jalapeño pepper, garlic powder, cumin and chili powder. Cook, uncovered, stirring occasionally, 4 minutes or until vegetables are crisp-tender. Stir in green onions, cilantro, if desired, and brown sugar.   *Makes 6 servings*

316 WARM FRESH FRUIT SAUTÉ

¼ cup unsalted butter
3 tablespoons orange-flavored liqueur *or* freshly squeezed orange juice
3 tablespoons water
1½ tablespoons sugar
¾ cup Chilean seedless red or green grapes, cut into halves
2 Chilean peaches or nectarines (about ½ pound), thinly sliced
½ cup Chilean raspberries or sliced strawberries
Mint leaves (optional)
Lemon Crème Fraîche (recipe follows) or vanilla ice cream

Melt butter in large skillet over medium-high heat. Stir in liqueur, water and sugar. Bring mixture to a simmer. Add grapes and peaches; reduce heat to medium. Cook, basting with sauce until fruits are just warmed through, about 2 to 3 minutes, being careful not to overcook. Add berries during last 30 seconds of cooking. (If using frozen berries, add them partially frozen.) Serve warm fruit in shallow bowls or on small plates; garnish with mint, if desired. Spoon on Lemon Crème Fraîche or serve with small scoop of vanilla ice cream.
Makes 4 servings

LEMON CRÈME FRAÎCHE: In small bowl, stir together 1 cup whipping cream (not ultra-pasteurized), 1 tablespoon fresh lemon juice and finely grated peel of 1 lemon. Let mixture stand at room temperature until slightly thickened, 4 to 8 hours. Refrigerate until serving. Mixture will thicken more when chilled. Sweeten to taste with sugar or mild honey.

Favorite recipe from **Chilean Fresh Fruit Association**

Spicy Southwestern Vegetable Sauté

GARDEN DELIGHTS

317 MOO SHU VEGETABLES

7 dried Chinese black mushrooms
2 tablespoons vegetable oil
2 cloves garlic, minced
2 cups shredded napa cabbage, or green cabbage, or preshredded cabbage or coleslaw mix
1 red bell pepper, cut into short, thin strips
1 cup fresh or rinsed drained canned bean sprouts
2 large green onions, cut into short, thin strips
1 tablespoon teriyaki sauce
1/3 cup plum sauce
8 (6- or 7-inch) flour tortillas, warmed

1. Place mushrooms in small bowl; cover with warm water. Soak 20 minutes to soften. Drain; squeeze out excess water. Discard stems; slice caps.

2. Heat oil in wok or large nonstick skillet over medium heat. Add garlic; stir-fry 30 seconds.

3. Add cabbage, mushrooms and pepper; stir-fry 3 minutes. Add bean sprouts and onions; stir-fry 2 minutes. Add teriyaki sauce; stir-fry 30 seconds or until hot.

4. Spread about 2 teaspoons plum sauce on each tortilla. Spoon heaping 1/4 cupful of vegetable mixture over sauce. Fold bottom of tortilla up over filling, then fold sides over filling. *Makes 8 side-dish servings*

318 STIR-FRY VEGETABLES

1 tablespoon peanut oil
3/4 cup *each* (or combination of any):
　　snow peas
　　broccoli, cut into 1-inch pieces
　　carrots, cut into 1-inch strips
　　green onions, cut into 1-inch pieces
　　celery, cut into 1-inch pieces
　　mushrooms, sliced (drained if canned)
　　bamboo shoots, sliced (drained if canned)
　　water chestnuts, sliced (drained if canned)
1/4 cup dry-roasted Texas peanuts
1/4 cup molasses
1/4 cup soy sauce
1 1/2 tablespoons cornstarch
1 large clove garlic, minced
1/8 teaspoon ground ginger
　　Dash ground red pepper
1/4 cup sherry
2 cups uncooked rice, cooked and kept hot

Heat oil in medium skillet or wok. Add vegetables. Cook until onions begin to turn translucent, about 3 to 5 minutes. Add peanuts, molasses, soy sauce, cornstarch, garlic, ginger and pepper; cook, stirring, until thickened. Cover; cook over low heat 5 to 10 minutes, stirring occasionally. Add sherry; heat through. Serve over rice.
Makes 8 servings

Favorite recipe from **Texas Peanut Producers Board**

Moo Shu Vegetables

Noodles & Rice

319 BEEF "CHOW FUN" STIR–FRY

½ pound boneless tender beef steak
(sirloin, rib eye or top loin)
7 tablespoons KIKKOMAN® Stir-Fry Sauce,
divided
6 ounces uncooked extra wide egg
noodles
6 tablespoons beef broth
¼ teaspoon white pepper
2 tablespoons vegetable oil, divided
1 clove garlic, minced
1 teaspoon minced fresh ginger root
1 onion, chunked
1 pound romaine lettuce, washed and cut
crosswise into 1-inch strips

Cut beef across grain into thin slices 1-inch wide; coat with 1 tablespoon stir-fry sauce. Let stand 30 minutes. Meanwhile, cook noodles according to package directions in lightly salted water; drain. Combine remaining 6 tablespoons stir-fry sauce, broth and pepper in small bowl; set aside. Heat 1 tablespoon oil in hot wok or large skillet. Add beef and stir-fry 1 minute; remove. Heat remaining 1 tablespoon oil in same pan. Add garlic and ginger; stir-fry 10 seconds, or until fragrant. Add onion; stir-fry 2 minutes. Add romaine; stir-fry 2 minutes longer. Reduce heat to medium. Add noodles and stir-fry sauce mixture; cook and stir until noodles are thoroughly heated, about 2 minutes. Stir in beef; heat through. Serve immediately.

Makes 4 servings

Beef "Chow Fun" Stir-Fry

320 GLASS NOODLES WITH PEANUT SAUCE

4 tablespoons soy sauce, divided
2 teaspoons dry sherry
1 pound boneless chicken, skinned and cut into matchstick pieces
¼ cup creamy peanut butter
2 tablespoons rice vinegar
1 tablespoon low-fat chicken broth or water
2 teaspoons sugar
1½ teaspoons sesame oil
10 ounces dried rice stick noodles
1 tablespoon vegetable oil
2 teaspoons minced fresh ginger
1 teaspoon minced garlic
½ medium red onion, thinly sliced
½ cucumber, peeled, seeded and cut into matchstick pieces
1 medium carrot, shredded
¼ cup unsalted dry-roasted Texas peanuts, coarsely chopped

Combine 1 tablespoon soy sauce and sherry in small bowl. Add chicken; stir to coat. Set aside 30 minutes.

For peanut sauce, combine peanut butter, remaining 3 tablespoons soy sauce, vinegar, chicken broth, sugar and sesame oil in another small bowl; set aside.

Bring 4 cups water to a boil in medium saucepan. Add noodles, stirring to separate strands. Cook, stirring, 30 seconds or until noodles are slightly soft. Drain in colander and rinse under cold running water. Drain well; cut noodles into halves and set aside.

Heat wok or wide skillet over high heat. Add vegetable oil, swirling to coat sides. Add ginger and garlic; cook, stirring, until fragrant, about 5 seconds. Add chicken; stir-fry 1 minute or until opaque. Add onion; stir-fry 1 minute. Add cucumber, carrot and peanut sauce; cook, stirring, until slightly thickened. Remove from heat. Add noodles and toss until evenly coated. Sprinkle with peanuts.   *Makes 4 servings*

NOTE: This dish may be prepared in advance and displayed.

Favorite recipe from **Texas Peanut Producers Board**

321 VEGETABLE FRIED RICE

1 teaspoon vegetable oil
1½ cups small broccoli florets
½ cup chopped red bell pepper
2 cups chilled cooked white rice
1 tablespoon low-sodium soy sauce
½ cup shredded carrot

1. Heat oil in large nonstick skillet over medium heat. Add broccoli and pepper; stir-fry 3 minutes or until crisp-tender.

2. Add rice and soy sauce; stir-fry 2 minutes. Add carrot; heat through. Serve rice mixture on kale-lined plates.
Makes 4 side-dish servings

Vegetable Fried Rice

322 PASTA WITH PIECES OF JADE

1 cup frozen peas, thawed
1 cup heavy cream
½ cup grated Parmesan cheese
½ teaspoon salt
½ teaspoon dried thyme leaves
½ teaspoon black pepper
2 dashes hot pepper sauce
8 ounces uncooked linguine
1 tablespoon vegetable oil
6 ounces green beans, stemmed and cut into halves
6 ounces broccoli florets, cut into bite-size pieces
4 ounces snow peas, stemmed and cut into halves
½ red bell pepper, roasted, peeled and cut into thin strips
1 clove garlic, minced
Additional grated Parmesan cheese

1. Purée peas in blender or food processor. Add cream, ½ cup cheese, salt, thyme, black pepper and pepper sauce; blend until smooth. Set aside.

2. Place 6 cups water in wok or large saucepan; bring to a boil over high heat. Add linguine; cook 8 minutes or until *al dente*, stirring occasionally. Drain, set aside.

3. Heat oil in wok over high heat. Add green beans and broccoli; stir-fry 5 to 6 minutes or until crisp-tender. Add snow peas, roasted bell pepper and garlic; stir-fry 1 to 2 minutes or until all vegetables are crisp-tender.

4. Pour pea mixture over vegetables, stirring until hot. Add linguine to wok; toss to combine. Sprinkle with additional cheese.

Makes 4 servings

323 THAI PEANUT NOODLE STIR-FRY

1 cup chicken broth or low-sodium chicken broth
½ cup GREY POUPON® Dijon Mustard
⅓ cup creamy peanut butter
3 tablespoons firmly packed light brown sugar
2 tablespoons soy sauce
1 tablespoon cornstarch
1 clove garlic, crushed
½ teaspoon minced fresh ginger
4 cups cut-up vegetables (red bell pepper, carrot, mushrooms, green onions, snow peas)
1 tablespoon vegetable oil
1 pound linguine, cooked
Chopped peanuts and scallion brushes for garnish

In medium saucepan, combine chicken broth, mustard, peanut butter, sugar, soy sauce, cornstarch, garlic and ginger. Cook over medium heat until mixture thickens and begins to boil; reduce heat and keep warm.

In large skillet, over medium-high heat, sauté vegetables in oil until tender, about 5 minutes. In large serving bowl, combine hot cooked pasta, vegetables and peanut sauce, tossing until well coated. Garnish with chopped peanuts and scallion brushes. Serve immediately. *Makes 4 to 6 servings*

Pasta with Pieces of Jade

NOODLES & RICE

324 FRIED RICE WITH HAM

2 tablespoons vegetable oil, divided
2 eggs, beaten
1 small onion, chopped
1 carrot, peeled and chopped
⅔ cup diced ham
½ cup frozen green peas
1 large clove garlic, minced
3 cups cold cooked rice
3 tablespoons reduced-sodium soy sauce
⅛ teaspoon black pepper

1. Heat 1 tablespoon oil in wok or large skillet over medium-high heat until hot. Add eggs; rotate wok to swirl eggs into thin layer. Cook eggs until set and slightly brown; break up with wooden spoon. Remove from wok to small bowl.

2. Heat remaining 1 tablespoon oil until hot. Add onion and carrot; stir-fry 2 minutes. Add ham, peas and garlic; stir-fry 1 minute.

3. Add rice; cook and stir 2 to 3 minutes or until rice is heated through. Stir in soy sauce and pepper until well blended. Stir in cooked eggs. *Makes 4 servings*

Prep and Cook Time: 18 minutes

325 ASIAN GARDEN NOODLES

8 ounces uncooked vermicelli
4½ teaspoons cornstarch
¼ teaspoon white pepper
1 cup ⅓-less salt chicken broth
3 tablespoons KIKKOMAN® Lite Soy Sauce
¾ teaspoon distilled white vinegar
1 pound fresh broccoli, trimmed
2 tablespoons vegetable oil
1 teaspoon minced fresh ginger root
2 medium carrots, cut diagonally into thin slices
1 medium onion, thinly sliced
1 tablespoon water
¼ pound fresh mushrooms, cut into quarters

Cook vermicelli according to package directions, omitting salt; drain and keep warm. Meanwhile, combine cornstarch, white pepper, broth, lite soy sauce and vinegar in small bowl; set aside. Remove flowerets from broccoli; cut into bite-size pieces. Peel stalks; cut diagonally into thin slices. Heat oil in hot wok or large skillet over high heat. Add ginger; stir-fry 10 seconds. Add broccoli, carrots and onion; sprinkle with water. Stir-fry 5 minutes. Add mushrooms; stir-fry 30 seconds longer. Add lite soy sauce mixture; cook and stir until sauce boils and thickens. Serve vegetables and sauce over vermicelli.

Makes 2 to 3 servings

Fried Rice with Ham

326 FRUITED WILD RICE WITH TOASTED NUTS

2 boxes (6.2 ounces each) fast-cooking long grain and wild rice
2 tablespoons walnut or vegetable oil, divided
1 package (2½ ounces) walnut pieces *or* ⅔ cup almond slivers
1 package (2¼ ounces) pecan pieces
2 cups chopped onions
12 dried apricots, sliced (about ½ cup)
½ cup dried cherries or dried cranberries
2 teaspoons minced fresh ginger
¼ teaspoon red pepper flakes
¼ cup honey
3 tablespoons soy sauce
1 tablespoon grated orange peel

1. Cook rice according to package directions.

2. Meanwhile, add 1 tablespoon oil to large nonstick skillet or wok. Heat skillet over medium-high heat 1 minute. Add walnuts and pecans; cook, stirring frequently, 8 minutes or until pecans are browned. Remove from skillet and set aside.

3. Add remaining 1 tablespoon oil and onions to skillet; cook 10 minutes or until onions begin to brown. Add apricots, cherries, ginger, pepper and reserved nuts; cook 5 minutes.

4. Whisk together honey, soy sauce and orange peel in small bowl; add to onion mixture. Toss with rice.

Makes 4 servings

NOTE: This dish can be served as a chilled rice salad. Spoon hot cooked rice evenly on large baking sheet to cool quickly, about 8 to 10 minutes. Toss with cooled nuts, onion mixture and honey mixture.

327 LINGUINE AND WALNUT VEGETABLE MEDLEY

½ pound uncooked linguine*
3 tablespoons vegetable oil
1 green bell pepper, cut into strips
1 red bell pepper, cut into strips
1 yellow squash, cut into strips
1 cup sliced mushrooms
⅓ cup broken walnuts
2 green onions, sliced
1 clove garlic, minced
1 teaspoon salt
½ teaspoon dried tarragon leaves
½ cup shredded mozzarella cheese

Pasta substitutions include capellini, fusilli, fettuccine and spaghetti.

Cook linguine according to package directions; drain. In large skillet, heat oil. Add remaining ingredients, except cheese. Stir-fry just until vegetables are crisp-tender. Serve over hot linguine. Sprinkle with cheese. *Makes 4 to 6 servings*

*Favorite recipe from **Walnut Marketing Board***

Fruited Wild Rice with Toasted Nuts

NOODLES & RICE

328 EGG NOODLES AND VEGETABLES WITH PESTO

1 package (16 ounces) enriched fine egg noodles
5 tablespoons olive oil, divided
10 cloves garlic
3 cups fresh basil leaves, lightly packed
3 cups fresh spinach, lightly packed
½ cup bottled fat-free Italian salad dressing
4 cups broccoli florets
4 cups cauliflower florets
2 large onions, cut into strips
2 cups sliced mushrooms
½ teaspoon red pepper flakes
2 pints cherry tomatoes, cut into halves
½ cup shredded Asiago cheese

1. Cook noodles according to package directions, taking care not to overcook. Drain; place in large bowl. Toss with 1 tablespoon oil.

2. To make pesto, place garlic in food processor; process briefly until chopped. Add basil; process using on/off pulsing action until finely chopped. Transfer to medium bowl. Process spinach until finely chopped. Add 3 tablespoons oil and salad dressing; process briefly to blend. Add to basil mixture in bowl.

3. Heat remaining 1 tablespoon oil in large nonstick skillet or wok over medium heat until hot. Add broccoli, cauliflower and onions. Cover and cook 5 minutes, stirring occasionally. Add mushrooms and pepper; cook, uncovered, 5 minutes or until vegetables are crisp-tender. Add vegetable mixture, tomatoes and pesto to noodles; toss until well blended. Serve with cheese. Garnish with fresh basil, if desired.

Makes 8 servings

329 TURKEY AND ORZO IN CILANTRO MUSTARD

1 cup uncooked orzo pasta
1 tablespoon butter or margarine
1 tablespoon olive oil
1 small onion, minced
2 cloves garlic, minced
1 package (about 1¼ pounds) PERDUE® FIT 'N EASY® Fresh Skinless & Boneless Thin-Sliced Turkey or Chicken Breast Cutlets, cut into thin strips
4 tablespoons chopped fresh cilantro, divided
2 tablespoons Dijon mustard
½ cup freshly grated Parmesan cheese

Cook orzo in boiling water according to package directions, about 10 minutes or until *al dente;* drain. Meanwhile, in large skillet over medium-high heat, heat butter and oil until butter melts. Add onion and garlic; sauté 1 minute. Add turkey; sauté about 2 minutes or until almost cooked through. Add 2 tablespoons water; cook 1 minute. Stir in 2 tablespoons cilantro and mustard.

In serving bowl, toss orzo with turkey mixture and cheese. To serve, garnish with remaining 2 tablespoons cilantro.

Makes 4 to 6 servings

Prep Time: 5 minutes
Cook Time: 12 minutes

Egg Noodles and Vegetables with Pesto

NOODLES & RICE

330 ALMOND FRIED RICE

2 tablespoons vegetable oil
¾ cup thinly sliced green onions and tops
½ cup diced red bell pepper
1 egg, beaten
3 cups cold, cooked rice
2 ounces diced cooked ham (about ½ cup)
2 tablespoons KIKKOMAN® Soy Sauce
½ cup slivered blanched almonds, toasted

Heat oil in hot wok or large skillet over medium-high heat. Add green onions and bell pepper; stir-fry 1 minute. Add egg and scramble. Stir in rice and cook until heated through, gently separating grains. Add ham and soy sauce; cook and stir until mixture is well blended. Just before serving, stir in almonds.   *Makes 4 servings*

331 FAR EAST FRIED BARLEY

12 ounces bacon, cubed
½ cup diced celery
¼ cup diced onion
¼ cup diced green bell pepper
4 eggs
3 cups cooked barley
2 tablespoons soy sauce

Fry bacon in large skillet or wok until crisp. Remove bacon and reserve 3 tablespoons drippings in skillet. Stir-fry celery, onion and bell pepper in bacon drippings until opaque. Remove vegetables and scramble eggs until set. Cut into small pieces and add vegetables, reserved bacon, barley and soy sauce.   *Makes 6 servings*

TIP: May be prepared ahead and reheated.

Favorite recipe from **North Dakota Barley Council**

332 CURRY COCONUT FRIED RICE

1 cup chopped red onion
2 tablespoons vegetable oil
¾ pound medium shrimp, peeled and deveined
¼ cup chicken broth
1 tablespoon curry powder
4 cups cooked long-grain rice
2 cups frozen mixed carrots and peas, thawed
1 tablespoon soy sauce
3 medium, firm DOLE® Bananas, sliced
½ cup flaked coconut, toasted

• Cook and stir onion in hot oil in large skillet over medium-high heat until crisp-tender.

• Add shrimp, chicken broth and curry powder; cook and stir until shrimp turn pink. Add rice, carrots and peas; cook and stir 3 to 5 minutes or until heated through.

• Stir in soy sauce. Add bananas; cook and stir 1 minute or until heated through. Sprinkle with coconut before serving.
        Makes 6 servings

Prep Time: 25 minutes
Cook Time: 20 minutes

Almond Fried Rice

333 QUICK SKILLET RICE GRATIN

2 tablespoons olive oil
1 onion, chopped
2 cloves garlic, minced
2 medium carrots, peeled and chopped
1 teaspoon dried thyme leaves
2 cups uncooked instant white rice
1 can (15½ ounces) kidney beans, rinsed
    and drained
1 teaspoon salt
    Black pepper to taste
⅓ cup grated Parmesan cheese

1. Heat oil in large skillet over medium-high heat until hot. Add onion and garlic; cook and stir 2 minutes. Add carrots and thyme; cook and stir 4 minutes more.

2. Add rice, 2 cups water, beans and salt; season to taste with black pepper. Stir well. Bring to a boil. Reduce heat to low. Sprinkle with cheese. Cover and simmer 5 minutes or until cheese is melted and all liquid is evaporated. *Makes 4 to 6 servings*

Prep and Cook Time: 15 minutes

334 STIR–FRIED WILD RICE

2 tablespoons vegetable oil, divided
1 egg, beaten
2 teaspoons minced garlic
1 teaspoon minced fresh ginger
½ cup chopped yellow onion
½ cup diced celery
½ cup frozen peas and carrots, thawed
½ cup cooked small shrimp
¼ cup diced cooked ham
2 green onions, chopped
4 cups cooked wild rice
¼ cup chicken broth
2 tablespoons oyster sauce
2 tablespoons soy sauce
2 teaspoons sesame oil
    Dash white pepper (optional)

1. Heat small nonstick skillet over medium heat until hot. Add 2 teaspoons vegetable oil and egg; tip skillet and spread egg thinly over bottom of skillet. Cook egg until barely set; turn and cook about 30 seconds. Remove egg and let cool. Cut into thin shreds.

2. Heat wok over medium-high heat until hot. Add remaining 1 tablespoon plus 1 teaspoon vegetable oil, garlic and ginger; stir-fry 10 seconds. Add yellow onion, celery, peas and carrots, shrimp, ham and green onions; stir-fry 2 minutes.

3. Reduce heat to medium-low. Add wild rice, chicken broth, egg shreds, oyster sauce, soy sauce, sesame oil and white pepper, if desired; toss to mix well.
Makes 4 to 6 servings

TIP: When cooking wild rice, use 1 part rice to 2½ to 3 parts liquid. Average cooking time ranges from 40 to 50 minutes.

*Favorite recipe from **California Wild Rice***

Quick Skillet Rice Gratin

335 VEGETABLE CHOW MEIN

Chinese Noodle Cakes (recipe follows)
3 tablespoons KIKKOMAN® Soy Sauce
4 teaspoons cornstarch
2 tablespoons vegetable oil
2 medium carrots, cut into julienne strips
1 medium onion, thinly sliced
2 teaspoons minced fresh ginger root
1 clove garlic, minced
6 ounces fresh bean sprouts
1 large stalk celery, thinly sliced
¼ pound fresh mushrooms, sliced

Prepare Chinese Noodle Cakes. Combine ¾ cup water, soy sauce and cornstarch; set aside. Heat oil in hot wok or large skillet over high heat. Add carrots, onion, ginger and garlic; stir-fry 1 minute. Add bean sprouts, celery and mushrooms; stir-fry 2 minutes longer. Stir in soy sauce mixture; cook and stir until sauce boils and thickens. Serve over noodle cakes.

Makes 4 to 6 servings

CHINESE NOODLE CAKES

8 ounces uncooked capellini (angel hair pasta)
4 tablespoons vegetable oil, divided

Cook capellini according to package directions. Drain, rinse under cold water and drain thoroughly. Heat 1 tablespoon oil in large nonstick skillet over medium-high heat. Add half of the capellini; spread slightly to fill bottom of skillet to form noodle cake. Cook 5 minutes, without stirring, or until golden on bottom. Lift cake with wide spatula; add 1 tablespoon oil to skillet and turn cake over. Cook 5 minutes longer, or until golden brown, shaking skillet occasionally to brown evenly; remove to rack and keep warm. Repeat with remaining capellini and oil. *Makes 4 to 6 servings*

336 BUNNY PASTA WITH GINGER BEEF

8 ounces uncooked BUCKEYE® FunnyBunny Pasta
3 tablespoons vegetable oil
1 tablespoon minced fresh ginger
1 teaspoon minced garlic
½ pound ground or thinly sliced beef
1 tablespoon all-purpose flour
½ cup low-sodium chicken or beef broth
2 tablespoons mirin
2 tablespoons chopped green onions
1 teaspoon red miso
1 teaspoon cornstarch (optional)

In boiling salted water, cook pasta according to package directions until *al dente.* Drain and divide equally into serving-size bowls.

In heated wok or deep skillet, add oil, ginger and garlic; stir-fry over high heat 30 seconds. Add beef and flour; stir-fry until meat turns brown. Pour chicken broth over beef. Add mirin, onions and miso; bring to a boil. (Whisk in cornstarch to thicken, if necessary.) Spoon beef mixture over pasta. Serve hot. *Makes 3 to 4 servings*

Vegetable Chow Mein

NOODLES & RICE

337 VERMICELLI WITH MINCED PORK

4 ounces uncooked Chinese rice
 vermicelli or bean threads
32 dried mushrooms
 3 green onions with tops, divided
 2 tablespoons minced fresh ginger
 2 tablespoons hot bean sauce
1½ cups chicken broth
 1 tablespoon soy sauce
 1 tablespoon dry sherry
 2 tablespoons vegetable oil
 6 ounces lean ground pork
 1 small red or green hot chili pepper,*
 seeded and finely chopped

*Chili peppers can sting and irritate the skin; wear
rubber gloves when handling peppers and do not
touch eyes.*

1. Place vermicelli and dried mushrooms in
separate bowls; cover each with hot water.
Let stand 30 minutes; drain. Cut vermicelli
into 4-inch pieces. Squeeze out as much
excess water as possible from mushrooms.
Cut off and discard mushroom stems; cut
caps into thin slices.

2. Cut one onion into 1½-inch slivers;
reserve for garnish. Cut remaining two
onions into thin slices. Combine ginger and
hot bean sauce; set aside. Combine chicken
broth, soy sauce and sherry; set aside.

3. Heat oil in wok or large skillet over high
heat. Add pork; stir-fry until no longer pink
in center, about 2 minutes. Add chili pepper,
sliced onions and bean sauce mixture. Stir-
fry 1 minute.

4. Add chicken broth mixture, vermicelli and
mushrooms. Simmer, uncovered, until most
of the liquid is absorbed, about 5 minutes.
Top with onion slivers. Garnish, if desired.

Makes 4 servings

338 ORANGE ASPARAGUS STIR–FRY

 1 pound uncooked mostaccioli, ziti or
 other medium pasta shape
 2 teaspoons vegetable oil, divided
12 ounces frozen small shrimp, thawed
 3 medium carrots, thinly sliced diagonally
 1 pound asparagus, diagonally cut into
 2-inch lengths
 1 bunch green onions, sliced
 1 cup fresh orange juice
 Salt and black pepper to taste

Prepare pasta according to package
directions. While pasta is cooking, warm
1 teaspoon oil over high heat in large
nonstick wok or skillet. Stir-fry shrimp until
firm, opaque and lightly browned, about 3
minutes. Remove and set aside. Add
remaining 1 teaspoon oil to wok; stir-fry
carrots 2 minutes. Add asparagus and
onions; stir-fry 3 to 4 minutes or until
asparagus is crisp-tender.

When pasta is done, drain well. Add pasta
and orange juice to wok and toss until hot,
about 2 minutes. Season to taste with salt
and pepper; transfer to serving bowl. Serve
immediately.   *Makes 4 servings*

Favorite recipe from **National Pasta Association**

Vermicelli with Minced Pork

339 RICE PILAF WITH DRIED CHERRIES AND ALMONDS

½ **cup slivered almonds**
2 **tablespoons margarine**
2 **cups uncooked converted rice**
½ **cup chopped onion**
1 **can (about 14 ounces) vegetable broth**
1½ **cups water**
½ **cup dried cherries**

1. To toast almonds, cook and stir in large nonstick skillet over medium heat until lightly browned. Remove from skillet; cool.

2. Melt margarine in skillet over low heat. Add rice and onion; cook and stir until rice is lightly browned. Add vegetable broth and water. Bring to a boil over high heat; reduce heat to low. Simmer, covered, 15 minutes.

3. Stir in almonds and cherries. Simmer 5 minutes or until liquid is absorbed and rice is tender. Garnish as desired.

Makes 12 servings

340 SWEET & SOUR TORTELLINI

1 **package (7 to 12 ounces) uncooked cheese tortellini**
½ **pound boneless tender beef steak (sirloin, rib eye or top loin)**
2 **teaspoons cornstarch**
2 **teaspoons KIKKOMAN® Soy Sauce**
1 **small clove garlic, pressed**
½ **cup KIKKOMAN® Sweet & Sour Sauce**
⅓ **cup chicken broth**
2 **tablespoons dry sherry**
1 **tablespoon sugar**
2 **tablespoons vegetable oil, divided**
1 **medium onion, chunked**
1 **small red bell pepper, chunked**
1 **small green bell pepper, chunked**

Cook tortellini according to package directions, omitting salt. Drain. Cut beef into thin bite-size squares. Combine cornstarch, soy sauce and garlic in small bowl; stir in beef. Let stand 15 minutes. Meanwhile, combine sweet & sour sauce, chicken broth, sherry and sugar; set aside. Heat 1 tablespoon oil in hot wok or large skillet over high heat. Add beef and stir-fry 1 minute; remove. Heat remaining 1 tablespoon oil in same pan. Add onion and bell peppers; stir-fry 3 minutes. Add beef, sweet & sour sauce mixture and tortellini. Cook and stir until beef, vegetables and tortellini are coated with sauce and tortellini are heated through.

Makes 4 servings

Rice Pilaf with Dried Cherries and Almonds

341 GREEK SKILLET LINGUINE

½ pound uncooked linguine
½ (3-ounce) package dehydrated sun-dried tomatoes
1 cup boiling water
3 tablespoons extra-virgin olive oil, divided
½ cup chopped onion
4 cloves garlic, minced
1½ pounds raw large shrimp, peeled and deveined
1¼ teaspoons dried oregano leaves
½ teaspoon salt or to taste
2 cans artichoke hearts, well-drained and cut into quarters
14 kalamata or black olives, pitted and coarsely chopped
2 tablespoons balsamic vinegar
⅓ cup crumbled feta cheese

1. Cook pasta according to package directions.

2. Meanwhile, place tomatoes in small bowl. Add 1 cup boiling water; let stand 10 minutes. Drain well and chop.

3. Add 1 tablespoon oil to large skillet. Heat over medium-high heat 1 minute. Add onion and garlic; cook and stir 3 minutes.

4. Add shrimp, oregano and salt to skillet; cook 4 to 5 minutes or until shrimp are opaque, stirring frequently. Add artichoke hearts, olives and reserved tomatoes. Stir gently; cook 3 minutes.

5. Remove skillet from heat. Gently stir in vinegar and remaining 2 tablespoons oil. Cover and let stand 5 minutes to absorb flavors.

6. Place pasta on serving platter. Spoon shrimp mixture over pasta and sprinkle with cheese. *Makes 4 servings*

342 MEXICAN TURKEY RICE

½ cup chopped onion
⅓ cup uncooked long-grain rice
1 clove garlic, minced
1 tablespoon olive oil
1 can (16 ounces) low-salt stewed tomatoes, coarsely chopped
½ cup reduced-sodium chicken broth
1 teaspoon chili powder
½ teaspoon dried oregano leaves
⅛ teaspoon red pepper flakes
⅓ cup chopped green bell pepper
1 pound fully-cooked oven-roasted turkey breast, cut into ¼-inch cubes

1. In large nonstick skillet over medium-high heat, cook and stir onion, rice and garlic in oil 3 to 4 minutes or until rice is lightly browned. Stir in tomatoes, chicken broth, chili powder, oregano and red pepper flakes. Bring to a boil. Reduce heat to low; cover and simmer 15 minutes.

2. Stir in bell pepper and turkey. Cover; cook 3 to 4 minutes or until mixture is heated through. *Makes 6 servings*

*Favorite recipe from **National Turkey Federation***

Greek Skillet Linguine

NOODLES & RICE

343 COUSCOUS CHICKEN SALAD

¼ cup plus 1 tablespoon olive oil, divided
1 yellow or orange bell pepper, chopped
1 small zucchini, chopped
1 green onion, finely chopped
1 pound chicken tenders, cut into bite-size pieces
2 cans (about 14 ounces each) chicken broth
10 ounces couscous
1 can (15½ ounces) chick-peas, drained
1 large tomato, seeded and chopped
½ cup chopped cilantro
⅓ cup lemon juice
1 teaspoon ground cumin
¼ teaspoon garlic salt
3 dashes hot pepper sauce
Radicchio leaves (optional)

1. Heat 1 tablespoon oil in wok or large skillet over high heat. Add bell pepper, zucchini and onion; stir-fry 2 minutes or until crisp-tender. Remove from wok and set aside in large bowl.

2. Add chicken and chicken broth to wok. Bring broth to a boil over high heat; reduce heat to medium and simmer 4 to 5 minutes or until chicken is no longer pink. Remove chicken from broth with slotted spoon. Place in bowl with vegetables; cool.

3. Add couscous to broth. Remove wok from heat. Cover and let stand 5 minutes or until all liquid is absorbed. Cool.

4. Combine chicken mixture, couscous, chick-peas, tomato and cilantro in large bowl.

5. Whisk together lemon juice, remaining ¼ cup oil, cumin, garlic salt and pepper sauce in small bowl. Pour over couscous mixture. Serve warm or chill 1 hour before serving in radicchio leaves, if desired.

Makes 6 servings

344 PASTA PEANUT STIR–FRY

1 pound uncooked linguine, spaghetti or thin spaghetti
1 teaspoon vegetable oil
4 carrots, cut into julienne strips
1 large cucumber, peeled and cut into julienne strips
1 bunch green onions, diagonally sliced into ½-inch lengths
½ teaspoon red pepper flakes
⅓ cup lime juice
¼ cup low-sodium soy sauce
¼ cup defatted low-sodium chicken broth
3 tablespoons smooth peanut butter
Black pepper to taste

Prepare pasta according to package directions; drain and transfer to serving bowl. Heat oil in large nonstick wok or skillet over high heat. Add carrots and stir-fry 2 to 3 minutes or until tender. Add cucumber, onions and red pepper flakes to wok; stir-fry 2 minutes.

Add lime juice, soy sauce, chicken broth, peanut butter and black pepper to wok. Bring to a boil. Pour vegetable mixture over pasta. Toss well and serve immediately.

Makes 4 servings

*Favorite recipe from **National Pasta Association***

Couscous Chicken Salad

345 TWO CHEESE MEDITERRANEAN STIR–FRY

6 ounces uncooked penne pasta
2 tablespoons extra-virgin olive oil, divided
4 cloves garlic, minced
½ pound mushrooms, cut into quarters
2 cups diced eggplant
1½ cups matchstick-size zucchini strips
1 green bell pepper, cut into 1-inch pieces
1 cup chopped onion
1½ teaspoons dried basil leaves
¾ teaspoon salt or to taste
⅛ teaspoon black pepper
4 plum tomatoes, cut into quarters and seeded
2 to 3 tablespoons capers, well-drained (optional)
3 ounces Provolone cheese, shredded
¼ cup grated Parmesan cheese, divided

1. Cook pasta according to package directions.

2. Meanwhile, place 1 tablespoon oil in large nonstick skillet or wok. Heat over medium-high heat 1 minute. Add garlic; cook 1 minute. Add mushrooms, eggplant, zucchini, bell pepper, onion, basil, salt and black pepper. Cook 15 minutes or until eggplant is tender.

3. Gently stir in tomatoes and capers, if desired. Reduce heat, cover tightly and simmer 5 minutes.

4. Remove skillet from heat; toss with remaining 1 tablespoon oil, Provolone cheese and 2 tablespoons Parmesan cheese.

5. Place cooked pasta on serving platter. Spoon vegetable mixture over pasta and top with remaining 2 tablespoons Parmesan cheese. *Makes 4 servings*

346 BRAISED VEGETARIAN E–FU NOODLES

7 ounces uncooked E-Fu noodles
4 ounces sliced straw mushrooms
2 ounces sliced button mushrooms
5 Chinese mushrooms, soaked and shredded
2 ounces shredded carrot
1 tablespoon vegetable oil
½ cup water
5 tablespoons LEE KUM KEE® Vegetarian Oyster Flavored Sauce
2 ounces snow peas, shredded
1 teaspoon LEE KUM KEE® Sesame Oil

1. Blanch noodles in boiling water until soft; drain.

2. In wok, sauté mushrooms and carrot in vegetable oil until fragrant.

3. Add noodles, water, Vegetarian Oyster Flavored Sauce and snow peas to wok; stir-fry until liquid evaporates. Sprinkle with Sesame Oil. *Makes 4 to 6 servings*

Two Cheese Mediterranean Stir-Fry

347 CHINESE–STYLE FRIED BROWN RICE

2 cups uncooked long-grain brown rice
3 tablespoons vegetable oil, divided
2 eggs, lightly beaten
1 medium yellow onion, coarsely chopped
1 slice (8 ounces) smoked or baked ham, julienned
1 cup frozen green peas, thawed
1 to 2 tablespoons soy sauce
1 tablespoon sesame oil
Fresh cilantro leaves for garnish

1. Combine rice and 3½ cups water in wok. Cover and bring to a boil over high heat. Reduce heat to low and simmer rice about 40 to 45 minutes or until tender and all water is absorbed, stirring occasionally with fork. Remove from heat and let stand, covered, 10 minutes.

2. With fork, fluff rice and spread out on greased baking sheet. Cool to room temperature, about 30 to 40 minutes. Rinse out wok.

3. Heat wok over medium heat about 30 seconds or until hot. Drizzle 1 tablespoon vegetable oil into wok and heat 15 seconds. Add eggs and cook 1 minute or just until set on bottom. Turn eggs over and stir to scramble until cooked but not dry. Remove eggs to bowl; set aside.

4. Add remaining 2 tablespoons vegetable oil to wok and heat 30 seconds or until hot. Add onion; cook and stir about 3 minutes or until tender. Stir in ham and increase heat to medium-high; stir-fry 1 minute. Add cooked rice, peas, soy sauce to taste and sesame oil; cook 5 minutes, stirring frequently. Stir in eggs and cook until heated through. Transfer to warm serving dish. Garnish, if desired. Serve immediately. *Makes 6 servings*

348 BROCCOLI SHRIMP PASTA

8 ounces linguine
3 cups fresh broccoli
1 tablespoon butter
1 (8-ounce) package frozen medium shrimp, thawed*
¼ cup sherry cooking wine
3 tablespoons soy sauce
2 tablespoons sliced almonds
1 tablespoon sesame seeds

Or substitute 2 cups cubed cooked chicken for shrimp.

Cook linguine according to package directions; drain.

Bring 2 quarts water to a boil. Place broccoli in water and cook 2 minutes; drain. Melt butter in skillet or wok. Sauté shrimp 2 minutes over medium-high heat. Add broccoli, sherry and soy sauce. Cook 2 minutes. Add almonds and stir.

Place linguine on serving tray. Spoon broccoli-shrimp mixture, including liquid, over top of linguine. Sprinkle with sesame seeds. *Makes 4 servings*

Favorite recipe from **North Dakota Wheat Commission**

Chinese-Style Fried Brown Rice

NOODLES & RICE

349 EASY CHICKEN LO MEIN

1 whole chicken breast, skinned and boned
1 tablespoon KIKKOMAN® Stir-Fry Sauce
4 ounces uncooked capellini (angel hair pasta)
⅓ cup KIKKOMAN® Stir-Fry Sauce
3 tablespoons water
2 tablespoons vegetable oil, divided
¼ pound fresh snow peas, trimmed and cut into julienne strips
1 large carrot, cut into julienne strips
⅛ teaspoon salt
2 teaspoons sesame seed, toasted

Cut chicken into thin strips; coat with 1 tablespoon stir-fry sauce in small bowl. Let stand 30 minutes. Meanwhile, cook capellini according to package directions, omitting salt. Drain; rinse to cool and drain thoroughly. Combine ⅓ cup stir-fry sauce and water; set aside. Heat 1 tablespoon oil in hot wok or large skillet over high heat. Add chicken and stir-fry 2 minutes; remove. Heat remaining 1 tablespoon oil in same pan. Add snow peas and carrot; sprinkle with salt. Stir-fry 4 minutes. Add stir-fry sauce mixture, chicken, capellini and sesame seed; cook and stir until all ingredients are coated with sauce and pasta is heated through.

Makes 4 servings

350 ANGEL HAIR NOODLES WITH PEANUT SAUCE

¼ cup Texas peanuts, puréed
2 tablespoons low-fat chicken broth or water
1 tablespoon soy sauce
1 tablespoon rice vinegar
10 ounces dried bean thread noodles
½ tablespoon vegetable oil
1 pound chicken breast, boned, skinned and thinly sliced
½ cucumber, peeled, seeded and cut into matchstick pieces
2 medium carrots, shredded

To make sauce, combine peanut purée, chicken broth, soy sauce and vinegar in small bowl; set aside.

Bring 4 cups water to a boil in medium saucepan. Add noodles, stirring to separate strands. Cook, stirring, 30 seconds or until noodles are slightly soft. Drain in colander and rinse under cold running water. Drain well; cut noodles into halves and set aside.

Heat wok or wide skillet over high heat. Add oil, swirling to coat sides. Add chicken and stir-fry 1 minute or until opaque. Add cucumber, carrots and sauce; cook, stirring to mix well. Remove from heat. Add noodles and toss until evenly coated. Sprinkle with extra peanuts, if desired.

Makes 6 servings

*Favorite recipe from **Texas Peanut Producers Board***

Easy Chicken Lo Mein

351 ORZO WITH CHICKEN AND CABBAGE

8 ounces uncooked orzo pasta
¼ cup rice vinegar
¼ cup chicken broth
2 tablespoons packed brown sugar
2 tablespoons soy sauce
1 teaspoon cornstarch
1 tablespoon sesame chili oil
2 cups thinly sliced red cabbage
1 tablespoon seasoned stir-fry or hot oil
1 pound boneless skinless chicken breasts or tenders, cut into bite-size pieces
4 ounces snow peas
4 green onions with tops (separating white and green parts), sliced into ½-inch pieces
1 tablespoon sesame seeds, toasted

1. Place 6 cups water in wok or large saucepan; bring to a boil over high heat. Add orzo; cook according to package directions until *al dente*, stirring occasionally. Drain; set aside.

2. Whisk together vinegar, chicken broth, brown sugar, soy sauce and cornstarch in small bowl; set aside.

3. Heat sesame chili oil in wok or large skillet over high heat. Add cabbage; stir-fry 2 to 3 minutes or until crisp-tender. Remove. Set aside on serving platter; keep warm.

4. Heat stir-fry oil in same wok over high heat. Add chicken; stir-fry 3 minutes. Add snow peas and white parts of green onions; stir-fry 1 to 2 minutes or until vegetables are crisp-tender. Add vinegar mixture, stirring until hot and slightly thickened. Add orzo and toss. Serve over cabbage. Sprinkle with green onion tops and sesame seeds.

Makes 4 servings

352 SZECHUAN SHRIMP & PASTA

8 ounces uncooked linguine
1 pound raw medium shrimp, peeled and deveined
2 teaspoons McCORMICK® Szechuan Style Pepper Blend, divided
2 tablespoons vegetable oil, divided
½ teaspoon McCORMICK® Ground Ginger
¼ teaspoon McCORMICK® Garlic Powder
1 red bell pepper, sliced into strips
8 ounces fresh snow peas or sugar snap peas
¾ cup water
¼ cup soy sauce
2 teaspoons cornstarch

1. Cook linguine according to package directions.

2. Sprinkle shrimp with 1 teaspoon Szechuan Style Pepper Blend. Heat 1 tablespoon oil in medium skillet over medium-high heat. Add shrimp; sprinkle with Ground Ginger and Garlic Powder. Stir-fry 3 minutes or until shrimp are pink. Remove and set aside.

3. Add remaining 1 tablespoon oil to skillet. Stir-fry pepper strips and snow peas 2 minutes or until vegetables are tender. Combine water, soy sauce, cornstarch and remaining 1 teaspoon Szechuan Style Pepper Blend. Add to vegetables in skillet; cook 1 to 2 minutes or until thickened, stirring occasionally. Return shrimp to skillet; heat through. Serve over linguine.

Makes 4 servings

Orzo with Chicken and Cabbage

NOODLES & RICE

353 JAMBALAYA STIR–FRY ON CAJUN RICE

1 cup uncooked converted rice
1 can (16 ounces) diced tomatoes, undrained
½ cup finely chopped celery
2 teaspoons chicken bouillon granules
1 bay leaf
8 ounces andouille sausage, cut into ¼-inch rounds*
1½ cups chopped onions
1 cup chopped green bell pepper
½ pound raw large shrimp, peeled and deveined
½ pound boneless chicken breasts, cut into 1-inch pieces
¾ teaspoon dried thyme leaves
¼ cup chopped parsley
1 teaspoon salt
½ teaspoon ground red pepper
½ teaspoon paprika
    Hot pepper sauce

*If unavailable, use kielbasa sausage.

1. Bring 1¾ cups water to a boil in medium saucepan. Add rice, tomatoes and their liquid, celery, bouillon granules and bay leaf. Return to a boil; reduce heat, cover tightly and simmer 20 minutes or until all liquid is absorbed.

2. Meanwhile, heat large skillet over medium-high heat 1 minute. Add sausage, onions and bell pepper; cook and stir 10 minutes.

3. Increase heat to high; add shrimp, chicken and thyme. Cook and stir 5 minutes. Add parsley, salt, ground red pepper and paprika. Stir to blend thoroughly.

4. Place rice on platter. Spoon shrimp mixture over rice and serve with pepper sauce. *Makes 4 servings*

354 PASTA CHICKEN STIR–FRY

1 pound uncooked mostaccioli, radiatore, medium shells or similar size pasta
1½ cups boiling water
¼ cup soy sauce
¼ cup white wine vinegar
1 tablespoon cornstarch
1 tablespoon chicken bouillon granules
1 tablespoon vegetable oil
1 pound chicken breast, cut into thin slices
3 carrots, sliced
8 ounces snow peas, stems removed
1 red bell pepper, cut into bite-size pieces
4 cloves garlic, minced
⅛ to ¼ teaspoon red pepper flakes
    Freshly ground black pepper to taste

Cook pasta according to package directions. While pasta is cooking, stir together boiling water, soy sauce, vinegar, cornstarch and bouillon granules in small bowl; set aside.

Heat large skillet or wok to medium-hot; add oil. Stir-fry chicken until almost done. Add carrots, snow peas, bell pepper and garlic; stir-fry until vegetables are tender. Reduce heat to medium-low; stir in red pepper flakes and soy sauce mixture.

When pasta is done, drain well. Add pasta to skillet; bring to a boil. Lower heat, cover and cook until pasta is heated through. Season with black pepper. Serve immediately.
Makes 6 servings

Favorite recipe from **North Dakota Wheat Commission**

Jambalaya Stir-Fry on Cajun Rice

NOODLES & RICE

355 GARDEN FRESH VEGETABLE AND HERB RICE

1 (16-ounce) can fat-free chicken broth with 1/3 less salt
1 cup uncooked RICELAND® Extra Long Grain Rice
1 cup sliced zucchini
1 cup fresh or frozen corn
1/2 teaspoon salt
1/8 teaspoon black pepper
1 medium tomato, chopped
1/3 cup chopped green onions
1 tablespoon chopped fresh basil *or* 1 teaspoon dried basil leaves

In medium saucepan, combine chicken broth, rice, zucchini, corn, salt and pepper. Bring to a boil over high heat; reduce heat to low. Cover; simmer 15 minutes. Stir in tomato, green onions and basil.

Makes 6 servings

356 LEE KUM KEE® FRIED RICE

2 tablespoons vegetable oil
2 eggs, beaten
2 cups cooled cooked rice
1/2 pound diced cooked chicken
1/2 cup mixed vegetables
5 tablespoons LEE KUM KEE® Oyster Flavored Sauce
1 tablespoon diced green onion

Heat skillet over medium heat. Add oil. Add egg and scramble. Stir in rice, chicken, vegetables and Oyster Flavored Sauce. Stir-fry until heated through. Sprinkle with green onion and serve. *Makes 4 servings*

357 PEPPER LOVERS' PASTA

1 (15-ounce) package BUCKEYE'S® Evergreen pasta
1 *each* red, green and yellow bell peppers, thinly sliced
1 bunch leeks, cleaned and thinly sliced
1/4 cup olive oil
3 ounces sun-dried tomatoes, sliced and puréed in blender or food processor
2 teaspoons minced garlic
2 teaspoons dried oregano leaves
1 teaspoon dried basil leaves
1 teaspoon dried thyme leaves
1 teaspoon salt
1/4 teaspoon black pepper
Additional black pepper

Cook pasta according to package directions until *al dente*. Sauté bell peppers and leeks in oil in large skillet until soft but still firm. Stir in puréed tomatoes, garlic, oregano, basil, thyme, salt, 1/4 teaspoon black pepper and drained pasta; toss to combine. Serve warm with additional black pepper.

Makes 4 to 6 servings

Pepper Lovers' Pasta

NOODLES & RICE

358 THIN NOODLES WITH CHICKEN AND VEGETABLES

6 ounces (about 3 cups) uncooked thin
    noodles or bean threads
1/2 cup chicken broth
2 tablespoons hoisin sauce
1 tablespoon vegetable oil
2 green onions, finely chopped
1 teaspoon minced fresh ginger
1 clove garlic, minced
1 pound boneless skinless chicken breasts,
    cut into bite-size pieces
1 package frozen vegetable medley,*
    thawed and drained
1/4 cup orange marmalade
2 tablespoons chili sauce
1/4 teaspoon red pepper flakes

*Use your favorite vegetable medley—for example, a
medley of cauliflower, carrots and snow peas.

1. Place 6 cups water in wok or large
saucepan; bring to a boil over high heat. Add
noodles; cook 3 minutes or until *al dente*,
stirring occasionally. Drain. Place noodles
in medium bowl; stir in chicken broth and
hoisin sauce. Set aside; keep warm.

2. Heat oil in wok or large skillet over high
heat. Add onions, ginger and garlic; stir-fry
15 seconds. Add chicken; stir-fry 3 to 4
minutes or until almost done. Add vegetables;
stir-fry until vegetables are hot and chicken
is no longer pink in center. Add marmalade,
chili sauce and pepper. Stir until hot. Serve
over noodles.   *Makes 4 servings*

359 STIR–FRIED WILD RICE

2 cups cooked wild rice (2/3 cup uncooked)
2 tablespoons vegetable oil
1 pound pork tenderloin, sliced 1/4 inch
    thick
1 medium onion, sliced
2 carrots, sliced 1/8 inch thick
1 bunch broccoli, florets removed and
    stalks sliced 1/8 inch thick
1 teaspoon cornstarch
1/2 teaspoon ground ginger
2 tablespoons low-sodium soy sauce

In heavy skillet, heat oil. Add pork and stir-
fry over high heat 2 minutes. Add onion,
carrots and broccoli slices. Stir-fry 5
minutes. Add broccoli florets and wild rice.
Blend cornstarch and ginger with soy sauce;
add to skillet. Cook and stir 1 minute or until
thickened.   *Makes 4 servings*

Favorite recipe from **Minnesota Cultivated Wild
Rice Council**

Thin Noodles with Chicken and Vegetables

NOODLES & RICE

360 THAI FRIED RICE

2½ cups water
1⅓ cups uncooked long-grain white rice
8 ounces ground pork or pork sausage
1 tablespoon vegetable oil
1 medium onion, thinly sliced
1 tablespoon finely chopped fresh ginger
1 jalapeño pepper,* finely chopped
3 cloves garlic, minced
½ teaspoon ground turmeric or paprika
2 tablespoons fish sauce
2 cups chopped cooked vegetables, such
  as broccoli, zucchini, red bell
  peppers, carrots, bok choy or spinach
3 eggs, lightly beaten
3 green onions, thinly sliced
½ cup cilantro leaves

Chili peppers can sting and irritate the skin; wear rubber gloves when handling peppers and do not touch eyes.

1. Bring water and rice to a boil in medium saucepan over high heat. Reduce heat to medium-low; cover and simmer 20 minutes or until water is absorbed.

2. Transfer rice to large bowl and fluff with fork. Let cool to room temperature, 30 to 40 minutes, stirring occasionally. Cover and refrigerate until cold, at least 1 hour or up to 24 hours.

3. When rice is cold, cook pork in wok or medium skillet over medium-high heat until no longer pink. Drain off excess fat; transfer pork to bowl and set aside.

4. Heat wok over medium-high heat. Add oil and swirl to coat surface. Add onion, ginger, jalapeño, garlic and turmeric; stir-fry 4 to 6 minutes or until onion is very tender.

5. Stir in fish sauce; mix well. Stir in cold rice, vegetables and pork; cook and stir 3 to 4 minutes or until heated through.

6. Push rice to side of wok and pour eggs into center. Cook eggs 2 to 3 minutes or just until set, lifting and stirring to scramble. Stir rice into eggs.

7. Stir in green onions. Transfer to serving bowl; sprinkle with cilantro. Garnish as desired. *Makes 4 servings*

361 FRIED NOODLES WITH CHICKEN MARINADE

4 tablespoons vegetable oil, divided
2 ounces shredded chicken fillet
5 ounces bean sprouts
4 ounces shredded carrot
12 ounces cooked noodles
6 tablespoons LEE KUM KEE® Chicken
  Marinade
2 ounces shredded ham
½ teaspoon salt
1 green onion, shredded

1. Heat 2 tablespoons oil in wok; stir-fry chicken until half done. Add bean sprouts and carrot; cook until tender. Remove to serving dish.

2. Heat remaining 2 tablespoons oil in wok. Stir-fry noodles, Chicken Marinade, ham and salt. Mix well; add to chicken mixture. Garnish with onion. *Makes 4 servings*

Thai Fried Rice

NOODLES & RICE

362 VEGETABLE LO MEIN

8 ounces uncooked vermicelli or thin
    spaghetti, cooked and drained
¾ teaspoon dark sesame oil
½ teaspoon vegetable oil
3 cloves garlic, minced
1 teaspoon grated fresh ginger
2 cups sliced bok choy
½ cup sliced green onions
2 cups shredded carrots
6 ounces firm tofu, drained and cubed
6 tablespoons rice wine vinegar
¼ cup plum preserves
¼ cup water
1 teaspoon low-sodium soy sauce
½ teaspoon red pepper flakes

1. Toss vermicelli with sesame oil in large bowl until well coated.

2. Heat vegetable oil in large nonstick skillet over medium heat. Stir in garlic and ginger; stir-fry 10 seconds.

3. Add bok choy and onions; stir-fry 3 to 4 minutes or until crisp-tender. Add carrots and tofu; stir-fry 2 to 3 minutes or until carrots are crisp-tender.

4. Combine vinegar, preserves, water, soy sauce and pepper in small saucepan. Heat over medium heat until preserves are melted, stirring constantly.

5. Combine noodles, vegetable mixture and vinegar mixture in large bowl; mix well.
Makes 6 side-dish servings

363 HARVEYS® BRISTOL CREAM® FETTUCINE AND VEGETABLES

1 pound fresh asparagus
1 cup sliced fresh mushrooms
½ cup finely chopped red bell pepper
¼ cup chopped onion
1 clove garlic, minced
3 tablespoons butter or margarine
2 tablespoons all-purpose flour
½ teaspoon salt
¼ teaspoon white pepper
1 cup milk
¼ cup HARVEYS® Bristol Cream®
¼ cup grated Parmesan cheese
8 ounces uncooked fettucine, cooked and
    drained

Snap off tough ends of asparagus. Cut asparagus into ¾-inch pieces. Cook in small amount of boiling water 2 to 3 minutes or until crisp-tender. Drain and set aside.

In small saucepan, sauté mushrooms, bell pepper, onion and garlic in butter until tender. Combine flour, salt and white pepper in small bowl; stir into vegetable mixture. Add milk and Harveys® Bristol Cream®. Cook and stir over medium heat until thickened and bubbly, stirring constantly. Stir in cheese.

Place hot fettucine in serving bowl. Add sauce and asparagus. Toss gently to coat evenly.
Makes 4 to 6 servings

Vegetable Lo Mein

364 MAJESTIC NOODLE NEST STIR–FRY

Noodle Nests (recipe follows)
⅓ cup KIKKOMAN® Stir-Fry Sauce
2 tablespoons dry sherry
2 tablespoons water
½ teaspoon cornstarch
¾ pound boneless lean pork
1 tablespoon KIKKOMAN® Stir-Fry Sauce
2 tablespoons vegetable oil, divided
1 carrot, cut diagonally into thin slices
1 medium onion, chunked
2 stalks celery, cut diagonally into thin slices
1 medium-size red bell pepper, cut into strips

Prepare Noodle Nests; keep warm. Blend ⅓ cup stir-fry sauce, sherry, water and cornstarch in small bowl; set aside. Cut pork across grain into thin slices; coat with 1 tablespoon stir-fry sauce. Heat 1 tablespoon oil in hot wok or large skillet over high heat. Add pork and stir-fry 3 minutes; remove. Heat remaining 1 tablespoon oil in same pan. Add carrot; stir-fry 1 minute. Add onion, celery and red pepper; stir-fry 3 minutes. Add stir-fry sauce mixture; cook and stir until mixture boils and thickens and meat and vegetables are coated with sauce. Serve over Noodle Nests.

Makes 4 to 6 servings

NOODLE NESTS: Cook 8 ounces capellini (angel hair pasta) according to package directions. Drain; rinse under cold water and drain thoroughly. Divide capellini into 4 to 6 individual nests. Heat 1 tablespoon oil in large nonstick skillet over medium-high heat. Add 2 or 3 nests. Cook 5 minutes, without stirring, or until golden on bottom. Lift nests with wide spatula; add 1 tablespoon oil to skillet and turn nests over. Cook 5 minutes longer, or until golden. Keep warm in 200°F oven. Repeat with remaining capellini. *Makes 4 to 6 servings*

365 SPAGHETTI WITH BEEF AND BLACK PEPPER SAUCE

7 ounces uncooked spaghetti
5 ounces shredded beef fillet
½ cup plus 2 tablespoons LEE KUM KEE® Black Pepper Sauce, divided
1 tablespoon vegetable oil
1 ounce shredded onion
1 ounce shredded green bell pepper
1 ounce shredded red bell pepper

1. Cook spaghetti in boiling water 10 minutes. Rinse with cold water and drain.

2. Marinate beef in 2 tablespoons Black Pepper Sauce 5 minutes.

3. Heat oil in wok. Sauté onion until fragrant. Add beef and stir-fry until cooked. Add spaghetti, bell peppers and remaining ½ cup Black Pepper Sauce. Stir well and serve. *Makes 4 to 6 servings*

Majestic Noodle Nest Stir-Fry

ACKNOWLEDGMENTS

The publisher would like to thank the companies and organizations listed below for the use of their recipes and photos in this publication.

Alpine Lace Brands, Inc.
American Lamb Council
BC-USA
BelGioioso® Cheese, Inc.
Birds Eye®
Blue Diamond Growers
Bob Evans Farms®
Buckeye Beans & Herbs
California Seafood Council
California Table Grape Commission
California Wild Rice Association
Chilean Fresh Fruit Association
Christopher Ranch Garlic
Delmarva Poultry Industry, Inc.
Del Monte Corporation
Dole Food Company, Inc.
Farmhouse Foods Company
Filippo Berio Olive Oil
Florida Department of Agriculture & Consumer Services, Bureau of Seafood and Aquaculture
Golden Grain/Mission Pasta
Grandma's Molasses, a division of Cadbury Beverages Inc.
Harveys® Bristol Cream®
Heinz U.S.A.
Hiram Walker
Holland House, a division of Cadbury Beverages Inc.
Hormel Foods Corporation
Hunt-Wesson, Inc.
Jones Dairy Farm
Kikkoman International Inc.
Kraft Foods, Inc.
Lawry's® Foods, Inc.

Lee Kum Kee (USA) Inc.
Lipton™
McCormick & Co., Inc.
McIlhenny Company
Mushroom Council
Minnesota Cultivated Wild Rice Council
MOTT'S® Inc., a division of Cadbury Beverages Inc.
Nabisco, Inc.
National Foods, Inc.
National Honey Board
National Onion Association
National Pasta Association
National Pork Producers Council
National Turkey Federation
Nestlé USA
Norseland, Inc.
North Dakota Barley Council
North Dakota Beef Commission
North Dakota Wheat Commission
Perdue Farms Incorporated
Plochman, Inc.
The Procter & Gamble Company
Quaker® Kitchens
Riceland Foods, Inc.
Specialty Brands, Inc.
StarKist® Seafood Company
The Sugar Association, Inc.
Sunkist Growers
St. Supéry Vineyards & Winery
Texas Peanut Producers Board
USA Rice Federation
Walnut Marketing Board
Washington Apple Commission

INDEX

INDEX

INDEX

INDEX

INDEX

INDEX

METRIC CONVERSION CHART

VOLUME MEASUREMENTS (dry)

1/8 teaspoon = 0.5 mL
1/4 teaspoon = 1 mL
1/2 teaspoon = 2 mL
3/4 teaspoon = 4 mL
1 teaspoon = 5 mL
1 tablespoon = 15 mL
2 tablespoons = 30 mL
1/4 cup = 60 mL
1/3 cup = 75 mL
1/2 cup = 125 mL
2/3 cup = 150 mL
3/4 cup = 175 mL
1 cup = 250 mL
2 cups = 1 pint = 500 mL
3 cups = 750 mL
4 cups = 1 quart = 1 L

VOLUME MEASUREMENTS (fluid)

1 fluid ounce (2 tablespoons) = 30 mL
4 fluid ounces (1/2 cup) = 125 mL
8 fluid ounces (1 cup) = 250 mL
12 fluid ounces (1 1/2 cups) = 375 mL
16 fluid ounces (2 cups) = 500 mL

WEIGHTS (mass)

1/2 ounce = 15 g
1 ounce = 30 g
3 ounces = 90 g
4 ounces = 120 g
8 ounces = 225 g
10 ounces = 285 g
12 ounces = 360 g
16 ounces = 1 pound = 450 g

DIMENSIONS

1/16 inch = 2 mm
1/8 inch = 3 mm
1/4 inch = 6 mm
1/2 inch = 1.5 cm
3/4 inch = 2 cm
1 inch = 2.5 cm

OVEN TEMPERATURES

250°F = 120°C
275°F = 140°C
300°F = 150°C
325°F = 160°C
350°F = 180°C
375°F = 190°C
400°F = 200°C
425°F = 220°C
450°F = 230°C

BAKING PAN SIZES

Utensil	Size in Inches/Quarts	Metric Volume	Size in Centimeters
Baking or Cake Pan (square or rectangular)	8×8×2	2 L	20×20×5
	9×9×2	2.5 L	23×23×5
	12×8×2	3 L	30×20×5
	13×9×2	3.5 L	33×23×5
Loaf Pan	8×4×3	1.5 L	20×10×7
	9×5×3	2 L	23×13×7
Round Layer Cake Pan	8×1½	1.2 L	20×4
	9×1½	1.5 L	23×4
Pie Plate	8×1¼	750 mL	20×3
	9×1¼	1 L	23×3
Baking Dish or Casserole	1 quart	1 L	—
	1½ quart	1.5 L	—
	2 quart	2 L	—